1 0 95

THE MYSTICISM OF
The Cloud
of Unknowing

THE MYSTICISM
OF THE
CLOUD OF UNKNOWING

WILLIAM JOHNSTON

FOREWORD BY
THOMAS MERTON

SOURCE BOOKS
TRABUCO CANYON CALIFORNIA

ANTHONY CLARKE
WHEATHAMPSTEAD HERTFORDSHIRE

NIHIL OBSTAT: P. Arrupe S.J. , *Censor*
IMPRIMATUR: P. Shirayanagi, *Delegatus Tokyo, 1965*

First Published in New York, Desclee,1967. This edition, first
published in Great Britain in 1974 and Reprinted 1980, 1984, 1987.
This printing, 1992.

Co-published by   SOURCE BOOKS
                      Box 794
                      Trabuco Canyon CA 92678
          and
                      ANTHONY CLARKE
                      16 Garden Court
                      Wheathampstead Herts. AL4 8RF

     ISBN   **0-940147-02-5**   (USA)

     ISBN   **0-85650-048-0**   (UK)

Library of Congress CIP Data
        1. Cloud of Unknowing. 2. Mysticism–History–Middles Ages,
        600-150. 3. Mysticism–Buddhism. I. Title
        BV5080.C6J65   1992
        248.2'2–dc20
                                              91-42388
                                                   CIP

Printed by KNI Inc. Anaheim CA, USA

CONTENTS

PART IV

UNION

FOREWORD
by
Thomas Merton

Mysticism will probably always be a disturbing subject. First of all, the concept of mystical experience is easily misunderstood. Aberrations have been palmed off as true mysticism. Or the word has been defined so loosely and with so little respect for truth that mystical experience has been confused with every kind of emotional, pseudo-religious, aesthetic or supposedly extra-sensory perception. Even when properly understood, and treated with perfect orthodoxy—as in this present book—mysticism tends to inspire apprehension even in religious minds. Why? Because the mystic must surrender to a power of love that is greater than human and advance toward God in a darkness that goes beyond the light of reason and of human conceptual knowledge. Furthermore, there is no infallible way of guaranteeing the mystic against every mistake: he can never be perfectly sure of any human technique. Only the grace of God can protect him and guide him. In other words, when we speak of mysticism, we speak of an area in which man is no longer completely in command of his own life, his own mind, and of his own will. Yet at the same time his surrender is to a God who is " more intimate to him than his own self" (intimior intimo meo, in St. Augustine's words) and therefore mysticism precludes real alienation. In mystical union God and man, while remaining no doubt metaphysically distinct, are practically and experientially " one Spirit " in the words of St. Paul (1 Cor 6, 16) quoted in this sense by Christian mystics down the centuries. But because there are also other " spirits " and because man does not possess within himself a natural faculty which can by its own powers pass final judgment on the transcendent experiences taking place within him, a counterfeit mysticism is not only possible but relatively common.

Mystical theology seeks to understand the highest union of man with God (outside of the beatific vision) and to help us to distinguish between experience that is truly supernatural and that which is not " from God. " Note that what is not supernatural and therefore not strictly mystical, is not necessarily evil. There is a natural metaphysical intuition of being, even of Absolute Being, or of the metaphysical ground of being. This intuition is certainly found in all the great world religions and in certain philosophies. Aristotle believed it to be the highest achievement possible to man, and the root of his true happiness. There is no difficulty in relating this metaphysical intuition to the Satori *of Zen.*

Whether there is in non-Christian religions a truly mystical or supernatural vision of God may still be debated, but the best theologians have admitted its possibility. Nor is there any real difficulty about this, in theory, since we know that men of good will in all religions, who follow the dictates of an upright conscience, can certainly attain to holiness and union with God because they receive grace from Him to do so. Union with God in love also implies a profound and existential grasp of His presence: indeed it should normally imply some such intuition, however vague this might be. Nor is this intuition, even when supernatural, necessarily " mystical " in the full sense of the word. The experience of living faith, the " sense of the presence of God " which many faithful Christians enjoy without being mystics, is a supernatural intuition of God's loving presence and care, granted with the gift of a mature faith.

One of the chief problems of mystical theology is to account for a loving, unitive and supernatural love of God that is beyond concepts, and to do so in language that does not in one way or other become completely misleading. The mystical theologian faces the problem of saying what cannot really be said. One of the ways of attacking this problem has been opened up by so called apophatic theology, the theology of " unknowing, " which describes the transcendent experience of God in love as a " knowing by unknowing " and a " seeing that is not seeing. " The language of apophatism is not peculiar to Christianity, and it had currency in Asia long before Christian times (for instance in Lao-tzu *and in the* Upanishads). *But it is also familiar in the*

Bible, in spite of the fact that in the Bible God is spoken of in poetic and concrete language which presents Him not as "formless" but as having very definite natural and even at times human "forms" together with human feelings. Yet the great theophanies of Moses and Elias are apophatic, and on Sinai Moses is enveloped in a dense cloud, in which he talks to God as to his friend, without seeing Him.

Mystical theology is negative in the sense that every positive statement is immediately qualified with: " but that is not it. " One cannot grasp the idea of " unknowing " as long as one clings to the notion of God conceived as a definite, that is to say " defined " or " limited "—therefore " finite "—object. Any experience of God as possessing some finite form or idea which we can grasp is an experience not of God but only of something that remotely resembles Him in an analogical way. There is nothing whatever in existence that even remotely resembles God as He is in Himself. And yet the " knowing " of God in " unknowing, " far from being unreal and uncertain, possesses the highest reality and certainty of any experience accessible to man. How is this possible? How can it be explained?

For centuries, mystics have groped for words in which to account for the supreme reality of this experience which not only illuminates a man's mind and fills his heart with new strength, but even radically transforms his whole life. But also they have warned men that the easiest way to be deluded and led into error is to seek experience for its own sake, and to want to possess and use what can never become our own private possession. The root of false mysticism is the yearning to " have experiences. " Spiritual ambition is an obstacle to mystic union. All this is said in classic and unforgettable pages by The Cloud of Unknowing, *the work of an anonymous fourteenth century English writer in the apophatic tradition, closely related to the Rheinland mystics. He is calmer, more prudent and more orthodox than the brilliant Meister Eckhart, as homely and humorous as Tauler, much more a man of solid common sense than Suso or any of them. Indeed, there has never been a book on mysticism that showed such realistic common sense as* The Cloud—*and the other writings of the same author. And yet, alas,* The Cloud *too must remain a closed book, mysterious and frightening, or simply confusing and inaccessible, to those who do not have the gift of appreciating such things.*

Nevertheless, there is a particular timeliness about a careful theological study of The Cloud *today. First of all we witness the meeting, or perhaps better the collision, of Zen and the West.* The Cloud, *as Father Johnston shows, has points in common with Zen, but the similarities must not be pushed too far. Certainly* The Cloud *provides a solid basis for dialogue between Christian and Eastern ways of contemplation.*

Then there is the current furor about the " death of God." This must be seen as a professedly religious concern, and indeed we are exhorted by some of the new theologians to embrace " Christian atheism" on the grounds that a truly contemporary man cannot be anything other than an atheist. It is clear that a lot of this supposedly new and radical theology sounds a great deal less strange and less new when it is seen against the background of apophatism. When the Anglican Bishop of Woolwich a few years ago discovered that God was not " out there " in the Milky Way somewhere, he was only discovering Christian theodicy. God never was " out there " or " up there " or anywhere in a particular place. In fact anyone who is acquainted with theological tradition is well aware that the God who has supposedly died in the minds of these new men is a god who never lived in the first place. Like the god demolished by atheism, he is a shadow and a contradiction. It is quite possible that the teaching of The Cloud of Unknowing *may help some Christian " atheists " to sort out a few simple ideas and recover their faith.*

Certainly The Cloud *is appropriate for an era which has become wary of religious clichés and of grossly inadequate imagery. Furthermore, the simplicity of* The Cloud *and of the way of prayer it teaches, will be a boon to those who can no longer cope with complicated and sentimental methods of meditating which appealed to an earlier age. Let us also frankly face the fact that for many Christians, some of the new liturgical experiments with all their unquestionable advantages, are often too noisy and too busy.* The Cloud *is an admirable antidote for a rather hectic and disordered communal piety which does not always quite come off. For that reason it will meet with a special kind of opposition, and will be condemned as quietism, illuminism, subjectivism, and so on. Never mind. That is an old, well-worn refrain and Father Johnston's book should take care of these routine objections.*

Next, and this is more serious still, there is the current rather massive trend toward the easy pseudo-mysticism of psychedelic drugs. This is not the place to discuss this trend or to pass final judgment in the crucial questions it raises. But The Cloud, *like all the great documents in the apophatic tradition, warns us that the appetite for experiences—or, more crudely, for kicks—is the greatest danger to the development of an authentic mystical life. Whether or not the use of such drugs is harmless in itself, and whether or not a positive human contribution is to be expected from them, it would seem that their use should* not *be recommended in the true mystical life. A sample quotation from St. John of the Cross should suffice, here, to show why:*

> *In order to come to this essential union of love in God the soul must have a care not to lean upon imaginary visions nor upon forms or figures or particular objects of the understanding; for these cannot serve it as a proportionate and proximate means to such an end; rather they would disturb it and* for this reason the soul must renounce them and strive never to have them. (Ascent of Mount Carmel, *II, xvi, 10)*

Here St. John of the Cross is speaking not only of illusory visions but of authentic spiritual experiences, supernatural and mystical ones included. He is teaching that one who seeks " essential union of love in God " which he describes as a " naked union of pure essences " will only be hindered by a desire for visions and experiences. This essential union is beyond all experience. Hence the desire and need for experiences will inevitably lead to an attachment to forms and objects, or to mental states and conditions, which are incompatible with perfect union. Obviously one cannot effectively " prevent " a true mystical experience which takes place with no initiative of our own. But even these must not, says St. John of the Cross, be desired or sought by one who is called by God to the most perfect union. If they happen, they are of course accepted. But one would do better not to desire them, and any effort to bring them on would end in illusion or frustration. As the present book shows, The Cloud *concurs perfectly with this traditional teaching.*

A final objection against apophatic mysticism will come from those who are suspicious of " introversion. " This term was used by mystics before it was appropriated by modern clinical psychology. The introversion of the mystics is metaphysical rather than psychological, and rightly understood it has nothing to do with the introversion of narcissistic withdrawal. However the term is a bit misleading, and we must admit that there does exist a real danger of silent and passive contemplation becoming a mere exercise in narcissistic self-indulgence. One must not rest in the simple pleasure of one's own being and become disinterested in other things, or in one's necessary work. This too The Cloud *explains sufficiently well. There is all the difference in the world between true contemplation and narcissistic repose in one's own self. True contemplation results in greater freedom of action and indeed makes action more spontaneous, more loving, and more effective. Narcissistic withdrawal ends in confusion, laziness, self-concern, sensitivity and other such morbid effects. By their fruits you shall know them.*

We can be grateful to Father Johnston for presenting the first extended and coherent theological treatment of all the works by the author of The Cloud, *seen in the light of a conscious comparison with Oriental ways of contemplation. He is in a good position to do this, as he is at Sophia University in Tokyo together with other Catholic authorities on Zen, Fr. H. Dumoulin and Fr. Enomiya Lassalle. His book is a most welcome and valuable contribution to mystical theology.*

PREFACE TO THE SECOND EDITION

Since this book was first written, interest in mysticism has grown rapidly in the West. We have seen an influx of oriental mysticism appealing to men and women in all walks of life. We have seen widespread interest in altered states of consciousness, in hypnosis, in dreams and in drugs. We find the bookstores filled with literature on Zen and Yoga, on Tibetan mysticism and the occult. We see that meditation (meditation that tends towards mysticism) is becoming part of modern culture and part of the educational system in the West.

Faced with this sudden inrush of mystical thought, many sincere and devout Christians are perplexed. What are they to think of this movement towards mysticism with all its seeming confusion? Is this progress or is it retrogress? Is it a quest for reality or a neurotic escape? Is it a passing fad or is it the wave of the future? Mysticism has always been a delicate subject fraught with pitfalls, abounding in perils, filled with illusion. The most orthodox tradition warns us about gnosticism, pantheism, monism, quietism, and the rest. Small wonder if the Christian is perplexed as he surveys the modern scene.

Now it seems to me that the modern Christian who would evaluate today's mystical climate and profit from it must begin by studying his own tradition. Here he will find a wealth of mystical doctrine which the West needs today. From the many mystical writers of the West I have chosen one: the anonymous author of *The Cloud of Unknowing, The Book of Privy Counselling* and several other satellite treatises. I have tried to show that we have here an eminently safe and reliable guide who will not lead his reader astray. Anyone aspiring to the practice of Christian mysticism and its comprehension can do no better than read the works of this author and reflect on their message.

If, however, the medieval author is a reliable guide it may be asked why I should write another book. And to this I would reply that this book is meant to be a work of mystical theology whereas the treatises of the medieval English author are primarily works of descriptive mysticism. Broadly speaking mystical writing can be divided into two categories—descriptive and theological. Works in the latter category attempt to evaluate mysticism, testing it with the yardsticks of reason and revelation. Christian tradition has always insisted that we can best evaluate mystical writings by examining their underlying theology.

Hopefully this book will be not only a theological commentary on *The Cloud* and its satellite treatises but also an introduction to the medieval tradition which gave them birth. Though almost ten years have elapsed since this book was written, I still recall with joy my explorations in the great schools of spirituality (Franciscan, Dominican, Cistercian, Benedictine) which flourished in the medieval world. I hope the reader will catch something of the spirit of this tradition. I also hope that the norms outlined in this book will help him evaluate from the Christian standpoint not only *The Cloud* but the other mystical writings, ancient and modern, eastern and western, which are brought to our attention today. In order to illustrate the theological exactness of this author I have simply selected four traditional and normative questions. The first concerns the author's attitude towards reason—because no truly Christian mystic has ever rejected reason for the cult of irrationality. The second is his treatment of love, which is the center of Christian perfection. The third question is about the author's Christology and the fourth about his doctrine concerning the relationship between the created universe and its Creator.

The foreword to the original book was written by Thomas Merton. I met the great Trappist at Gethsemani in the summer of 1965, and we talked about East and West, about mysticism and Zen. Already at that time Merton was eager to visit Japan but somewhat frustrated that his plans were not working out. Yet he saw that there was something providential in all the frustration. Providential indeed it was; for Merton was never to set foot on Japanese soil. Some years later while we in Sophia University were preparing for his visit we learned of his sudden and tragic death in Bangkok. Those are days I will not easily forget.

Merton observes that *The Cloud* provides a solid base for dialogue between Christian and Eastern ways of contemplation.

This, I believe, is true. And I hope that a theological discussion of the mystical doctrine of this medieval author will further understanding between the schools of spirituality in the East and in the West.

William Johnston
Sophia University, Tokyo
January, 1975

ACKNOWLEDGMENTS

The author wishes to thank the following publishers for permission to use quotations in this book from copyrighted material:

Geoffrey Bles, London, for permission to quote from *The Degrees of Knowledge* by Jacques Maritain.

Burns and Oates, Ltd., London, for permission to quote from *The Cloud of Unknowing*, edited by Justin McCann.

Bruno Cassirer, Oxford, for permission to quote from *Buddhism* by E. Conze.

E. P. Dutton Co., New York, for permission to quote from Ruysbroeck's *The Adornment of the Spiritual Marriage, The Sparkling Stone, The Book of Supreme Truth*, translated by C. A. Wynschenk, edited by E. Underhill.

Faber and Faber, London, and Harcourt, Brace & World Inc., New York, for permission to quote from *The Four Quartets* by T. S. Eliot.

Grove Press, New York, and Hutchinson Publishing Group Ltd., London, for permission to quote from *Essays in Zen Buddhism* by Daisetz Suzuki, and *An Introduction to Zen Buddhism* by Daisetz Suzuki, preface by C. G. Jung.

Harper Torchbooks, New York, for permission to quote from *Meister Eckhart, a Modern Translation* by R. B. Blakney.

Harper & Row, New York, for permission to quote from *Grey Eminence* and *Doors of Perception* by Aldous Huxley.

The Newman Press, Westminster, Maryland, for permission to quote from *The Complete Works of St. John of the Cross*.

Oxford University Press, Oxford, for permission to quote from *Mysticism Sacred and Profane* by R. C. Zaehner.

Pantheon Books, New York, for permission to quote from *A History of Zen Buddhism* by H. Dumoulin.

Philosophical Library, New York, for permission to quote from *Buddhism and Zen* by Senzaki and McCandless.

Julian Press, New York, for permission to quote from *The Cloud of Unknowing*, introduction, commentary and translation by Ira Progoff.

Routledge & Kegan Paul, London, for permission to quote from *The Graces of Interior Prayer* by A. Poulain.

Charles Scribner & Sons, New York, for permission to quote from *From Glory to Glory*, texts from Gregory of Nyssa.

Sheed and Ward, Inc., New York, for permission to quote from *The Complete Works of Saint Teresa*, translated and edited by E. Allison Peers from the critical edition of P. Silverio de Santa Teresa, C. D., published in three volumes; *The Mystical Theology of St. Bernard* by Etienne Gilson; *The Theology of the Spiritual Life* by Joseph de Guibert.

The author would also like to express his deep gratitude to Professors A. Evangelista and P. Nemeshegyi for their guidance and help in his work, as well as to Father James Walsh who kindly read the manuscript and made many valuable suggestions.

ABBREVIATIONS

C.	The Cloud of Unknowing.
H.D.	Denis Hid Divinity.
P.	The Epistle of Prayer.
P.C.	The Book of Privy Counsel.
St.	An Epistle of Discretion of Stirrings.
Sp.	A Treatise of Discretion of Spirits.
S.W.	A Treatise of the Study of Wisdom that Men Call Benjamin.

INTRODUCTION

THE BACKGROUND

In the fourteenth century, England gave birth to a spiritual writer who was at once a mystic, a theologian, and a director of souls. He wrote anonymously and his identity has not been established; but usually he is referred to, from the name of his most famous work, as " the author of *The Cloud of Unknowing.* "

This Englishman belongs to a mystical trend known as " apophatic " because of its tendency to emphasize that God is best known by negation: we can know much more about what God is *not* than about what He is. His is a doctrine that follows a long tradition stretching from Gregory of Nyssa and the pseudo-Dionysius to the Rhineland mystics whence it later crosses the Pyrénées to reach a great climax with St. John of the Cross in sixteenth-century Spain. [1]

The Cloud of Unknowing, the most celebrated work of the English author, is a book of considerable literary beauty written with a simplicity of style that, however, does not conceal the wealth of theological learning lying beneath the surface. But even more profound and metaphysical (and, for that reason, more difficult reading) is *The Book of Privy Counsel*, which appears to be the work of his maturity and may have been written to clear up some points left obscure in the earlier treatise. [2] In addition to these two works, there are attributed

---

[1] The word *apophatic* is used by Dionysius who speaks of θεολογία ἀποφατική, or " negative theology, " in opposition to θεολογία καταφατική, or " positive theology. "

[2] See C. 130:14. N. B.: References throughout are to the critical texts of Professor Hodgson (Early English Text Society). In the actual quotations, however, I have used some modernization for which I have been greatly helped by the work of Justin McCann.

to the same author the *Epistle of Prayer* (in the later *Privy Counsel* the author makes reference to this work as well as to *The Cloud*, making their common authorship indisputable) and the *Epistle of Discretion of Stirrings*. In these four treatises the author, in clear-cut and direct prose, covers in some detail the main problems of the mystical life. His doctrine is direct and traditional; it stresses the essentials of the interior life; it is distinguished by a humanity, a sense of humor, and a psychological shrewdness that tell us much about the personality of the man who speaks to us through the pages.

The same author has left us three translations. The *Denis Hid Divinity* is a rough translation of a Latin version of the *Mystica theologia* of the pseudo-Dionysius; *A Treatise of the Study of Wisdom that Men Call Benjamin* is based upon the *Benjamin Minor* of Richard of St. Victor; and *A Treatise of Discretion of Spirits* is a paraphrase of two sermons of St. Bernard.[3] I have called these works " translations " but it might be more accurate to call them adaptations; for the English author freely adds his own ideas and omits what he considers unnecessary. This is made clear in the opening paragraph of *Hid Divinity* where he says of the work of Dionysius, " in translation of it I have not only followed the naked letter of the text, but for to declare the hardness of it, I have followed the sentence of the Abbot of St. Victor, a noble and worthy expositor of this same book. " (H.D. 2:8)[4] And since in his other translations he follows a similar policy of adding and omitting as he thinks fit (indeed, many of the more significant words and phrases are his own additions), it can reasonably be assumed that they, like the original works, express his true mind and can be used in the analysis of his thought.

These seven treatises form the basis of the present work.

Apart from evidence of common authorship deriving from similarity of style and vocabulary, there is in all these works (with the possible exception of the *Discretion of Spirits*) a similarity of doctrine that makes it difficult to doubt but that

[3] Sermons XXIII and XXIV, *PL* clxxxiii, cc 600-605.
[4] This Abbot of St. Victor is Thomas Gallus, subsequently Abbot of Vercelli and known as " Vercellensis. "

they came from the pen of the same man. [5] The similarity
will, I think, become clear as this work develops. At present
it is sufficient to say that in all cases the mysticism taught is
highly introspective. That is to say, even though the metaphor
of a cloud in the sky is central to the principal treatise, the
main endeavor of the author is not so much to fix our eyes
on an outer world charged with the presence of God in all
things, but rather to direct our eyes into the depth of our
own soul in the darkness of which " mirror " we will find God.
This way of thinking occupies the opening pages of *Privy
Counsel* where the author, instructing his disciple to empty
his mind of all thoughts and images so that it may remain in
supraconceptual darkness, says: " Let that darkness be thy
mirror and thy mind wholly. " (P.C. 136:7) The mind is a
mirror; void of images and thoughts but filled with faith, it
is in darkness; and in the darkness one sees God.

This darkness, which wholly fills the mind when, void of
discursive reasoning and conceptual thinking, it is grounded
in supernatural faith—this darkness is the cloud of unknowing.
And out of this darkness of faith there arises the " blind
stirring of love "—also called the " naked intent of the will "—
that darts upward (or, more correctly, downward) toward
God who, by grace, is in secret and silence in that deeply
mysterious part of the soul that is called " the sovereign point
of the spirit. " The thought of the English author constantly
centers around the darkness of the mystical mind vivified by
the blind stirring of ardent love. *Hid Divinity* and the *Study
of Wisdom* give the theoretical or theological basis; the other
treatises add practical advice as to how this theory can be
applied to the mystical life. Notable for its practicality is the
Discretion of Stirring, which vividly describes how the " blind
stirring of love " guides the contemplative in his daily life,
instructing him when to be silent and to speak, when to fast
and when to eat and so on. It is here, while describing the
experimental nature of divine love, that the author gives us

---

[5] Similarity in style and vocabulary is thoroughly treated in the introduction
to the two volumes of Professor Hodgson. I do not mean to question the common
authorship of the *Discretion of Spirits* but merely to remark that the similarity
in doctrine is here less evident.

some of his most colorful prose vivid with acute psychological insight.

Manuscripts of the author's works are rather numerous, the oldest dating back to the beginning of the fifteenth century with clear indications that the original is of earlier origin. Since the author seems to have known the work of Richard Rolle and since Walter Hilton seems to have known *him*, the historians conclude that he wrote in the late fourteenth century. This is corroborated by the style that moreover indicates that the treatises were written in the North-East Midlands. [6]

No one has succeeded in putting a name on the author, though numerous suggestions have been made; nor has any definitive conclusion been reached about the religious order to which he belonged—if indeed he was a religious. So successful was his humble desire to remain unknown. [7]

Internal evidence reveals a man richly endowed with that " high and glorious wisdom " that emanates from his work. That he himself was a mystic can scarcely be doubted. " And there is no doubt that he wrote it chiefly out of the experience he had in himself, " writes Augustine Baker of *The Cloud*, " and otherwise could not have written what he hath done and as he hath done. " [8] Indeed, the sureness of touch with which he writes indicates clearly enough that he himself experienced that sapiential repose in silence which he describes with a serene authority arising, one feels, not only from deep theological study but also from silent communion with God at the sovereign point of his own spirit.

Delicacy of the Subject

An interesting feature of the author's work is his constant stressing of the extreme delicacy of his subject together with

---

[6] See Professor Hodgson's first volume p. lxxxiv; also Knowles [1] p. 70. (For further details about books quoted in these notes, see bibliography.)

[7] At one time it was suggested that the author of *The Cloud* was Walter Hilton, but this is no longer accepted (See Eric Colledge [1], pp. 64ff.; Knowles [1], pp. 68ff.). The author addresses some of his treatises to a young disciple, but again it is not known if this man is real or fictitious. He may be introduced as part of a literary device like the Timothy of Dionysius.

[8] McCann, p. 152.

a great fear of misunderstanding. It is not that the thing itself is difficult. Contemplation is the simplest thing in the world for those called by God to engage in this " working "; for even the most ignorant of men, he tells us, can forget everything to remain in utter silence, bathed in the love of God. To do this one need be no scholar; and the author expresses surprise that some people should consider his work abstruse and difficult. " For I hold him too lewd and too simple that cannot think and feel that himself is—not what himself is, but that himself is. For this is plainly proper to the lewdest cow, or to the most unreasonable beast—if it might be said, as it may not, that one were lewder or more unreasonable than another—for to feel their own proper being. Much more is it proper to man, the which is singularly endued with reason above all other beasts, for to think and for to feel his own proper being. " (P.C. 137:26) The work of contemplation, then, which is an experience of the meeting of one's own being with the being of God in utter simplicity, is no complicated affair in itself.

Yet *The Cloud* begins and ends with stern recommendations that this book be not given indiscriminately to all and sundry but only to those determined to devote themselves totally to the service of Christ:

> I charge and I beseech thee, with as much power and virtue as the bond of charity is sufficient to suffer, whatsoever thou be that this book shalt have in possession, whether by property, by keeping, or by hearing as a messenger, or else by borrowing, that inasmuch as in thee is by will and advisement, thou neither read it, write it, nor speak it, nor yet suffer it to be read, written, or spoken, by any other or to any other, unless it be by such a one or to such a one as hath (to thy supposing) in a true will and by a whole intent purposed him to be a perfect follower of Christ. And that not only in active living, but also in the sovereignest point of contemplative living the which is possible by grace to come to in this present life by a perfect soul yet abiding in this deadly body. (C. 1:8)

Moreover, all who read *The Cloud* are begged in charity to do so with great caution lest, in a matter of great delicacy, they be led into error; they should read it several times to grasp the true meaning—this is no book for " curious learned or unlearned men. " [9]

This cautious advice is taken quite literally by Augustine Baker who, while he has no hesitation in recommending the reading of *The Cloud* to the contemplative religious he is directing, yet insists that it must be read with care. He re-echoes the author in recommending that it be read several times for fear of error. In general, he feels about mystical works that " all are not fit to read them, " and he adds that " it may be questioned whether they be fit at all to be printed and published. " [10]

In short, the work of contemplation itself is supremely simple; but treatises on the subject are fraught with danger. Wherein lies this danger?

For one thing there is the fact that the mystical life demands a call or vocation. Scattered references throughout the English author's work indicate his awareness that premature excursions into the mystical life can lead to ludicrous, even disastrous, results. Not infrequently the author voices his concern lest some naive person may consider himself mystically in the cloud of unknowing when in fact his obscure state of darkness arises from some more commonplace source. Consequently, he feels the need of telling the inexperienced reader to beware.

Yet I do not think that this is the main problem. What troubles the author most (as he says explicitly in the quotations given) is that people, misunderstanding his doctrine, may be led into error. Anyone who has studied even a little mystical theology will realize that the subject is full of pitfalls: the mystic—and the mystical theologian—must choose his words with the utmost care, for a slight deviation from accuracy may lead to, or be interpreted as, pantheism or gnosticism or any one of a variety of ideologies to which the writer does not in fact subscribe. The English author had undoubtedly heard of the condemnation of Eckhart and was anxious to avoid a similar fate; but his scrupulously exact choice of words arises,

---

[9] This point is greatly emphasized by the author. See C. 2:9; C. 2:19; C. 130:3.

[10] McCann, p. 152. Augustine Baker, however, has no hesitation in recommending the book to his contemplative nuns: " To none of you that give yourselves to prayer and to the reading of good books would I forbid the reading of this book; but do rather commend unto you the reading of it. " (McCann, p. 154)

it seems to me, less from fear for his personal safety (undue preoccupation with which is hardly in keeping with the character of the man) than from a horror of leading people into error of which he had a genuine dislike. In short, he realizes that when one comes to analyze and theorize about this simple union with God called contemplation, tempests of misunderstanding and misinterpretation can all too easily arise.

But if misunderstanding was a real danger in fourteenth-century England where there was no conflict of cultures, how much greater in our modern world in which mystics of East and West are ranged side by side in inexpensive anthologies of mysticism and sold in translations throughout the world? Extracts from *The Cloud* now appear together with the *Upanishads*, the *Vedanta*, and the exponents of Zen. The similarity in process common to all forms of mysticism is readily noted, with the resulting tendency to interpret Buddhist mystics from a Christian background and Christian mystics from a Buddhist background. The author of *The Cloud* might well be surprised to find himself in such company. The very similarity of all forms of mysticism might make him even more grave in his cautious warnings to beware. " Beware of error here, I pray thee; for ever the nearer men touch the truth, the more wary must men be of error. " (C. 69:17) It is precisely when one comes nearest to the truth that one must make that rapier-like distinction separating the height of wisdom from the depth of foolishness.

MYSTICISM EAST AND WEST

With the introduction of Eastern religions into the West in the last century, many rationalist scholars uttered a joyful " eureka " at the discovery of a mysticism divorced from the encumbrance of sacraments and dogma but essentially the same as that of the great Christian mystics of the West. It was from this time that it became customary to quote Eckhart side by side with the *Upanishads* on the assumption that all who emptied their mind of images and concepts to remain in mystic silence were doing exactly the same thing. With the passage of time and deeper investigation, however, it became clear that the problem was not so simple as appeared at first sight; the experiments of Aldous Huxley with mescalin made people ask if all types of mysticism were, after all, quite the same. " Always it is *assumed*, " wrote R. C. Zaehner, " that mysticism is ' essentially one and the same '; rarely is any attempt made to substantiate the assumption, and rarely are the equally significant differences analyzed. We are greatly indebted to Mr. Huxley in that, in *The Doors of Perception*, he has carried the popular view to its logical conclusion; for since he has proved that preternatural experience of the most vivid kind can be acquired by the taking of drugs and since the state of the drug-taker's consciousness bears at least a superficial resemblance to that of the religious mystic in that time and space appear to be transcended, must it not follow that this experience is ' one and the same ' as that of the generally accredited mystics?

" Huxley could, and should, have gone farther. Mescalin is clinically used to produce artificially a state akin to schizo-phrenia, more specifically the manic phase of the manic-depressive psychosis. It must therefore follow, if we accept the fatal ' platitude ', that not only can ' mystical ' experience be obtained artificially by the taking of drugs, it is also naturally present in the manic. It must then follow that the vision of God of the mystical saint is ' one and the same ' as the hallucination of the lunatic. There would appear to be no way out, unless the original ' platitudinous ' premise is unsound. " [11]

Thus far Zaehner. And in the pages that follow he demonstrates rather convincingly that there are considerable differences in the various kinds of mysticism. And obviously in all this there is much common sense; for even a superficial reading of St. Teresa will show that within Christianity there are many grades and types of mystical experience; and Zen, too, admits of many varieties of enlightenment. It is difficult, then, to sympathize with those who lump everything together (including experiments with mescalin) to hold that they are " essentially one and the same "; and modern scholars have become increasingly conscious of the differences. While no one denies that in all forms of genuine mysticism there is a somewhat

[11] Zaehner, Introduction, p. xii.

similar psychological pattern justifying the generic term " mysticism " for a certain mental activity common to many countries and to many cultures, it becomes increasingly clear that the search for a *rapprochement* must be carried out at a deeper level than was at first envisaged: intelligent Christians become increasingly wary of premature attempts to baptize Buddhism, as true Buddhists become less eager to claim that Christianity and every other religion can be gathered under the all-embracing mantle of Zen.

For in attempting any synthesis between East and West we must never overlook the great fact of tradition. Every great mystic, as every genius, is like a huge iceberg with only a fraction of its vast bulk protruding from the waters. Below the surface lies the great mass of tradition upon which the whole thing rests. If we take the words of Oriental or Occidental mystics at their face value without reference to the tradition that gave them birth, we are in great danger of deceit.

For the author of *The Cloud* is like this huge iceberg, resting on a tradition that goes back not only to the Judaic civilization of the Old Testament but also to Aristotle and the Greeks; and the same can be said for Dogen and Hakuin and the rest, whose thought can only be understood in the light of its origin in China and in India. Those engaged in translating Christian mystics into Japanese assure us that it is precisely the mystical words common to both cultures (" nothing, " " the void, " " emptiness, " and so on) that are the most untranslatable; for in both worlds such words are surrounded by a nuance stemming from centuries of peculiar, mystical usage. If we casually take similar words and phrases from both and conclude that the underlying thought is the same, there arises the danger that the Buddhist remains a Buddhist using a Christian vocabulary, or that the Christian remains a Christian using a Buddhist vocabulary—and in this way little progress is made. [12]

TRADITION AND THE AUTHOR OF *The Cloud*

If, then, the modern reader wishes to read *The Cloud* and its accompanying treatises with that sympathetic charity the

[12] See, for example, *Spurious Parallels to Buddhist Philosophy* by Edward Conze in *Philosophy East and West*, Vol. XIII, No. 2.

author demands, he must keep in mind the society from which they sprang and the tradition that gave them birth.

The author belongs to a century made famous in the annals of spirituality by the names of Richard Rolle, Juliana of Norwich, and Walter Hilton in England; by Meister Eckhart, John Tauler, and Henry Suso in Germany; by Jan Ruysbroeck in Flanders; by Jacopone da Todi and Catherine of Siena in Italy. This is the age associated with the names of Angela de Foligno and Thomas à Kempis. It is an age in which, in spite of troubles and rumbling presages of a coming storm, Europe was deeply religious: faith penetrated to the very hearts of the people and influenced not only their art, music, and literature but every aspect of their lives. " Merry England " was saturated with a religious faith that breaks forth in *Piers Plowman* and the *Canterbury Tales*: Chaucer may laugh good-humoredly at the foibles of nuns and friars, but he accepted the established religion with an unquestioning mind. Such was the society in which the author of *The Cloud* lived and wrote: both he and his public took for granted a Church, a faith, and a sacramental life that many of his modern readers will less easily recognize.

Moreover, this English author was a thoroughgoing medieval, steeped in the spirit of his times and imbued with its tradition. So many of his words, phrases, and ideas are also found in *The Imitation of Christ*, in the *De adhaerendo Deo*, in the writings of the Rhineland mystics, and the other devotional treatises of the time that one immediately sees him as part of a great current of medieval spirituality. He was aware, too, of what was being said and thought throughout Christendom, for there was no " splendid isolation " at that time; British monks and scholars frequenting the great centers of learning throughout Europe.

If proof were needed of his traditionalist character, one has but to mention his constant reference not only to the Scriptures but also to Augustine, Dionysius, Gregory, Bernard, Aquinas, Richard of St. Victor, and the rest. Modesty and an A Kempis-like fear of vanity forbid him from quoting these authors at length, but he cannot escape referring to their works and reflecting their thought. And again, the wealth of tradition underlying his writings breaks through in the figures and illustrations that fill his pages. The "cloud of unknowing" itself, the Martha-Mary motif, the picture of Moses ascending the mountain, the notion of the soul as a mirror in which one can see God, the comparison of mystical prayer to sleep, the "naked intent of the will, " the "chaste and perfect love of God, " the "sovereign point of the spirit "—all these phrases are pregnant with tradition, used by so many Christian authors that it is well-nigh impossible to state categorically from whom the English author is borrowing or from whom he chiefly draws his inspiration.

But when one comes to study this author in his historical setting, there arises another point that here deserves mention, namely, his striking similarity to St. John of the Cross. Quite a few commentators have adverted to this, the English author being spoken of as a St. John of the Cross two centuries before his time. [13] For it is true that almost every detail of his doctrine is paralleled in the later Spanish mystic—and not only the doctrine but even the words and phrases are in many cases identical. How account for this remarkable affinity?

One obvious answer is that both writers are Christian mystics attempting to describe a similar experience; so what more natural than that they should speak in the same way? Yet this, however true, does not explain everything; and there is another point to be remembered. St. John of the Cross, we know, far from being a solitary voice in the wilderness, is the heir to a great tradition. Through his pages, speak Augustine, Dionysius, the Victorines, Tauler, Ruysbroeck, and the rest; and we know, moreover, that he was an unrelenting Thomist, educated by the Dominicans at the University of Salamanca. In other words it is, once again, the great stream of tradition that has formed the minds of these two men, both being part of an apophatic current that has flowed through Christian culture, breaking down the barriers of space and time separating fourteenth-century England and sixteenth-century Spain; nor have its surging waves lost their power in the twentieth-century world.

[13] This similarity has been pointed out by such widely different personalities as Dom Chapman, Aldous Huxley, Garrigou-Lagrange, and David Knowles.

SCOPE OF THE PRESENT WORK

The pages that follow attempt to study the mystical doctrine
of the author of *The Cloud* against its background of medieval
theology and in the light of Christian tradition, giving special
attention to the relationship between the Englishman's
mysticism and Christianity as lived by the simplest person
who believes. Mysticism is often regarded as something
esoteric, something different from the ordinary religious belief
of the mass—but Augustine Baker, who knew and loved *The
Cloud* so well, insists that its mysticism is "ordinary." By
this he seems to have meant that it can be reduced to a system,
being no more than an intensification of the ordinary Christian
life. Consequently, in this work I have attempted to systema-
tize the author's thought, considering it in the light of the
theology of the time.

    In the course of this study I have occasion to refer to Zen—
and that for two reasons. First, because with the so-called
"Zen boom" witnessed in the last decade, comparisons
between Zen and the doctrine of *The Cloud* have been made
and I feel it necessary to consider them. Secondly, since Zen
fills the atmosphere in which these pages are written, it is
natural that comparisons should suggest themselves. I would
like to stress, however, that it is not my intention here to
make original contribution to the existing Zen scholarship:
I am more concerned with Zen-influenced attempts to interpret
The Cloud than with the phenomenon of Zen itself. I have
already referred to the differences between Oriental and
Occidental mysticism, differences stemming from widely
diversified traditions; but I have no intention of going to the
extreme of asserting that there is no similarity, no meeting
point between East and West in this line. Such a position would
be untenable.

    That as a psychological process there can indeed be a great
similarity between many forms of mysticism is recognized by
St. Thomas himself who, defining *contemplatio* more widely
than the English author as "a simple intuition of the truth"
(simplex intuitus veritatis), includes within its scope the
contemplation of a variety of thinkers from Aristotle to

Augustine and from Plotinus to Richard of St. Victor. His *contemplatio* covers not only the experiences of the Christian mystics but also those of the Greeks; and this would indicate that Aquinas holds for a basic psychological similarity in all great intuitive experiences irrespective of whether or not the subject was a Christian. Obviously enough, the human psychology will usually work according to a fixed pattern, nor does faith provide man with utterly new psychic processes— unless, of course, God makes some special intervention which is a somewhat unusual case not to be catered for in a *systematic* study of mysticism. This being so, there seems to be no reason why the definition of St. Thomas should not apply equally well to Zen and other genuine intuitive experiences.

Yet St. Thomas did not hold that all contemplation was essentially one and the same. For him there was an all-important element distinguishing the teaching of Aristotle from that of the Gospel—and this element was supernatural faith and love. It was precisely this that constituted the apex of Christian wisdom, separating it from any wisdom accessible to the unaided human powers. But for him, though love gives a new and powerful motivation, the gifts of God do not normally do violence to any psychological process but penetrate the human psychology like a powerful ray enlightening the delicate mechanism of an engine without disturbing its ordinary working. In this way of thinking, it is possible for God's invitation to the mystical life to come in an ordinary way; that is, when God, providentially intervening in the life of man, faithfully follows His own psychological laws and draws up man's love to the cloud. In short, the supernatural can often be ordinary. It can, of course, also be extraordinary, when God dispenses from or transcends the ordinary laws of psychology; but is the mysticism of *The Cloud* of this nature? To what extent does this supernatural faith and love that *elevate* nature interfere with its ordinary working?

It is hoped that the pages which follow will help toward the understanding of this good Englishman who, maligned by scrupulous theologians of the fourteenth century, could be no less misinterpreted in the twentieth.

PART I

Knowledge

THE PROBLEM OF UNKNOWING

In East and West the language of the mystics is full of paradox. Concepts of " light " and " darkness, " " vision " and " blindness, " " all " and " nothing, " " knowledge " and " ignorance " keep recurring with a frequency that is sometimes bewildering. The author of *The Cloud*, then, is true to type in constantly playing on the paradoxical theme of " knowing " and " unknowing. " Toward the end of *The Cloud* he strikes the keynote of his message with an appeal to Dionysius:

And therefore St. Denis said, " The most godly knowing of God is that which is known by unknowing. " (C. 125:11)

We know God, yet we do not know Him; we know Him by unknowing; we know Him in darkness; we know Him by love. The idea that runs like a refrain through the work of the English author is expressed in the terse words: " ...for why he may well be loved, but not thought. " (C. 26:3) And at the beginning of *The Cloud* he writes:

For of all other creatures and their works — yea, and of the works of God himself — may a man through grace have fulness of knowing, and well can he think of them; but of God himself can no man think. And therefore I would leave all that thing that I can think, and choose to my love that thing that I cannot think. (C. 25:18)

Since God cannot be known by any activity of the reasoning power, the English author tells his disciple to bury all conceptual thinking and rational discourse beneath a cloud of forgetting; he keeps emphasizing that no amount of syllogistic thinking will bring a man to God as He is in Himself. Therefore, forgetting everything, he should think of nothing. Forget, forget, forget, is the advice of the author. Empty your mind of all images, and thus you will allow to rise in your heart "the blind stirring of love" that will pierce the cloud of unknowing bringing to you a knowledge, supraconceptual and dark, that is the supreme wisdom. Normally, in the abandonment of conceptual knowledge, the mind will be dark though filled with love; sometimes, however, God may pierce the cloud with a "beam of ghostly light" filling the contemplative with an intense and inexpressible joy, knowledge, and love.

Such, in brief, is the doctrine of the English author. Read against a background of twentieth-century thought, his words are open to a variety of interpretations. It is well known that in Zen Buddhism there are many parallels to the above in thought and expression [1]; and, moreover, since the fourteenth century, Western idealism has had much to say about knowing and unknowing. First of all, then, I would like to set forth some of the interpretations that have been made, or might be made, in our time; then I shall try to outline the traditional doctrine in which the English author must have been educated, for it filled the air of the fourteenth century in which he lived.

SOME MODERN INTERPRETATIONS

REJECTION OF DOGMA

It has already been said that there is a strong parallel between the unknowing of *The Cloud* and the unknowing of Zen.

---

[1] See, for example, Seng-chao, in the treatise *On Prajña Not Being Knowledge.* Prajña, he says, is "the illuminating power of not-knowledge" that reveals true reality. See Dumoulin [1], p. 59.

Japanese writers generally distinguish between Zen and Zen Buddhism. The latter is a religion containing doctrine, a philosophy of life, and axioms for its practice; Zen, on the other hand, " is. " Its whole center is the enlightenment, or *satori*, about which no one can speak unless he himself has had the experience—and even he can say very little. It crashes upon the mind like a peal of thunder or a flash of lightning; it is " a turning point in one's life, " " a mental revolution, " " a fiery baptism of spirit, " but its content is inexpressible in human language. [2] The descriptions given by Zen masters are not unlike that of the beam of ghostly light piercing the cloud of unknowing. Zen, however, is divorced from all schemes of thought, all philosophies of life, all religious dogma—according to Dr. Suzuki, it should not even be called mysticism. And since it is so divorced from all religion, it can be practiced (and is practiced) by people who hold no allegiance to Zen Buddhism: it is practiced by a variety of people from atheists to Catholic priests. [3]

Since, then, Zen claims to be above all dogma and creed (Suzuki describes it as a wafting cloud [4]), some people may be tempted to conclude that Christian mysticism also is above all creeds, dogma, and ritual. Indeed, this transference from Zen to Christian mysticism is made by Suzuki himself. Speaking of the vocabulary of Christian mysticism, " flame of love, a wonderful love shed in the heart, embrace, the beloved, bride, bridegroom, spiritual matrimony, Father, God, the Son of God, God's child etc., " he continues:

[2] " As satori strikes at the primary fact of existence, its attainment marks a turning point in one's life. The attainment, however, must be thorough-going and clear-cut in order to produce a satisfactory result. To deserve the name ' satori ' the mental revolution must be so complete as to make one really and sincerely feel that there took place a fiery baptism of the spirit. " (Suzuki [1], Essay V, *Satori*, v, p. 231).

[3] Suzuki insists that Zen is divorced from history and from metaphysics. Dumoulin, however, denies this, saying that Suzuki's own works contain much material which refutes his thesis that Zen is without metaphysics... (Dumoulin [1], p. 271). Indeed, it seems impossible to cut off an experience from the philosophy and tradition that gave it birth. This is true also of Christian mysticism.

[4] " We may say that Christianity is monotheistic, and the Vedanta pantheistic; but we cannot make a similar assertion about Zen. Zen is neither monotheistic nor pantheistic; Zen defies all such designations. Hence there is no object in Zen upon which to fix the thought. Zen is a wafting cloud in the sky. " (Suzuki [4], p. 41).

We may say that all these terms are interpretations based on a definite system of thought and really have nothing to do with the experience itself. [5]

The conclusion reached is that the Trinity, the Incarnation, and other dogmas are interpretations built on the personal philosophy of the mystic; but his experience might well be expressed in Buddhist philosophical terms or in any other— for " enlightenment " is above and superior to all dogmatic formulations.

Applying this way of thinking to *The Cloud*, some recent writers have made its author a rebel against dogma and (a fortiori) against the Church. After all, does he not clearly tell his disciple to " forget " the Church's dogmas? Does he not even instruct him to abandon meditation on the Passion of Christ? What can the cloud of forgetting be except a ruthless cutting away of those religious dogmas that ordinary Christians esteem so much?

Mr. Aldous Huxley, who shows considerable insight into the kind of prayer taught in *The Cloud*, seems to subscribe to this way of thinking. He contrasts those mystics who were truly Catholic with those " of the Dionysian tradition " (in which he includes the English author of *The Cloud*) who abandoned their mystical vocation:

> The contemplatives of the Dionysian tradition ... had adapted dogma to their own experience, with the result that, in so far as they were advanced mystics, they had ceased to be specifically Catholic. To a non-Christian, this seems the supremely important, the eminently encouraging fact about mysticism — that it provides the basis for a religion free from inacceptable dogmas, which themselves are contingent upon ill established and arbitrarily interpreted facts. [6]

Here the author of *The Cloud* (being in " the Dionysian tradition ") insofar as he is an advanced mystic ceases to be specifically Catholic, adapting dogma to his own experience.

In this interpretation, Aldous Huxley is not, of course, alone. Another commentator, who makes interesting com-

[5] Suzuki [2], p. 19.
[6] Huxley [1], p. 97.

parisons between the prayer of *The Cloud* and Zen, seems to hold the opinion that the English author uses Christian dogma as a point of departure (just as a believer of another religion might use the teachings of *his* faith) but that the enlightenment itself has nothing to do with the preparatory doctrine. The Bible and the teaching of the Church are (in his opinion) accessories, not intrinsically connected with the mystical experience to which the author is leading; they have only a transitory significance and the aim of his work is " to lead beyond all theological conceptions and doctrines, and beyond all attachment to religious objects and observances. " [7]

It is true, of course, that the author is leading to a type of knowledge that is without images and is above concepts; but do his references to Jesus and to the nature of God have only transitory significance?

In short, the problem is: Is the mystical prayer taught by the author of *The Cloud* something divorced from the dogmas of the Church? Or is it, perhaps, a deeper penetration into those very mysteries expressed in human language by the Church's dogmatic formulation?

REASON AND IRRATIONALITY

Another point in the English author's works that may give rise to a variety of interpretations is his tendency to attack the discursive intellect and the use of the natural faculties. Reasoning and thinking and the use of one's " wits " are of no use in bringing one to the knowledge and love he is teaching. Not only are they of no use; they are a positive hindrance, and the would-be contemplative must give them up; for (as Richard of St. Victor has said) when contemplation is born, reason dies. [8] Mystical prayer is above any natural activity of man's human faculties.

Once again, statements very similar to the above are made in Zen. Suzuki seems to mean something rather similar when he says that " satori is not a conclusion to be reached by

[7] Progoff, p. 26.
[8] " And as soon as a soul is touched with very contemplation... surely and verily right then dieth all man's reason. " (P.C. 150:13)

reasoning and defies all intellectual determination. Those who have experienced it are always at a loss to explain it coherently or logically ";[9] and he says of Zen: " There is nothing here suggestive of cool reasoning and quiet metaphysical or epistemological analysis.... Therefore, the outcome also defies intellection or conceptualization. "[10] The problem arises when he goes further, making statements that (taken, at any rate, at their face value) deny the very validity of human reasoning. Take, for instance, the following:

> According to the philosophy of Zen, we are too much of a slave to the conventional way of thinking, which is dualistic through and through. No interpenetration is allowed, there takes place no fusing of opposites in our everyday logic. What belongs to God is not of this world, and what is of this world is incompatible with the divine. Black is not white, and white is not black. Tiger is tiger; and cat is cat; and they will never be one. Water flows, a mountain towers. This is the way things or ideas go in this universe of the senses and syllogisms. Zen, however, upsets this scheme of thought, and substitutes a new one in which there exists no logic, no dualistic arrangement of ideas. [11]

Some phrases used by the author of *The Cloud*, if read side by side with Suzuki, might lead to the conclusion that he too rejects " the conventional way of thinking, " that he does not trust " this universe of senses and syllogisms, " that he leads to a state " in which there exists no logic, no dualistic arrangement of ideas. " It might be thought, then, that he teaches that there are two truths: a relative and inferior truth found in the knowledge of everyday life, and an absolute, real truth found at the summit of the mystical life shattering the conceptions we have received from the ordinary use of senses and intellect.

This interpretation is all the more inviting if one reflects (as a commentator on *The Cloud* has pointed out [12]) that just as the author's mysticism is preceded by " pious meditation " on the Passion of Christ, so the Zen enlightenment is preceded by the *kōan*.

[9] Suzuki [2], p. 16.
[10] *Ibid.*
[11] Suzuki [1], p. 255.
[12] Progoff, p. 33.

Now the *kōan* is, in the words of Professor Dumoulin, " one great mockery of the rules of logic. " [13] An example of one of these paradoxical questions to which there is no logical answer is: " A monk asked T'ung-shan, ' Who is the Buddha? ' ' Three chin of flax. ' " And the explanation of this is given in a noted Zen textbook, *Hekiganshu:*

> There are some people these days who do not truly understand this kōan; this is because there is no crack in it to insert their intellectual teeth. By this I mean that it is altogether too plain and tasteless. Various answers have been given by different masters to the question, " What is the Buddha? " One said, " He sits in the Buddha Hall. " Another said, " The one endowed with the thirty-two marks of excellence. " Still another, " A bamboo-root whip. " None, however, can excel T'ung-shan's " three chin of flax, " as regards its irrationality which cuts off all passage of speculation. [14]

Much has been written about the psychology of the *kōan*; in the interpretation of C. G. Jung, for example, the keynote in the above would be that the irrationality of the answer " cuts off all passage of speculation " and prepares the mind for a deeper intuition. It is not my intention to enter into that here, but merely to ask if in the advice given by the author of *The Cloud* and in his constant disparagement of logical thinking there is anything akin to this apparent denial or destruction of logical thinking. Moreover, the comparison of the *kōan* with the " pious meditations " of *The Cloud* has repercussions on the question of dogma and mysticism already treated; for the Zen masters claim that there is no connection between the content of the *kōan* and the enlightenment to which it leads. If, stretching the comparison, it is stated that there is no connection between discursive meditation on the Passion and the enlightenment of Christian mysticism, we are back again to the rejection of dogma.

---

[13] Dumoulin [1], p. 129.
[14] Suzuki [1], p. 71, 72. Also: " The worst enemy of Zen experience, at least in the beginning, is the intellect which consists in discriminating subject from object. The discriminating intellect, therefore, must be cut short if Zen consciousness is to unfold itself, and the kōan is constructed eminently to serve this end " (*Ibid.*, p. 71).

THE PROBLEM OF TECHNIQUE

A final problem arises from the similarity in technique in the works of the English author and in Zen. Ejo, the greatest disciple of the Zen master Dogen, gives practical advice that reminds one of the cloud of forgetting:

> Abandon your body and soul into the abundance of light sent from above and give no thought to them. Do not seek for enlightenment nor reject illusion; do not try to avoid distractions nor attach yourself to them nor dwell on them. Just sit with perfect composure. If you do not prolong distractions voluntarily, how should they occur by themselves? Only sit like the great void or fire, breathing naturally; do not concern yourself with anything whatever; just keep sitting. Even though there may arise eighty-four thousand distractions, if you take no heed of them and leave them alone, every distraction will be turned into the divine light of Prajña. This principle applies not only to the state of sitting but also to that of walking. You would be led by light at every step. I do not mean that you would use discretion at every step but that you would be like a completely dead man twenty-four hours a day, entirely devoid of selfish will and discretion. [15]

The technique here advocated is not unlike that of the English author; and that this technique has been more highly developed in the Orient than in the West can be seen from the following words of Dogen:

> Put your right hand on your left thigh, palm up, and let it hold the four fingers of your left hand so that the left thumb may press down the right thumb. Hold your body straight. Lean not to the left nor the right. Do not tip forward nor bend to the back. Your ears should be at right angles to your shoulders, and your nose must be on a straight line with the navel. Keep your tongue at the roof of your mouth and close your lips and teeth firmly. Keep your eyes slightly open, and breathe through your nostrils.
> Before you begin meditation, move your body from right to left a few times, then take several slow, deep breaths. Hold your body erect, allowing your breathing to become normal again. Many thoughts will crowd into your mind... just ignore them and they will soon vanish. Do not allow the mind to

[15] Quoted in Akiyama, pp. 167-168.

become negative, or you will fall asleep. Think that which you cannot think. In other words, think nothing. This is the proper way to meditate according to Zen teaching. [16]

The above with its command to " think nothing " is a highly developed form of the cloud of forgetting; the psychological similarity is inescapable. The problem is that our modern age, preoccupied as it is with psychology, inclines to see only technique, overlooking other aspects of mystical prayer. Is the prayer of the author of *The Cloud only* a technique? Or is there something more important in it?

TRADITIONAL CHRISTIAN TEACHING

I have tried to emphasize that in order to understand the author of *The Cloud* it is necessary to keep in mind that he did not belong to the twentieth century but to fourteenth-century England. While Japanese thought has always shown a tendency to disparage discursive reasoning (and especially metaphysical thinking) of which Zen is one expression [17] the thought-stream in which the English author is situated contains a glorification of dialectical thinking going back to Aristotle and the Greeks; and in this stream, authors like the Victorines and A Kempis who inveigh against the vanity of natural learning (the validity of which they never question) are often reacting against certain currents in the thought of their time.

As for " contemplation " and " contemplative life, " when the English author uses these words he is employing a vocabulary that has a long and complicated history in European thought: it is no small task to distangle the various meanings of " contemplation. "

---

[16] Senzaki, p. 22.

[17] Speaking of the way of thinking of the Japanese, Nakamura devotes one chapter to *Irrationalistic Tendencies* that he lists in the following way: " (1) The tendency to be illogical (to neglect logical rules). (2) Lack of the ability to think with logical coherence. (3) Immaturity of logic in Japan. (4) Some hopes for development of logical thinking in Japan. (5) Intuitive and emotional tendencies. (6) Lack of ability of forming complicated ideas. (7) Fondness for simple symbolic expressions. (8) The lack of knowledge concerning the objective order. " (Nakamura, p. 5 [Contents])

CONTEMPLATION

Plato and Aristotle had spoken of contemplation (θεωρία) and the contemplative life (βίος θεωρητικός) as the acme of human endeavor. In the *Symposium* Plato speaks of the ascent of the mind to the source of all goodness and beauty; and Aristotle, following his master's teaching, treats of contemplation as the highest activity of man in the *Nicomachean Ethics*. In his description of the joys of the contemplative life the Stagirite, usually so dry and scientific, verges on poetry— in the highest moment of contemplation man is like God: it is sad that he must return to the humdrum life of mortal men, for in this moment man is akin to Mind (νοῦς) itself; namely, God. Obviously, Aristotle was no mystic in the Christian sense of the word, nor is his contemplation religious; but his way of thinking, as well as the way of thinking of his master, Plato, was to exercise great influence on subsequent Christian thought. This influence comes in great part through neoplatonism: for Plotinus, contemplation is a return to the One from which man emanated and, though it seems to involve not only intellection but also love, it is philosophical rather than religious in nature.

Influenced by this way of thinking, the Fathers of the Church (notably Origen and Clement of Alexandria) use the word contemplation (θεωρία) for the consideration of Christian truths. Their contemplation demands faith, for it is a penetration of the mysteries of the life of Christ; it has two divisions only later clearly distinguished—a contemplation accessible to anyone with faith and another special form of prayer subsequently called infused contemplation.

This latter has always been regarded as a special gift of God, being a high form of union with Him. Theologically, this kind of prayer was regarded as the climax in the soul's ascent to God and was treated as such by the great theologians from Augustine and Bernard to Bonaventure and Aquinas. With the German mystics of the Rhineland, however, this mystical theology was separated from the ordinary theology, being treated as a special science or branch of sacred learning.

Broadly speaking, then, we can say that there are three

kinds of contemplation: one is philosophical and its peak-point is a metaphysical experience of being; the second has for its object Christian dogmas the inner meaning of which it savors with the light of faith; the third is a high form of union with God, conferred gratuitously upon His intimate friends. A consideration of these three kinds of contemplation helps us to understand the traditional relationship between reason, dogma, and mysticism.

REASON, DOGMA, MYSTICISM

Corresponding to these three grades of contemplation were three kinds of wisdom: metaphysical, dogmatic, and mystical.

The first kind of wisdom is the science by which, with Aristotle, one can rise from the knowledge of creatures by causality to the Supreme Being who is the source of existence; this is " natural theology, " found also in St. Paul. [18] While it gives true analogical knowledge of God, it does not bring us to God as He is in Himself; that is to say, the mind does not here attain directly to God but only through creatures, His effects, so that we can say that God is " unknown "—He is unknown as He is in Himself.

The second kind of wisdom, being built on Divine revelation, rises above natural knowledge. This is the wisdom of faith that comes from hearing *(ex auditu)* and is grasped by the human faculties that (aided by the infused light which is called *lumen fidei)* penetrate deeply into the mysteries of revelation: the believer has a deeper knowledge than the catechumen who knows everything but does not yet believe.

The third kind of wisdom is mystical: this is experimental knowledge of God as He is in Himself, the apophatic mystics speak of it as silent, supraconceptual, dark, infused by God Himself. This is the highest wisdom man can attain to in this life; in comparison with it (in the words of the author of *The Cloud)* natural knowledge is " but feigned folly formed in fantasy, as far from the very certainty when the ghostly sun shineth, as the darkness of the moonshine in a mist at

[18] Rom 1:20.

midwinter's night from the brightness of the sunbeam in the clearest time of midsummer day. " (P.C. 146:2) Mystics will often say that *by comparison* with what they have seen in prayer, scientific knowledge and theology are like " ignorance " or (as St. Thomas himself said) like " straw. "

The point to be stressed here, however, is that in the Catholic tradition all three kinds of knowledge or wisdom are valid and their object is precisely the same; so far from contradicting, they complement one another. If some of the interpretations of *The Cloud* quoted above were true, then the author would reject the first two wisdoms in favor of the third; or he might hold for an illusory world and a real world found through enlightenment. But this is far from the medieval way of thinking. The traditional position was that there is only one truth, known imperfectly by reason, more clearly by faith, more clearly still by mystical experience, and perfectly in the beatific vision. Faith does not contradict reason but builds on it; mystical knowledge does not contradict reason or revelation but builds on them. Far from being a rejection of dogma, it is a supraconceptual penetration of those mysteries that are formulated conceptually (and, for that reason, imperfectly) in dogma.

A figure of the mystic is Moses who, ascending into the darkness, draws nearer to God but never rejects the knowledge he had while below with his people. It is simply that he comes closer to that same God whom he previously knew from afar by reason and revelation; and in the same way the mystic denies nothing of reason or of faith but approaches in love the same God the truths about whom these dogmas express. The mystical life, in short, is no more than a development of the ordinary Christian life: it is its highest point.

Almost all the greatest mystics describe the peak-point of their experience as some kind of fruition of that mystery expressed in the central Christian dogma: the Blessed Trinity. This is true not only of Augustine, Bernard, Bonaventure, and so on, but also of the mystics of " the Dionysian tradition ": Dionysius himself begins his *Mystica theologia* with a Trinitarian invocation, and this Trinitarian line is followed by Eckhart, Ruysbroeck, and the other apophatic mystics. It is against this background of the unity of truth that we must read the author of *The Cloud.*

Technique

Technique in mysticism was not unknown to medieval Christianity, though it was less highly developed than in the Orient. The technique of emptying the mind of all images was always considered a necessary condition for the development of mystical prayer; but the medievals were aware that mystical prayer was not *only* a question of technique which was its less important aspect. Emptying the mind of ideas was only a preparation for the reception of infused knowledge and love from God; and anyone who was not receiving this infused gift should not presume to remain in silent emptiness. This point was made especially by Ruysbroeck with whose thought the author of *The Cloud* may well have been familiar. The Flemish mystic speaks of a form of rest that may be purely natural, not induced by the action of God on the soul. " When a man is bare and imageless in his senses, and empty and idle in his higher powers, he enters into rest through mere nature; and this rest may be found and possessed within themselves in mere nature by all creatures, without the grace of God, whenever they can strip themselves of images and activity. " [19] Ruysbroeck does not consider this rest wrong in itself, but it has its dangers. " This rest is in itself no sin; for it exists in all men by nature, whenever they make themselves empty. But when a man wishes to practise and possess it without acts of virtue, he falls into spiritual pride and a self-complacency, from which he seldom recovers. " [20] His contrast between this vacancy and mystical prayer is worth quoting at length:

> Such a rest is nought else than an idleness, into which the man has fallen, and in which he forgets himself and God and all things in all that has to do with activity. This rest is wholly contrary to the supernatural rest, which one possesses in God... And in this natural rest one cannot find God, but it certainly

[19] *Adornment of the Spiritual Marriage,* c. LXVI.
[20] *Ibid.*

leads a man into a bare vacancy, which may be found by... all men, how wicked soever they may be, if they can live in their sins without the reproach of their conscience, and can empty themselves of every image and of all activity. In this bare vacancy the rest is pleasant and great. [21]

From this it can be seen that the technique of emptying the mind of thoughts and images is of no use, is even dangerous, unless that same mind is filled with a very special love of God. The tradition that underlies *The Cloud* and to which the author frequently refers is that no one can come to this mystical rest who has not spent a long time in ordinary meditation on the mysteries of Christ, devoting himself to penance and works of virtue. As to the moment when one could be permitted to abandon discursive meditation and allow one's mind and heart to be filled with the dark prayer of silence, there were many tests to discern this vocation. One finds oneself unable to meditate, the faculties being somehow hindered and filled with a silent longing for God; dissatisfied with the pleasure afforded by created things, one longs for solitude that alone provides peace and rest.

By signs such as these, the soul and its director may know that *God is leading it* to the life of contemplation and that it is licit to remain silent, all images buried beneath a cloud of forgetting. But, as can be seen, the loving action of God is the all-important thing; the emptying of the mind is no more than the small co-operation of the creature with his Creator.

Such is the background to the mystical life of fourteenth-century Europe. We must now consider how the English author fits into this framework. We shall first consider his paradoxical statement that, on the one hand, God cannot be known and, on the other hand, He can be known by unknowing. Then we shall examine the meaning of the cloud and the dark knowledge that it symbolizes. Finally, we shall consider the relationship of this dark knowledge to two fundamental dogmas: the Incarnation and the Church.

[21] *Ibid.*

2

THE CLOUD OF FORGETTING

KNOWLEDGE BY NEGATION

It has already been said that the English author belongs to the apophatic school of mysticism, greatly influenced by Dionysius the Areopagite. Toward the end of *The Cloud* he pays his debt to Dionysius in the following words:

> And truly, whoso will look in Denis' book, he will find that his words clearly confirm all that I have said or shall say, from the beginning of this treatise to the end. (C. 125:13)

Recent scholars have pointed out, however, that he was less Dionysian than he himself supposed. One reason for this is that no medieval could get an objective view of the writings of the Areopagite. Only comparatively recently was it established with certainty that Dionysius was a Syrian monk of the early sixth century; for the medievals he was St. Paul's convert writing to Timothy with an authority close to that of the Scriptures themselves. [1] His writings had influenced not

---

[1] Recent study shows that pseudo-Dionysius took part of his doctrine from Gregory of Nyssa—and this doctrine goes back to Origen and Clement of Alexandria. As for the Indian influence on neoplatonism, this is a question that has not yet been decided. In general, history of the relationship between India and the Mediterranean indicates mutual influence; but it is not easy to say which way this influence worked. Modern scholars point to Gnostic and Hellenistic influences on the development of Buddhism.

only the Greek mystics, notably Maximus the Confessor in the eighth century, but also after the translation of John Scotus Erigena in 877 they made an incalculable impact on the whole Latin Church. Commentaries were multiplied; Sts. Albert, Thomas, and Bonaventure received Dionysian influence; even Dante sang the praises of the Areopagite. Consequently, the Dionysius who came to the author of *The Cloud*, like the Aristotle who sometimes comes to modern scholastics, was overlaid with a tradition some of which he himself might not have recognized. Moreover, the English author makes no secret of the fact that he will not follow the " naked letter " of Dionysius' book; he intends to interpret it himself and to make use of other interpreters. He almost certainly did not read the original text of Dionysius but used the Latin translation of Joannes Sarracenus together with the commentary of Thomas Gallus, Abbot of Vercelli.

Yet, granted that Dionysius has been somewhat embellished in the years that elapse between the sixth century and the fourteenth, it still remains true that his basic ideas are fundamental to the thought of the author of *The Cloud*. We shall, therefore, first briefly set forth his doctrine.

NEGATIVE KNOWLEDGE AND DIONYSIUS

According to Dionysius, there are two ways in which man can know God: one is the way of reason (λόγος); the other is the way of mystical contemplation (μυστικὸν θέαμα). Rational knowledge of God is obtained through speculative theology and philosophy; but mystical knowledge is greatly superior to this, giving a knowledge of God that is intuitive and ineffable. Hence, it is called " mystical " or " hidden. " Dionysius speaks much of the transcendence of God, stressing the fact that by reasoning we know little about Him; but he never denies the power of discursive reason to come to the knowledge of God, merely emphasizing the superiority of mystical knowledge.

In fact, he teaches two ways of knowing God by reason— one affirmative and the other negative. We can affirm of God all the good that can be affirmed of His creation, saying that He is holy, wise, benevolent, that He is light and life. All these things come from God, so we can affirm that the source possesses their perfections in a higher way. But (and this is the point stressed by Dionysius) there is also a negative way of knowing God; since he is above all His creatures. He is wise, but with a wisdom different from that of men; His beauty, goodness, and truth are different from those we know. So, in a sense, God is unlike anything we know: we must keep in mind that the ideas we have of Him are totally inadequate to contain Him.

But there is yet a higher way of knowing God. " Besides the knowledge of God obtained by processes of philosophical and theological speculation, there is that most divine knowledge of God which takes place through ignorance "; in this knowledge the intellect is illuminated by " the insearchable depth of wisdom. " Such knowledge is not found in books nor can it be obtained by human effort, for it is a divine gift. Man, however, can prepare himself to receive it; and this he does by prayer and purification. Here is his advice:

> Do thou, then, in the intent practice of mystic contemplation, leave behind the senses and the operations of the intellect, and all things that the senses or the intellect can perceive, and all things which are not and things which are, and strain upwards in unknowing, as far as may be, towards the union with Him Who is above all things and knowledge. For by unceasing and absolute withdrawal from thyself and all things in purity, abandoning all and set free from all, thou shalt be borne up to the ray of divine Darkness that surpasseth all being. [2]

The point of Dionysius is that since the human senses and intellect are incapable of attaining to God, they must be " emptied " of creatures or purified in order that God may pour His light into them. In this sense they are in complete darkness in regard to created things but they are at the same time filled with light from God. Hence, we can say that " The Divine Darkness is the unapproachable light in which God is said to dwell. " When the faculties are emptied of all human knowledge there reigns in the soul a " mystic silence " leading

[2] *De myst. theol.*, I, 1.

it to the climax that is union with God and the vision of Him as He is in Himself.

Such is the doctrine that flows through the apophatic mystics to the time of St. John of the Cross. It is important to note three things: first, that Dionysius recognizes the validity of reason and theology; second, he asserts that reason and philosophy give very inadequate knowledge of God; third, his " unknowing " or ignorance means that one must (in time of prayer) abandon human, conceptual knowledge for the reception of divine, infused knowledge.

NEGATIVE KNOWLEDGE AND *Hid Divinity*

Hid Divinity, the middle English translation of *Mystica theologia*, follows Dionysius in teaching how God may be known in the highest possible way. *Affirming Divinity* (the English translation of *Theologia affirmativa*) has been treated of elsewhere, so the present work, the author tells us, will deal with *Denying Divinity (Theologia negativa)* and *Hid Divinity*.

Advancing on Dionysius, the English author asserts that in addition to affirming and denying there is another extremely important element in " hid divinity, " namely, love. This is the most important factor in all contemplative prayer—it has been clearly put into Dionysian thought by Thomas Gallus and others. Indeed, following the commentary of Thomas Gallus, the English author makes some additions to the text to remind his reader that love, or " affection " as he calls it, rises up to God when intellect stays behind:

> Thou shalt be drawn up *above mind in affection* to the sovereign-substantial beam of the godly darkness, all things thus done away. (H.D. 3:16)

In his opening, too, he has spoken of " affection above mind, " as if to tell us that love soars up to God beyond the powers of the mind, attaining to a higher knowledge. This point is of great importance: " denying divinity " in the mystics can only be understood in the light of a higher knowledge that comes from love. It is precisely because of his love, his

" singularity of affection, " that Moses can climb the mountain in the darkness of unknowing; and it is because of his love that he is able to " feel in experience the presence of him that is above all things "; it is only because of love that he is allowed to abandon all natural knowledge, to deny it, to shut it out. The passage in which the author states this is worth quoting, for it shows how all natural knowledge is abandoned by Moses only because he experiences God in love:

> In this time it was that Moses *in singularity of affection* was separated from these before said chosen priests, and entered by himself the darkness of unknowing, the which darkness is verily hid; in *the which he shuts out all knowable knowing.* And surely he is made (in a manner that is invisible and ungropable) for *to feel in experience the presence of him that is above all things,* not having feeling nor thinking of no being nor yet of himself. But, in avoiding of all knowing that is still unknowing, he is knitted unto him in the best manner; and in that that he knoweth nothing, he is made to be knowing above mind. (H.D. 5:15)

Here is an example of knowledge acquired by negation. In love, or " affection, " Moses abandons all knowledge, even knowledge of himself, and in this way he is " knitted " unto God. But just as Moses shuts out knowable knowledge for a higher wisdom obtained by love, so the contemplative is justified in forgetting only in order to obtain a higher knowledge and love:

> And yet, nevertheless, not covered; but verily and clearly he appeareth open, not to all, but to them only the which pass above both all unclean and clean things, and the which come above all ascensions of all holy ends or terms set unto man or to angel, and the which forsake all divine lights and all heavenly sounds and words and enter *with affection* into darkness, where verily he is, as the Scripture showeth, the which is above all. (H.D. 4:19)

From this it is clear that the contemplative must abandon all knowledge, however holy, in order to enter with love into the darkness where God is.

Hid Divinity describes the way to God by negation in various metaphors. One is that of the man trying to make an image out of a piece of wood that is at the exact center of a huge block. Such a man must keep cutting away until he reaches the center; and in the same way we must keep denying our concepts of God if we are to come to the true supraconceptual knowledge of Him found in darkness.

The fundamental point is that our ordinary faculties, or " wits, " sensible and intellectual, are incapable by themselves of representing God to us; that is why their ordinary use must be abandoned. God is above anything we can picture in our imagination or conceive in our mind. The fourth and fifth chapters of *Hid Divinity* give a formidable and detailed catalog of the things God is *not* like. First of all, no sensible thing resembles God, so that " we remove from him all bodily things, and all these things that pertain to body, or to bodily things— as is shape, form, quality, quantity, weight, position, visibility, sensibility... For he is neither any of these things nor hath any of these, or any or all these sensible things. " Again, He is like nothing we can conceive in our mind—and once again there follows the remarkable catalog of the spiritual things that God is not like. Such is the negative theology that underlies apophatic mysticism.

Negative Knowledge in *The Cloud*

Hid Divinity gives the theory; *The Cloud* puts more emphasis on the practice. [3] The cloud of forgetting is nothing else but the abandonment of all images and concepts to allow the soul to love mystically. The blind stirring of love has begun to burn in the breast of the contemplative; it is leading to a higher knowledge (for God can be *known* by love) and therefore the soul must be careful not to smother this little love with meditations and conceptual thinking. Images are now a barrier between the soul and God; that is why they must be forgotten:

> And if ever thou shalt come to this cloud and dwell and work therein as I bid thee, thou must, as this cloud of unknowing is above thee, betwixt thee and thy God, right so put a cloud

[3] But see C. 124:4ff.

of forgetting beneath thee, betwixt thee and all the creatures that ever he made. Thou thinkest, peradventure, that thou art full far from God, because this cloud of unknowing is betwixt thee and thy God; but surely, if it be well conceived, thou art full further from him when thou hast no cloud of forgetting betwixt thee and all the creatures that ever be made. (C. 24:1) [4]

His statement here that one is far from God unless surrounded by the cloud of forgetting is re-echoed by St. John of the Cross who, declaring that the worst deceptions enter the soul by way of knowledge and memory, goes on: " Thus if the memory enter into darkness with respect to them all, and be annihilated in its oblivion to them, it shuts the door altogether upon this evil which proceeds from the devil, and frees itself from all these things, which is a great blessing. " [5] And just as St. John of the Cross is completely radical in his demand that everything must be forgotten (or that " nothing " must remain), so the English author admits of no exceptions:

As often as I say " all the creatures that ever be made, " so oft do I mean, not only the creatures themselves, but also all the works and the conditions of the same creatures. *I except not one creature*, whether bodily creatures or ghostly; nor yet any condition or work of any creature, whether they be good or evil. But, to speak shortly, all should be hid under the cloud of forgetting in this case. (C. 24:9) [6]

It can easily be seen how the above is a practical application of the theory of *Hid Divinity*; one is reminded of the catalog of things that are not like God. Furthermore, the author, like St. John of the Cross, is not satisfied if the contemplative forget

---

[4] For an understanding of this doctrine, it is important to note that the mind is emptied of creatures only to be filled with God. On this point the doctrine of Eckhart is similar but more neoplatonic: " Where the creature ends, there God begins to be. God asks only that you get out of his way, insofar as you are creature, and let him be God in you. The least creaturely idea that ever entered your mind is as big as God. Why? Because it will keep God out of you entirely. The moment you get (one of your own) ideas, God fades out and the Godhead too. It is when the idea is gone that God gets in. " (Eckhart, p. 127) Unlike the author of *The Cloud*, Eckhart here seems to suggest that if creatures are abandoned, God will *necessarily* flow into the soul.

[5] *Ascent*, III, IV, 1.

[6] See also C. 34:23.

temporal things; he must also abandon knowledge of things holy and spiritual; for good and pious thoughts about the Passion of Christ, about Our Lady and the saints, about one's wretchedness and so on may not always help toward union. [7] Such reflections are good in themselves; they are excellent in beginners—in fact, no one can come to contemplation without long practice in such pious meditations and reflections. But once the contemplative life has begun, once the blind stirring of love has risen in the heart, then these reflections are only an obstacle that can all too easily extinguish the tiny flame or draw the contemplative away from the work of supraconceptual love, the one thing necessary, the contemplation of Mary Magdalen. In a passage of great psychological interest, the author describes how the contemplative, quietly immersed in the prayer of silent love, may be torn away by some thought attracting him under the appearance of good. This pious and holy thought may take him away from a more important work of union, " scattering " him disastrously:

> For peradventure he will bring to thy mind divers full fair and wonderful points of his kindness, and say that he is full sweet and full loving, full gracious and full merciful. And if thou wilt hear him, he coveteth no better; for at the last he will thus chatter ever more and more till he bring thee lower, to the thought of his passion.
> And there will he let thee see the wonderful kindness of God; and if thou listen to him, he desireth nought other. For soon after he will let thee see thine old wretched living; and peradventure, in seeing and thinking thereof, he will bring to thy mind some place that thou hast dwelt in before this time. So that at the last, ere ever thou knowest, thou shalt be scattered thou knowest not where. The cause of this scattering is: that first thou didst wilfully listen to that thought, and then thou didst answer him, receive him, and let him have his way. (C. 27:3) [8]

---

[7] " Wherefore, the soul that is pure, cautious, simple, and humble must resist revelations and other visions with as much effort and care as though they were very perilous temptations. For there is no need to desire them; on the contrary, there is need not to desire them, if we are to reach the union of love. " (*Ascent*, II, XXVII, 6)

[8] For a somewhat similar psychological description, see St. John of the Cross, *Living Flame*, Stanza III, 63.

The contemplative should not listen to a thought, nor should he argue with it. " Tread him fast down with a stirring of love " is the advice of the author.

NEGATIVE KNOWLEDGE AND *Privy Counsel*

At the beginning of *Privy Counsel* the English author, in clear-cut terms, tells his disciple to empty his mind of all concepts, to forsake good and evil thoughts alike in order that his act of love may go naked to God:

> When thou comest by thyself think not before what thou shalt do after, but forsake as well good thoughts as evil thoughts. And pray not with thy mouth, unless thou likest right well... And look that nothing remain in thy working mind but a naked intent stretching unto God, not clothed in any special thought of God, in himself, how he is in himself, or in any of his works, but only that he is as he is. (P.C. 135:13)

The metaphor of the " naked " will or intent occurs often in *Privy Counsel*—the contemplative is to be naked nor should his love be " clothed " in any thought or image. This strikes a sterner note than the cloud of forgetting which is, after all, a rather pleasant image; the notion of nakedness, on the other hand, gives some indication of the terrible renunciation demanded by the abandonment of conceptual knowledge. This violent element of naked knowledge and love will be treated of later; suffice it here to give one example of the suffering of the cloud of forgetting:

> But look, as I oft said, that it be naked, for fear of deceit. If it be naked, then will it be full painful to thee in the beginning to abide therein any while. And that is, as I before said, because thy wits find no meat therein unto them. But no matter thereof, for I would love it the better. Let them fast awhile, I pray thee, from their natural delight in their knowledge. (P.C. 171:18)

Deprived of their " meat, " the natural faculties suffer in this process of forgetting, for the memory is purified, emptied, voided of all forms.

CHARACTERISTICS OF THE ENGLISH AUTHOR

THE ROLE OF GRACE

It will be clear from what has been said that the main element in the negative approach to God in the mystical life is love: discursive meditation is abandoned that love may develop. Yet this love is not something any man can stir up in his heart at will; it is a gift of God; it is the work of grace. This is made clear by such words as the following:

> And therefore lift up thy love to the cloud. Or rather (if I shall say thee sooth) let God draw thy love up to that cloud; and strive thou through the help of his grace to forget all other things. (C. 34:19)

In other words, God does the main work; the work of man is only to forget—and even this cannot be done without the help of grace. So far is contemplation from mere technique. " Almighty God with his grace must always be the chief stirrer and worker, either with means or without, and thou, or any other like unto thee, but the consenter and the sufferer. " (P.C. 155:8) The work of the contemplative is simply to dispose himself, to be increasingly passive, and to allow God to work within his very will for " this devout stirring of love... is wrought in his will not by himself but by the hand of Almighty God. " (C. 61:17) The author emphasizes this in oposition to those who " in confusion of their erring presumption, that in the curiosity of their learning or their natural wit will always be principal workers themselves, God suffering or only consenting; when verily the contrary is true in things contemplative. " (P.C. 162:14) In the active life, it is true, man has much to do with his natural faculties, but in this work everything is done by God:

> So that, in things active, man's learning and his natural knowledge shall principally abound in working — God graciously consenting... But in things contemplative, the highest wisdom that may be in man, as man, is far put under, so that

God be the principal in working, and man but only consenter and sufferer. (P.C. 163:5)

So it is that as the soul approaches nearer and nearer to God, " Jesu " becomes the " chief worker " while human activity changes into a silent passivity or expectancy. But only, it is to be noted, when " Jesu " is positively working in the soul may the negative technique of forgetting be practiced.

VOCATION TO CONTEMPLATION

The author is well aware of the dangers of entering the cloud of forgetting before one's time. One of his reasons for insisting that his book may not be given to everyone is his fear that some naive young person, filled with good will, on hearing of mystical things may imagine that he is called to the contemplative life and end up in a condition that is " madness and no wisdom. "

Even good people must be careful not to enter this path prematurely; they must wait for the call of God. The Good Shepherd calls into the sheepfold those whom He will and He does so quite gratuitously; for " there is no soul without this grace which is able to have this grace: none, whether it be sinner soul or innocent soul. For it is neither given for innocence, nor withholden for sin. " (C. 69:13) Those not called must patiently and humbly wait outside. Indeed, the author protests that he himself cannot teach contemplation, nor can any man:

> And if thou ask me by what means thou shalt come to this work, I beseech Almighty God of his great grace and his great courtesy to teach thee himself. For truly I do well to let thee know that I cannot tell thee. And this is no wonder. Because it is the work of only God, specially wrought in whatever soul he liketh, without any merit of the same soul. For without it no saint nor angel can think to desire it. (C. 68:20)

Thus the grace is given by God alone " as he liketh, where he liketh, and when he liketh. " (C. 69:10)

But how is one to discern this vocation? How is one to distinguish this call from God from such psychological stirrings as may rise in the heart of any man? In both *The Cloud* and *Privy Counsel* the English author devotes considerable attention to this point. [9] He stresses the necessity of " counsel, " or spiritual direction, obedience to the Church, fidelity to Holy Scripture, and he insists that the would-be contemplative " should be such a one as doth all that in him is, and... hath done long time before, for to able him to contemplative living, by the virtuous means of active living. For else it accordeth nothing to him. " (C. 2:5) When he has meditated long on the Passion, Our Lord calls him to a higher degree of union with Him [10], to a union beyond imagery, typified by a constant longing for God and dissatisfaction with creatures. " All thy life now must always stand in desire, if thou shalt advance in degree of perfection. This desire must always be wrought in thy will, by the hand of Almighty God and thy consent. " (C. 15:14) Any stirring might rise in the heart of man from ordinary grace, and to distinguish the contemplative stirring, the author makes a point to which he continually returns: the difference between stirrings that come *from within* and those that come *from without*. If the stirring arises only when one reads books about or hears talks about the mystical life, it is only an ordinary grace: one must then wait for the true calling.

The true contemplative call comes from within; it impedes the ordinary use of the faculties; it is even a hindrance in one's daily life, somehow interfering with one's work—" it reaveth thee from thy quotidian exercise and goeth between thee and it " (P.C. 166:17)—which the contemplative performs (and here the author uses an interesting phrase) " not without difficulty but without great difficulty. " (C. 126:15) As St. John of the Cross speaks of " an inclination and desire to be alone " with " the memory centered upon God, " so the English author in a few terse phrases points to the same longing for God, the same passion for silence that characterizes contemplation:

Thou lovest to be alone and sit by thyself; men would hinder thee, thou thinkest, unless they wrought with thee; thou

---

[9] See *The Cloud*, pp. 130 ff., and *Privy Counsel*, pp. 164 ff.
[10] Meditation is necessary, but it must be abandoned when the call comes to something higher. See C. 27:16.

wouldst not read books nor hear books but only of it. (P.C. 167:3)

As for the cloud of unknowing itself, sometimes it is like a cloud above one's head, separating oneself from God; but at other times the contemplative seems to be somehow immersed in the cloud, and then it becomes a symbol for an inability to meditate or make discursive prayer: the contemplative, surrounded by the mist, is able to cry out to God only in silent love.

Such are the tests by which the contemplative may know if he is permitted to enter the way of negation, surrounding himself with the cloud of forgetting. The signs of God are clear enough; so clear indeed that the contemplative may appear absent-minded and may be ridiculed by " actives. " But the author of *The Cloud*, following the " Martha, Martha! " of Our Lord, addresses these " actives ":

Actives, actives! make you as busy as ye can... And meddle you not with contemplatives. Ye know not what aileth them. Let them sit in their rest and in their play, with... the best part of Mary. (C. 55:1)

From all this it can be seen that contemplation, far from being a mere technique, is a call from God.

THE CLOUD OF FORGETTING:
THEOLOGICAL JUSTIFICATION

Granted that he has the vocation, the contemplative enters the cloud of unknowing and puts between self and all creatures a cloud of forgetting. But this immediately poses another problem: If ordinary conceptual knowledge of God and creatures is true and valid, why should it be abandoned? It could be argued that the person who rejects conceptual knowledge and reasoning because it is illusory is, paradoxically, logical; but the person who esteems it and accepts its validity should not throw it away.

And the answer to this is that the author instructs his disciple to empty his mind of conceptual knowledge in time of prayer in order to make him capable of receiving a higher knowledge infused by God in love. Because (and this is the pivotal point) conceptual knowledge of God is totally inadiequate and imperfect. We shall now consider this imperfection of conceptual knowledge of God.

IMPERFECTION OF CONCEPTUAL KNOWLEDGE

In an assertion that has a somewhat Aristotelian or Thomistic flavor, the author declares that conceptual knowledge is, in this life, accompanied by a phantasm or mental image, and if we apply this image to spiritual things (and especially to God), then we fall into error. He has been saying that " love may reach to God in this life, but not knowing, " and then he goes to explain why it is that in this life we cannot know God:

> And all the while that the soul dwelleth in this deadly body, evermore is the sharpness of our understanding in beholding of ghostly things, but most especially of God, mingled with some manner of fantasy; for which reason our work should be unclean, and unless much wonder were, it should lead us into much error. (C. 33:11)

It will be noted here that the danger of error comes from " the deadly body " and, in particular, from the " fantasy "; just as St. John of the Cross says that the memory should be voided of forms and figures because " the more it leans upon the imagination the farther it is going from God, and the greater is the peril wherein it walks, since God is incomprehensible and therefore cannot be apprehended by the imagination. " [11]

Our conceptual knowledge is taken from the world around us; it comes through the senses and is accompanied by an imaginative picture; it is, moreover, quidditive or essential, which means that when I use the concepts " good " or " merciful, " I limit existence to that particular mode that is

[11] *Living Flame*, Stanza III, 44.

goodness or mercy. If, therefore, we apply it to God univocally, it will contain some falsehood; for as *Hid Divinity* has repeatedly asserted, God is above everything we can imagine. Not only is He above any picture we can have of Him in our phantasm, He is above any thought we can entertain in our mind. Thus, if we say that God is " good " or " merciful, " this is true, as the " affirming divinity " has taught us; but if we have in our imagination the phantasy of goodness and mercy as found in creatures, and if we apply this also to God, then we fall into anthropomorphism and what we say is false. If, on the other hand, we have the mental restriction that " God is good and merciful, but not in the sense of goodness and mercy in any creature whatever, " then our statement is correct: the negative knowledge has supplemented the positive. This is simply what St. Thomas means when, following Augustine and Boethius, he says that God, by reason of His eminence, escapes any form that can be held in the human mind—" Quamcumque formam intellectus concipiat, Deus subterfugit illam per suam eminentiam. " [12]

Hence the author (whose avowed intention is to lead his disciple to a perfect knowledge of God as He is in Himself) opposes quidditive knowledge in favor of existential knowledge. At the beginning of *Privy Counsel* he orders the disciple to put away all essential or quidditive knowledge, telling him to think not of *what* God is but *that* God is. And this is a theme running through the whole book: Leave all essences; do not think of *what* you are; do not think of *what* God is; it is enough to think *that* you are and *that* God is. Here are his words at the beginning of *Privy Counsel*:

> And look that nothing remain in thy working mind but a naked intent stretching unto God, not clothed in any special thought of God, in himself, how he is in himself, or in any of his works, but *only that he is as he is*. Let him be so, I pray thee, and make him on no otherwise. (P.C. 135:19)

The author continues to stress that mystical knowledge is not essential but existential. It is the meeting of two existences,

[12] In *I Sent.*, dist. 22, q. 1.

the existence of God and the existence of man. There must be no quidditive discourse about the nature or essence either of God or self:

> That that I am, Lord, I offer unto thee, without any looking to any quality of thy being, but only that thou art as thou art, without anymore. (P.C. 136:4)

Thus prayer is reduced to a wonderful simplicity without words, without images. " And therefore think of God in this work as thou dost on thyself, and on thyself as thou dost on God: that he is as he is and thou art as thou art, so that thy thought be not scattered nor separated, but oned in him that is all. " (P.C. 136:11) This is the void, the nothingness of the mystics.

ESSENCE AND EXISTENCE

The author, then, is leading his disciple to existential knowledge of God. It might be argued, however, that one does not really know a being until one knows its quiddity, or essence: it is not much to know *that* a being is unless we also know *what* it is. And is it not so with God? Of little value to know that He exists if we cannot know His essence. And to this valid objection the author answers scholastically that in God essence and existence are identical, so that to know His existence is to know His essence. To follow his reasoning here one must recall then that essence, being a way of existence, limits the existence of the creature; it is a potency to which existence is the act. If, for instance, I exist as a man, my existence is limited to that form of existence we call humanity; and so it is restricted.

Now in God there can be no limit, no restriction, no potency, no mode or way of existence. God is the source; He contains every perfection; He is existence itself. Consequently, His existence and His essence are identical: *that* He is and *what* He is are the same:

> For there is no name, nor feeling, nor beholding more, nor so much, according unto everlastingness (the which is God), as is

that the which may be had, seen, and felt in the blind and the lovely beholding of this word *is*. For if thou say: " Good " or " Fair Lord " or " Sweet, " " Merciful " or " Righteous, " " Wise " or " All-witting, " " Mighty " or " Almighty, " " Wit " or " Wisdom, " " Might " or " Strength, " " Love " or " Charity, " or what other such thing that thou say of God: all it is hid and enstored in this little word *is*. For that same is to him only to be, that is all these for to be. And if thou add a hundred thousand such sweet words as these: good, fair, and all these other, yet went thou not from this little word *is*. And if thou say them all, thou addest not to it. And if thou say right none, thou takest not from it. (P.C. 143:19)

From this the author deduces his central idea that it is quite unnecessary to make discursive reflections about what God is; the contemplative should not think about His goodness and mercy and so on, for he, by vocation, is called to touch in love that very existence which is the essence of God. The logical conclusion, therefore, is drawn:

And therefore be as blind in the lovely beholding of the being of God as in the naked beholding of the being of thyself, without any curious seeking in thy wits to look after any quality that belongeth to his being or to thine. But, all curiosity left and far put back, do worship to thy God with thy substance, all that thou art as thou art, unto all him that is as he is, the which only of himself without more is the blissful being both of himself and of thee. (P.C. 144:1)

And in making this existential prayer in love, the contemplative necessarily puts all creatures beneath the cloud of forgetting; because now quiddities or essences are gone and the soul is " empty, " " void, " " silent, " " in darkness, " " thinking of nothing "—all these words of the mystics come down to the same thing, expressed by the author of *The Cloud* in the words: " all that thou art as thou art, unto all him that is as he is. "

The above doctrine, widespread in the fourteenth century, is found in St. Thomas.

The Angelic Doctor could hardly be called apophatic; yet he has his share of Dionysian influence. He, too, asserts repeatedly that we do not know what God is (" nos non scimus de Deo quid est "); St. Thomas says that although we cannot know *what* God is, we can know *that* He is ("quamvis maneat ignotum quid est, scitur quia est ") . And in another striking phrase he follows Dionysius saying that at the term of our knowledge we know God as unknown (" in finem nostrae cognitionis Deum tamquam ignotum cognoscimus. " [13]) What does St. Thomas mean by all this?

Obviously he does not mean that we cannot at all know the essence of God; for about this essence he has written in detail. When he says that " we do not know what God is " he means that our concepts do not attain to God univocally or (in other words) that through conceptual knowledge we do not know God as He is in Himself. But St. Thomas does hold that " we can know God by ignorance, by a certain union with the divine which is above the nature of the mind, " and he writes:

> For it is then above all that the mind dwells more perfectly in the knowledge of God, when it is known that His essence is above everything that can be apprehended in the present state of this life. And so, though the deity remains unknown according as it is in itself, there is (to a higher degree than ever) knowledge of God according as He is. [14]

Negative knowledge, then, leads to a superior knowledge. But what is the nature of this superior knowledge of God? Jacques Maritain, stating that this negative knowledge can be viewed either metaphysically or mystically, writes as follows:

> Insofar as the " via negationis " announces that God is like nothing created, it is one of the ways of metaphysical knowledge or ordinary theology, and indeed its most exalted moment. *But insofar as " theologia negativa " constitutes a species of knowledge, a wisdom of a higher order* (and that is what is meant once it is distinguished from ordinary theology) *it is nothing if not mystical experience.* [15]

In short, the negative theology of St. Thomas opens the door to a wisdom of a higher order that is mysticism.

---

[13] St. Thomas is here quoting Dionysius: *Myst. theol.*, c. 1.
[14] Quoted by Maritain, p. 237.
[15] Maritain, p. 237.

REASON AND IRRATIONALITY

Now we are in a position to understand more clearly the author's attacks on ratiocination that make him resemble so closely Dr. Suzuki. To understand his way of thinking, three points need to be kept in mind.

First, his sporadic attacks on philosophers and theologians are more often aimed at their vanity than at their doctrine; this was not an uncommon theme of spiritual writers of the day.

Second, he never utters one word which might indicate that he doubts the validity of ordinary knowledge derived from sense and intellect. In fact, he says quite clearly that one can have knowledge of all creatures; but " of God can no man think. " Therefore it is only a question of our knowledge of God.

Third, in his attacks on reasoning and logical thinking he is no more than pounding home with emphasis the Thomistic doctrine of analogy which says that by reason we can know God only indirectly through creatures. By reason, our knowledge of God is illative, going from effect to cause; this is what he means when he says:

> By reason we may trace how mighty, how wise and how good he is in his creatures, but not in himself. (St. 72:19)

That God can be known through reason he here clearly states; and, of course, he speaks of causality and admits the value of " affirming divinity. " But, speaking to contemplatives, he feels the need of emphasizing that human reasoning cannot know God intuitively, univocally, as He is in Himself; " for one is he in himself, and another be his works. " To know Him as He is in Himself is the real knowledge; this is the true knowledge, and it can be gotten only by the grace of God that comes from love. All the logical thinking and ratiocination in the world will not bring the mind to an intuitive grasp of God—hence his attacks on those who think that the " natural wits " will give a kind of knowledge that, in fact, can be given only by God.

CONCLUSION

To sum up: The English author is in the Dionysian tradition, an apophatic mystic who emphasizes the knowledge of God by negation. In order to understand his negative theology, one must keep in mind the great stress he puts upon love and his constant assertion that love can know God. The *via negativa* is, in his thought, no more than a preparation for a *via amoris*; the cloud of forgetting is no more than a means to the cultivation of " the blind stirring of love "; the rejection of concepts is to allow the flame of love to burn brightly in the heart of the contemplative. Thus conceptual knowledge may be abandoned only when it is determined by clear-cut signs that the Good Shepherd is issuing an invitation to a higher loving knowledge.

Consequently, there is no question of conceptual knowledge and reasoning being false or illusory; in fact, there is an " affirming divinity " by which the mind can truly know God. But the knowledge of God obtained in this way is very imperfect. Nor does it attain to God as He is in Himself but only as He is in creatures. It is imperfect because, drawn from creatures, it is accompanied by a phantasy, is circumscribed and quidditive—such knowledge cannot be applied to God univocally but only analogously. The knowledge in favor of which it is abandoned is supraconceptual, existential, mystical; it is given by God Himself.

In short, when the English author says that we cannot know God, he means that our ordinary conceptual knowledge of God is analogous and does not attain to God as He is in Himself; when he says that we know God by unknowing, he means that in order to know God mystically by love one must abandon (that is, not know) imaginative and conceptual knowledge.

3

THE CLOUD OF UNKNOWING

DARK KNOWLEDGE

THE CLOUD

Mystical knowledge is dark; it is obscure; it is knowledge found in a cloud. At the beginning of *The Cloud*, the author, in a few succinct words, sketches a picture of the contemplative at the outset of the mystical life finding himself in a cloud, unable to think discursively, stretching out in love toward something or Someone whom he scarcely knows—or, rather, he knows *that* He is without being clear about *what* He is. The words of the English author run as follows:

> For at the first time when thou dost it, thou findest but a darkness, and as it were a cloud of unknowing, thou knowest not what, saving that thou feelest in thy will a naked intent unto God. This darkness and this cloud, however thou dost, is betwixt thee and thy God, and hindereth thee, so that thou mayest neither see him clearly by light of understanding in thy reason, nor feel him in sweetness of love in thine affection. And therefore shape thee to bide in this darkness as long as thou mayest, evermore crying after him whom thou lovest. For if ever thou shalt see him or feel him, as it may be here it must always be in this cloud and in this darkness. (C. 16:19)

Here the soul, filled with love, is plunged deep in the darkness of the cloud; its faculties are " hindered " so that it cannot see clearly nor feel sweetly; but from the mist of the cloud it cries out after Him whom it loves like the spouse in the Canticle: " Whither hast thou hidden thyself, And hast left me, O Beloved, to my sighing? " For this cloud is like that of which St. John of the Cross writes saying that " as this dark night has hindered its [i.e., the soul's] faculties and affections in this way, it is unable to raise its affection or its mind to God, neither can it pray to Him thinking, as Jeremias thought concerning himself, that *God has set a cloud before it through which its prayer cannot pass.* " [1]

The English author goes to some trouble to explain that the cloud he speaks of is a mystical grace in which the faculties are impeded and the soul rests silently in God. Always afraid of being misinterpreted, he seems to fear lest some of his readers, amateurs in the spiritual life, may simply close their eyes, visualize a cloud in the sky, and then imagine that they are in " the cloud of unknowing. " Things are not so simple as that; and so he writes:

> And ween not, because I call it a darkness or a cloud, that it is any cloud congealed of the vapours that fly in the air, or any darkness such as is in thine house on nights, when thy candle is out. For such a darkness and such a cloud mayest thou imagine with curiosity of wit, for to bear before thine eyes in the lightest day of summer; and also contrariwise in the darkest night of winter thou mayest imagine a clear shining light. Let be such falsehoods; I mean not thus. For when I say darkness, I mean a lack of knowing; as all thing that thou knowest not, or hast forgotten, is dark to thee; for thou seest it not with thy ghostly eye. And for this reason it is called, not a cloud of the air, but a cloud of unknowing; which is betwixt thee and thy God. (C. 23:13)

Here the author is clear. He means a psychological condition in which the mind is dark from a " lack of knowing ": on the one hand it has abandoned all knowledge of creatures, burying

---

[1] *Dark Night*, II, VIII, 1.

them beneath the cloud of forgetting, and on the other it cannot know God with clear and distinct knowledge.

To be in this cloud is a wonderful grace of God; yet here one sometimes suffers greatly. One suffers because this cloud is an impediment, an obstruction, as something blotting out the light of the sun, as something keeping the contemplative away from God whom he loves and wants to see. It is suffering, too, because the natural faculties want to be active; they crave knowledge and, deprived of their object, left without clear knowledge of God or creature, they suffer. [2] It is then like that cloud of St. John of the Cross who, speaking of the distress of the impeded faculties, says that " a thick and heavy cloud is upon the soul, keeping it in affliction, and, as it were, far away from God. " [3]

Yet even when it makes one suffer, this is a " high and wonderful cloud. " The person in the cloud is nearer to God than anyone else alive; all the saints in heaven rejoice at what he is doing; the souls in purgatory are benefited; all men are wonderfully helped. [4] For, though sometimes bitter to the natural man, this darkness leads one to God like that of which St. John of the Cross will later sing: " O Night that guided me! O Night more lovely than the dawn! " Moreover the darkness is not always bitter; it was not so for Mary when she sat at the feet of Christ in the cloud of unknowing:

> Thither regarded she with all the love of her heart. For from thence she would not remove for nothing that she saw or heard spoken or done about her; but sat full still in body, with many a sweet, secret, and a listy love set upon that high cloud of unknowing betwixt her and her God... In this cloud it was that Mary was occupied with many secret settings of love. And why? Because it was the best and the holiest part of contemplation that may be in this life. And from this part she would not remove for nothing. (C. 47:12)

Such is the beautiful (if sometimes bitter) cloud of contemplative prayer.

---

[2] " Let them fast awhile, I pray thee, from their natural delight in their knowledge. " (P.C. 171:22)

[3] *Dark Night*, II, XVI, 1.

[4] See C. 16:10.

MYSTICAL SLEEP

From this it can be seen that the cloud is an image to express that prayer of silent repose in unknowing later called by St. Teresa the prayer of quiet, or (when the faculties are more deeply united with God) the prayer of union. It can be expressed in many figures; one more which the author uses (and which is deeply traditional) is that of sleep:

> And well is this work likened to sleep. For as in a sleep the use of the bodily wits is ceased, that the body may take his full rest in feeding and strengthening of the bodily nature: right so in this ghostly sleep the wanton questions of the wild ghostly wits, imaginative reasons, be fast bound and utterly voided, so that the silly soul may softly sleep and rest in the lovely beholding of God as he is, in full feeding and strengthening of the ghostly nature. (P.C. 152:3)

Here the soul is silently attentive to God at the deepest part of its being while " the wild ghostly wits " are ignored or, rather, " fast bound and utterly voided, " that is, deprived of images by the cloud of forgetting and filled with God in love. This, too, will be echoed by a future mystic: " In this spiritual sleep which the soul has in the bosom of its Beloved, it possesses and enjoys all the calm and rest quiet of the peaceful night, and it receives in God, together with this, a profound and dark Divine intelligence. " [5] In short, this mystical sleep is yet another description of the cloud of unknowing.

SILENCE AND WORDS

Normally, this prayer of the cloud and of spiritual sleep is made in deep silence without words. Sometimes, however, words may be used; but not often, for this prayer " is best when it is in pure spirit, without special thought or any

---

[5] *Canticle*, Stanzas XIII and XIV, 22. See also St. Francis de Sales: " Now this repose sometimes goes so deep in its tranquillity, that the whole soul and all its powers fall as it were asleep, and make no movement nor action whatever, except the will alone, and even this does no more than receive the delight and satisfaction which the presence of the well-beloved affords. " (Quoted by Poulain, Chapt. IX, *Extracts*, 37)

pronouncing of word; unless it be seldom, when for abundance of spirit it bursteth up into word. " (C. 78:20) That is to say, from the midst of this silent prayer, words may well up in the heart; and then they should be used; but these are not words thought out by men but words given by God. " And therefore take thou none other words to pray in... but such as thou art stirred by God to take. " (77:21) Such words will be very short (and the shorter the better) like " love, " " God, " and so on. They will fly straight to God like the stirrings he has compared to sparks flying up from burning coal. The soul using such tiny words is like the man who calls out " Fire! ":

> And rightly as this little word Fire stirreth rather and pierceth more hastily the ears of his hearers, so doth a little word of one syllable, when it is not only spoken or thought, but secretly meant in the depth of the spirit... And rather it pierceth the ears of Almighty God than doth any long psalter unmindfully mumbled in the teeth. And therefore it is written, that " short prayer pierceth heaven. " (C. 74:23)

Such is the prayer of the cloud. It is a prayer of silent union with God during which there may rise up in the heart momentary words; it is a prayer of darkness and unknowing.

DARK KNOWLEDGE AND DOGMA

It has already been indicated that the dark knowledge of the cloud has sometimes been interpreted as a rejection of dogma, the cloud of forgetting being a means of voiding the mind of clear-cut propositions and concepts. In this way the English author has been taken as a rebel against dogma.

In answer to this it could be argued that the truth of Christian dogma underlies almost every statement the author makes. His exhortation to enter the cloud is no more than an urging to the perfect following of Christ; [6] he constantly expresses dislike of heresy; he often refers to the Mystical Body; [7] his whole doctrine on the purification of the soul is

---

[6] See the opening pages of *The Cloud*. This subject is treated at length in the next chapter.

[7] See " The Cloud and the Church," pp. 80 ff.

built on an extremely accurate and orthodox teaching on original sin; [8] he keeps referring to redemption through the blood of Christ; [9] he has a clear statement about the Last Judgment. [10] He follows Dionysius in *Hid Divinity* by invoking the Blessed Trinity and, outlining the main tenets of the faith, he tells us that God is One, that the " sovereign-substantial Jesu " has become man, and he holds firmly " all other things that be expressed in the Scripture. " (H.D. 7:22) These are not the words of a man who thinks that all these doctrines have no more than relative value, that they are a sort of jumping-off place for a knowledge in which they will all be jettisoned. If anything is to be said for his sincerity (which few will doubt), he has an unshakable fidelity to the teaching of the Church.

Furthermore, he has an interesting aside in which he asserts clearly his belief that the unknown God encountered in the cloud is the God of Christian revelation. He is speaking of how distracting thoughts may rise in the mind asking the contemplative what he is looking for; then he writes:

> And if he [i.e., the distracting thought] ask thee, " What is that God? " say thou, that it is God that made thee and bought thee, and that graciously called thee to his love. (C. 26:16)

This is to say that the God whom the contemplative seeks in the cloud is the God of Scripture and dogma, the God who is Creator and Redeemer and Sanctifier. The text is all the more interesting as being unmistakably Trinitarian. " God that made thee " is the Father; that " bought thee " is the Son; " that graciously called thee to his love " is the Holy Spirit. This means that the contemplation of the author is directed to the triune God of revelation; it is centered on the principal Christian dogma: the Blessed Trinity. Moreover, the author has an interesting habit of using triple words that recall the Trinity, as when, for example, he speaks of God " mightily, wisely and goodly succouring " the soul. (P.C. 149:16) Here again, traditionally the Father is mighty; the Son (the Word) is wise; and the Holy Spirit is good. Or again, he speaks of

[8] See Part III.
[9] *Ibid.*
[10] C. 104:17.

God's " almighty-hood, his unknown wisdom, and his glorious goodness " (P.C. 149:9)—with the same Trinitarian ring. [11]

All this indicates that in the darkness of the cloud the soul encounters the Blessed Trinity. It is true that if asked, " What is that God? " the contemplative might say first that he scarcely knows, or that what he feels is inexpressible in human language; but, if pressed, he answers in the words of Christian dogma: the Creator, the Redeemer, the Sanctifier. One recalls here the words of Maritain who, asserting that true mysticism culminates in a Trinitarian experience, continues: " The reason is that from the very outset, its [i.e., the soul's] contemplation—if it is authentically mystical—has proceeded from a living faith and from supernatural gifts and has led the soul, not to the One of the philosophers, not to God unknown as if from without and by his effects, but to God attained in his own divine essence, to the Deity Itself and as such, who in his absolutely proper and intimate life, is a Trinity of Persons, a resplendent and tranquil society of Three in the same indivisible essence of light of love. " [12]

Dark contemplation, then, is communion with the Blessed Trinity. But to explain more fully how this can be so, it is necessary to enter into the relationship between this dark knowledge and faith.

DARKNESS AND FAITH

THE APOPHATIC TRADITION

When the mind is barren of images and clear, distinct concepts have been abandoned, the soul will be in some kind of darkness. There is, however, a philosophical cloud of unknowing entailing a supraconceptual grasp of, or rest in, being: the problem that now confronts us, therefore, is to analyze the darkness and the cloud of which the English author speaks,

---

[11] See also C. 28:3.
[12] Maritain, p. 378. The Trinitarian aspect of the English author's doctrine is developed in the last section of this work.

asking what are its special characteristics, what differentiates it from other kinds of mental darkness. [13]

In his commentary on *The Cloud*, Augustine Baker asserts that the darkness and the cloud of the English author symbolize faith; but he probably came to this conclusion less from a study of the text itself than from his general study of apophatic mysticism (for Baker was widely read in the mystics) which taught him that all these mystics from Gregory of Nyssa to St. John of the Cross, when they speak of the cloud and darkness, mean the obscurity of faith: traditionally the cloud is a symbol of faith. Gregory of Nyssa had spoken of how the mind leaves conceptual knowledge to enter the darkness of faith just as Abraham " after he had purified his mind of all such concepts... took hold of a faith that was unmixed and pure of any concept. " [14]

This teaching is summed up by Jean Daniélou in words that recall strikingly the doctrine of the English author of *The Cloud*. " For God, " writes Daniélou interpreting Gregory, " is beyond every representation. This does not, however, mean that there is no contact with God, but merely that this contact is not by way of the understanding but by faith. It is only in the obscurity of faith that the soul can grasp the transcendent Godhead. And thus we are directly on the way that leads to St. John of the Cross. God, as He is in Himself, is Darkness for the intellect, but can be grasped by faith. In this way it is clear that the knowledge of God in the darkness is not merely negative. It is truly an experience of the presence of God as He is in Himself, in such wise that this awareness is completely blinding to the mind, and all the more so, the closer it is to Him. In fact one might almost say that the darkness expresses the divine presence, and that the closer He comes to the soul, the more intense is the darkness. The image of darkness is merely a way of expressing the fact that the awesomeness of the divine essence is more than human nature can endure. " [15]

---

[13] There are various kinds of supraconceptual states. Suzuki speaks of *dhyana* in which the mind is emptied of all concepts, and " when all forms of mental activity are swept clean from the field of consciousness that is now like a sky devoid of every speck of cloud, a mere broad expanse of blue, *dhyana* is said to have reached its perfection. " (Suzuki [1], p. 246)

[14] Gregory of Nyssa, p. 35.

[15] Introd., *ibid.*, p. 32.

Daniélou has said that with the doctrine of Gregory the way leading to St. John of the Cross is opened; but this is a way that passes through the Rhineland and Ruysbroeck; it is in this path that the author of *The Cloud* stands. After him St. John of the Cross, voicing a long tradition, will say in unmistakable terms that the cloud of unknowing is the darkness of faith; for faith is " a black and dark cloud to the soul " paradoxically giving light in the night.

And, from his study of apophatic mysticism, Augustine Baker concludes, not unreasonably, that the cloud of the English author is the darkness of faith.

Faith, the " Ground " of Contemplation

Turning now to the English author, an analysis of his dark knowledge shows that it contains three elements: faith, love, and wisdom. Faith, or " belief " (as it is usually called), is the ground; love, " the naked intent of the will, " rises from this faith and goes directly to God; " ghostly wisdom " is the " fruit of this working. "

At the beginning of *Privy Counsel* the author, having told his disciple to empty his mind of all concepts, to banish good thoughts as well as evil thoughts, makes a significant statement: " Let that belief be thy ground. " (P.C. 135:24) [16] That is to say, faith is the foundation of the whole thing. There is to be no " subtlety of wit, " no natural learning, but only a naked love that springs from faith—" this naked intent, freely fastened and grounded in very belief. " And later, when he is looking for a really contemplative soul, he exclaims:

> But where shall such a soul be found, so freely fastened and founded in the faith... and so lovely led and fed in the love of our Lord. (P.C. 149:6)

Here again, faith is the ground and out of faith there springs love.

But what is this faith that fills a mind void of concepts and natural learning? The English author does not say too much

[16] Hodgson points to textual difficulties here, but the substantial meaning is clear enough.

by way of explanation, for he is writing no thesis on theology; but some light may be thrown on the matter by a glance at the doctrine of St. Thomas whose teaching on faith dominated the century and which was subsequently, at Trent, accepted as the official teaching of the Church.

THE LIGHT OF FAITH

In the doctrine of St. Thomas, faith is not a reasoning process whereby one, having heard a preacher or read the Gospel, assents to its content; faith is an infused gift of God, enabling one to see His eternal truth in the Scriptures or in the dogmatic formulations that come to us through men *(ex auditu)*. " Fides est principaliter ex infusione... sed quantum ad determinationem est ex auditu. "[17] I give my assent to certain propositions conveyed to me by the Church not because of their intrinsic probability but because of the authority of God Himself who enlightens my mind to see His word in these formulas; just as, for example, I believe that Christ is present in the Eucharist not because of anything I see with my eyes or reason with my intellect but because of the enlightenment of God enabling me to grasp beneath appearances the reality that is Christ. Now the light that God pours into my mind at the moment of belief is not anything conceptual (faith gives no more *conceptual* knowledge than study) but is a supraconceptual enlightenment. And being supraconceptual it is " obscure " or " dark "; not in the sense that it is uncertain but because it is not clear and distinct.

The " darkness " of this " light " of faith fills the pages of the mystics. The light of faith, they say, is so bright that it blinds and darkens the intellect, just as the sun blinds the person who looks at its dazzling beauty—" even as the philosopher teaches, saying that even as the ray of the sun is dark and black to the eye of the bat, even so the lofty and bright things of God are dark to our understanding. "[18] This way of speaking, found throughout Gregory, Ruysbroeck, and

---

[17] *IV Sent.*, D. 4, Q. 2, a. 2.
[18] *Canticle*, Stanza XXXVIII, 10.

St. John of the Cross, [19] appears also in the author of *The Cloud*. He is speaking of how the mind is dark and empty, seemingly filled with " nothing "; and then he goes on to say that, in fact, this nothing is a wonderful enlightenment:

This nought may better be felt than seen; for it is full blind and full dark to them that have but a little while looked thereupon. Nevertheless (if I shall trulier say) a soul is more blinded in feeling of it for abundance of ghostly light. (C. 122:9)

In other words, this cloud of darkness is an intensely bright light, blinding the mind of the contemplative.

But this blinding light enables one to *see* God's truth hidden in the propositions of Scripture and dogma; that is why the author seems to regard faith as a kind of vision, for in *Hid Divinity* he declares that we hold " in sight of belief " that God is above all things. (H.D. 4:9) [20] And in another passage he writes:

For if ever thou shalt *see* him [i.e., by faith] or *feel* him [i.e., by love] it must always be in this cloud and in this darkness. (C. 17:7)

Here he says that by faith we see the truth of God in an obscure way; and when we have seen it, love brings us to God Himself.

All this is in conformity with the doctrine of St. Thomas who says that the act of faith does not terminate at any proposition but at the reality that it contains (" actus autem credentis non terminatur ad enuntiabile sed ad rem ") [21]; beneath the human words in which dogma is expressed there lies hidden a great reality, and it is to this that the mind assents.

[19] Ruysbroeck: " The divine light... dazzles her [the soul's] eyes, even as the bat is blinded by the sun's rays. " (Quoted by Poulain, Ch. VI, *Extracts*, 31) Also St. John of the Cross: " Hence it follows that for the soul this excessive light of faith which is given to it is thick darkness; for it overwhelms that which is great and does away with that which is little, even as the light of the sun overwhelms all other lights whatsoever, so that when it shines and disables our power of vision, they appear not to be lights at all. " (*Ascent*, II, III, 1)

[20] The words " in sight of belief, " not in the Latin, are added by the English author himself.

[21] *Summa*, II^a^-II^æ^, q. 1, a. 2, ad 2. It is for this reason that St. Thomas speaks of faith as " inchoatio quaedam vitae aeternae. " (*De Ver.*, q. 14, a. 2, c.)

And St. John of the Cross, faithful disciple of St. Thomas, declares of faith that " such is the likeness between itself and God that there is no other difference, save that which exists between seeing God and believing in Him. " [22]

Now faith is purest when it is naked; that is, when we assent to the truth of revelation not because of its intrinsic probability, not because of any human authority, not because of any reasoning process, not because of miracles; but because of the authority of God (" propter auctoritatem ipsius Dei revelantis. ") [23] It is in this time that the mind has no other prop or support except God. Consequently, it is in darkness; but the darkness is a blinding light, for it is the infused gift of faith. [24]

FAITH AND EXTERNAL REVELATION

It remains to say something about the faith that comes from hearing *(ex auditu)* and its relationship to this dark supraconceptual knowledge.

The great truths about the life of God (about the Blessed Trinity, the Incarnation, and so on) were taught by Christ and His Apostles and are expressed in the Bible and the teaching of the Church in certain conceptual definitions and dogmas which, it has been pointed out, the author of *The Cloud* accepts unconditionally, making them the warp and woof of his doctrine. However, he realizes that these definitions, being expressed in human language, are imperfect; they are inadequate to contain perfectly the great truths that they express—the dogmatic expression of the Trinity, for example, is a weak and stammering, yet true, expression of the great reality that is the life of God. It is precisely the light of faith that enables the believer to see in these human formulations the tremendous truth of the triune God. Therefore these conceptual formulations are little, insofar as they cannot exhaust the reality they express; they are great, as truly pointing to something that is infinite. This can be said of the

---

[22] *Ascent*, II, IX, 1.
[23] See Denzinger, 1789.
[24] By faith here I mean the living faith that also includes love.

Scriptures and of the whole revelation of Christ; and this is what the author says in *Hid Divinity*:

> For this reason it is that the godly Bartholomew, the Apostle of Christ, saith in his writing that Christ's divinity [i.e., revelation] is both much and it is least; and that the gospel is broad and much, and eftsoon he saith, it is strait and little. (H.D. 4:12) [25]

In short, the words and sentences used about God in theology and Scripture are great because they are true, but they are little because so imperfect. St. John of the Cross says something similar in emphasizing that the things of God are totally removed from any concepts or images we may have of them:

> Wherefore, if one should speak to a man of things which he has never been able to understand, and whose likeness he has never seen, he would have no more illumination from them whatever than if naught had been said of them to him. I take an example: If one should say to a man that on a certain island there is an animal which he has never seen, and give him no idea of the likeness of that animal, that he may compare it with others that he has seen, he will have no more knowledge of it, or idea of its form, than he had before, however much is being said to him about it. [26]

From what he hears the man knows *that* the animal is, but he does not know *what* it is because the concepts he has received through the senses until now do not fit this object. In the same way, essential or quidditive knowledge alone does not attain to God as He is; to attain to Him as He is we need the infused light of faith—which does not come through the senses and is supraconceptual. And the dark knowledge of the cloud of unknowing is grounded on this.

FAITH AND LOVE

It should be noted, however, that faith is only one element in this dark knowledge of God: it is the ground. The principal

[25] " This reference has not yet been traced. Nothing is known of any genuine writings of St. Bartholomew the Apostle. " (Hodgson, *Notes to H.D.*, p. 124)
[26] *Ascent*, II, III, 2.

element is love that rises in the darkness; but since love is always based on knowledge (*"ignoti nulla cupido"* was a scholastic dictum) and since it cannot be based on natural reasoning and conceptual knowledge, which is useless for attaining to God as He is in Himself, it must, for every Christian, be based on faith—and, for the contemplative, on naked faith. Having seen the truth in *faith*, the soul comes to *love* God—and in love it " touches " the essence of Him the truth about whom it has seen in the Scriptures and teaching of the Church. Touching Him it finds a new *wisdom* that is also dark and about which more will be said later.

CONCLUSION

Keeping all this in mind we can return to a problem posed earlier when it was said that Zen is an experience cut off from all dogma and all philosophy, and that certain commentators felt that the author of *The Cloud* also teaches a rejection of the dogmas of the Church.

In evidence of this theory, Aldous Huxley quotes the following passage:

> Yea, and what more? Weep thou never so much for sorrow of thy sins, or of the passion of Christ, or have thou never so much thought of the joys of heaven, what may it do thee? Surely, much good, much help, much profit, and much grace will it get thee. But in comparison of this blind stirring of love, it is but little that it doth, or may do, without this. This by itself is the best part of Mary. (C. 39:4)

In considering this passage, three things should be noted. First, the author praises meditation wholeheartedly as something that brings much good, much help, and much profit. [27] Second, he says that *by comparison* with the prayer of contemplative love it is little. Third, meditation on the words of

[27] The author reiterates that meditation is necessary for beginners. It is just that he is not writing for beginners, and so he says: " Of these three [i.e., Reading, Thinking, and Praying] thou shalt find written in another book by another man much better than I can tell thee; and therefore it needeth not here to tell thee the qualities of them... And prayer may not well be gotten in beginners and profiters without thinking coming before. " (C. 71: 14)

Scripture and the dogmas of the Church is a means to help us, enlightened by the grace of God, to see in the revelation of Christ the great truths hidden therein: principally the truths of the Blessed Trinity and the work of Redemption. When these truths are grasped meditation is finished, for the words and the actions and the miracles of Christ were ordained to revealing these truths. And when these truths are seen by the mind, the will goes out in love to that which they express—and this is the blind stirring of love. Far from being an escape from faith, this faith is its very ground.

In the darkness of a mind enlightened by naked faith (that is, without support of any human reasoning or of any imaginative forms in the memory), the will adheres in love to God who has revealed Himself in Christ and in His Church. The cloud of forgetting ensures that no other consideration, however holy, will influence the contemplative; no new revelation or message from God will be accepted; no vision will be trusted; no supernatural communication will be received—for all creatures have been forgotten and the author has said, " I except not one creature, whether bodily creatures or ghostly, " thus emphasizing that nothing under God will hamper the naked faith of contemplation. It is this faith that must be the ground of contemplation according to the English author.

We may conclude, then, that the cloud of unknowing is that dark and obscure knowledge and love that fills the mind of the contemplative when, void of images and discursive reasoning, it rests silently in God in mystical sleep. The knowledge now suffusing the mind is only that of a *faith* which, nakedly divorced from any human consideration whatsoever, finds God's truth in His revelation in Christ; and from this knowledge springs a *love* that touches the very essence of God, bringing yet a higher *wisdom*. This darkness of *faith* and *love* and *wisdom* is in reality a dazzling light that blinds the mind of the contemplative, thus leaving him in the mists of the cloud.

4

THE CLOUD AND CHRIST

THE PROBLEM

It has been said in the last chapter that the contemplative in the cloud of unknowing comes to know God as revealed in Scripture and the teaching of the Church, rising from this to love Him as He is in Himself.

If this interpretation is correct, the dogma of the Incarnation should be central to the mysticism of *The Cloud* and its accompanying treatises, since God revealed Himself to us in Christ. Yet it is precisely on this point that doubts have been cast, the assertion being made that *The Cloud* is theocentric rather than Christocentric, Christ being relegated to a place of secondary importance. This interpretation is, again, sometimes influenced by a desire to compare the teaching of the English author with certain mystical tendencies in Buddhism which, stressing the necessity of emptying the mind of all images to remain in silent rest, use such phrases as, " If you encounter the Buddha, slay him, " or " When you have spoken the name of Buddha, wash your mouth. " [1] Since the English author

---

[1] " O you, followers of Truth, if you wish to obtain an orthodox understanding [of Zen], do not be deceived by others. Inwardly or outwardly, if you encounter any obstacles, lay them low right away. If you encounter the Buddha, slay him; if you encounter the Patriarch, slay him; if you encounter the Arhat or the parent or the relative, slay them all without hesitation: for this is the only

seems to include the humanity of Christ in the list of things to be put down beneath the cloud of forgetting, it is tempting to reach the conclusion that both Buddhists and Christians are saying the same thing, urging some communion with the imageless Godhead in the rejection of any human mediator. Whereas in fact both the forgetting of the humanity of Christ and the slaying of the Buddha are extremely delicate points that can be spoken about only with great caution. Here I will not venture to discuss what Buddhists mean by this saying (for this would take us too far from our subject), but it is necessary to discuss the teaching of the author of *The Cloud* on a point of such vital importance.

DEVOTION TO CHRIST THE MAN

The pages of the English author are by no means lacking in devotion to Christ the man, in that " familiar friendship with Jesus " that we find in A Kempis: it would be a mistake to think of him as teaching a religion of pure spirit, an angelism that rejects all sensible feeling and imagery. One has but to recall his picture of Mary, the ideal contemplative, who wept at the sepulcher for her Lord. " Sweet was that love betwixt our Lord and Mary. Much love had she to him. Much more had he to her. " (C. 55:8) So tenderly deep was his loving consideration that " he might not suffer any man or women— yes, not her own sister—to speak a word against her. " (C. 56:1) And the author exclaims: " This was great love: this was surpassing love. "

way to deliverance. Do not get yourself entangled with any object, but stand above, pass on, and be free. " (Quoted by Suzuki [1], p. 332) Such teaching in Buddhism has, no doubt, prompted Dr. Progoff to write of *The Cloud*: " But the individual who wishes to reach God as He is in Himself must overcome his attachment to all such beliefs, even the most hallowed. The author specifically extends this to the sacraments and to meditations upon the life of Christ. Sacred objects are not to become stopping places, lest we remain with them and forget that our one goal is God as He is in Himself.

" This teaching of *The Cloud of Unknowing* is reminiscent of one that is expressed in rather strong form in Zen Buddhism. There it is said, ' When you have spoken the name Buddha, wash your mouth out '! " (Progoff, p. 28, 29) The English author, it is true, bids the contemplative cease from discursive meditations on the Passion of Christ; but I cannot recall any passage where he speaks of detachment from " beliefs " or from the sacraments. On the contrary, belief is the " ground, " and the " well " of penance is the indispensable condition.

Nor is it completely true to say that the author has no devotion to the Holy Name. He may, it is true, choose his words with care in reaction against Richard Rolle, whose enthusiasm for " fire " and " mirth " and " melody " could be interpreted in a too carnal sense—and hence the author of *The Cloud* will insist that it is better to be in darkness than " to have the eye of the soul opened in contemplation or beholding of all the angels or saints in heaven or in hearing all the mirth and melody that is among them in bliss. " (C. 34:11) But together with this one must consider such passages as that which concludes the *Study of Wisdom* where the author introduces the Holy Name into the words of Richard of St. Victor:

> Thou shalt call together thy thoughts and thy desires, and make for thyself of them a church, and learn therein to love only this good word Jesu, so that all thy desire and thy thought be only set for to love Jesu and that unceasingly, as it may be here, so that thou fulfill what is said in the psalm: " Lord, I shall bless thee in churches, " that is, in thought and desires of the love of Jesu. And then, in this church of thoughts and desires, and in one head of studies and of wills, look that all thy thoughts and thy desires and thy studies and all thy wills be only set in the love and the praising of this Lord Jesu. (S.W. 45:13)

In this way, underlying and intertwined with silent mysticism is human love for Christ the man, He who is the " ghostly spouse " of the soul, brooking no rival and asking for all.

Yet it is also true that the English author wants the contemplative to put away all imaginative pictures of Christ. He tells him that such meditation is good in itself but that the time for it has now gone. That discursive prayer that forms mental pictures of Christ and His Mother or of scenes from the Gospel is inferior to the prayer of mystic silence in which one is attentive to the blind stirring of love.

TRADITIONAL DOCTRINE

First of all, let it be said that the author of *The Cloud* is here no revolutionary; he is no more than repeating the ordinary traditional spiritual teaching that had preceded him. Even St. Bernard (whose devotion to the humanity of Christ is proverbial) speaks of a spiritual love far superior to any devotion to Christ's humanity:

> In reality, although this devotion to the humanity of Christ be a gift, and a great gift, of the Holy Ghost, the love which inspires it is none the less sensible as compared with that other love *which is not so much connected with the Word made flesh as with the Word of Wisdom, the Word of Justice, the Word of Truth, the Word of Holiness.* [2]

When treating of the mystical union, St. Bernard prefers to speak of " The Word " rather than of " Christ, " just as St. Augustine prefers to speak of " God. " Moreover, St. Bernard is as clear as the author of *The Cloud* in his rejection of sensible imagery:

> Be careful to think of nothing corporal or sensible in this union of the Word with the soul. Let us call to mind here what the Apostle says, " He who is joined to the Lord is one spirit " (1 Cor 6:17). . . It is in the spirit that this union takes place: " In spiritu fit ista conjunctio. " [3]

Doctrine similar to the above can be found in A Kempis, in the *De adhaerendo Deo*, and in the other spiritual writers of the age—indeed of every age in Christian spirituality. If one more example may be permitted there is the word of Ruysbroeck:

> Certainly in this exercise a man should lay hold of good images to help him; such as the Passion of our Lord and all those things that may stir him to greater devotion. But in the possession of God, the man must sink down to that imageless Nudity which is God; and this is the first condition, and the foundation, of a ghostly life. [4]

We can conclude from such passages that the author of *The Cloud* is proposing nothing novel when he urges the contemplative to bury the thought of Christ's Passion beneath the thick cloud of forgetting.

---

[2] Quoted by Pourrat, Vol. II, pp. 66, 67.
[3] *Ibid.*, p. 67.
[4] *The Sparkling Stone*, c. II.

THEOLOGICAL FOUNDATION

But to what extent is all this theological? And in what sense is Christian spirituality Christo-centric?

The English author gives a clear, theological basis to what he says. The humanity of Christ is a creature (that is to say, Christ's body is something which was created in time, born of the Virgin Mary), and true charity does not terminate at the human nature of Christ but at the *person* of Christ, which is the person of God. Indeed, it is possible to become too attached to the physical body of Christ, such a thing being an obstacle to true charity that terminates in the divinity. Thus (the English author declares) Christ ascended into heaven in order that the disciples might not become too attached to His merely human qualities. And in proof of this argumentation he appeals to the authority of St. Augustine:

> An example of this showed Christ in his life. For if it had so been that there had been no higher perfection in this life but in the beholding and in the loving of his Manhood, I trow that he would not then have ascended unto heaven whiles this world had lasted, nor withdrawn his bodily presence from his special lovers on earth. But for there was a higher perfection the which a man may have in this life—that is to say, a pure ghostly feeling in the love of his Godhead—therefore he said to his disciples, the which grudged for to forgo his bodily presence (as thou dost in part and in manner for to forgo thy curious meditations and thy quaint subtle wits): that it was speedful to them that he went bodily from them: " Expedit vobis ut ego vadam. " That is: " It is speedful to you that I go bodily from you. " Upon this word saith the doctor thus: " That unless the shape of his Manhood be withdrawn from our bodily eyes, the love of his Godhead may not fasten in our ghostly eyes. " And thus say I unto thee, that it is speedful some time to leave off thy curious working in thy wits and to learn thee to taste somewhat in thy feeling ghostly of the love of thy God. (P.C. 170:24)

It can be seen from the above that there is no question of forgetting *Christ* but of forgetting the *humanity of Christ* in order to relish " the love of his Godhead " with one's " ghostly eyes. " Moreover, spiritual love is substituted for sensible love and the contemplative is compared to the Apostles when deprived of the physical or sensible presence of their Master.

The author has appealed to " the doctor, " St. Augustine. [5]
He might equally well have appealed to St. Thomas who
comments on the same text that the humanity of Christ is a
way of going to God and that " we ought not to rest in it as
in an end in itself, but through it we should reach out to
God "; [6] he says that Christ took away His physical presence
lest the hearts of the disciples be captivated by His purely
human qualities. And this is in keeping with what the same
saint has written in the *Summa*:

> Things concerning the Godhead are, in themselves, the strongest
> incentives to love and to devotion because God is lovable above
> all things. Yet, such is the weakness of the human mind that it
> needs a guide not only to the knowledge, but also to the love,
> of divine things by means of certain sensible objects known to
> us. Chief among these is the humanity of Christ... Accordingly,
> things relating to Christ's humanity are the chief incentive to
> devotion, leading us there as a guide, although devotion itself
> has for its principal object things that concern the Godhead. [7]

This is the traditional theology that the author of *The Cloud*
and others apply to the spiritual life. Ruysbroeck has said that
" never creature may be or become so holy that it loses its
created being and becomes God; even the soul of our Lord
Jesus Christ shall ever remain creature, and other than God. " [8]
Here, of course, Ruysbroeck is very accurate: he says that the
soul (not the Person) of Christ is not God; and this is a way
of speech he uses again. [9]

CHRIST THE WAY

The doctrine of St. Thomas that through the humanity of
Christ one goes to His divinity, a doctrine found also in the

[5] St. Augustine, Sermon cxliii: P.L., 38, 786; *In Joann. Evan.*, Tract XCIV:
P.L. 35, 1869.
[6] *In Joann.* 7, 32.
[7] IIª-IIæ, q. 82, a. 3, ad 9.
[8] *The Book of Supreme Truth*, c. II.
[9] " But before the Infinity of God, he must yield, and must follow after It
essentially and without end; for This no creature, not even the soul of our
Lord Jesus Christ, which yet received the highest union above all other creatures,
can either comprehend or overtake. " (Ruysbroeck, *The Book of Supreme
Truth*, c. VIII)

De adhaerendo Deo, which says that we must " pass by the wounds of His Humanity so as to reach the intimacy of His Divinity, " [10] is stressed by the English author when he insists that contemplation is preceded by meditation on the Passion. Furthermore, he stresses that Christ is the *only* way to contemplation of the divinity: there is no other path. " Whoso entereth not by this door, but climbeth otherwise to perfection... is not only a night thief, but a day skulker. " (P.C. 160:4) Such a person is in great danger if he tries " to climb to high things, not only above himself but above the common plain way of Christian men touched before, the which I call the teaching of Christ the door of devotion and the truest entry of contemplation that may be in this life. " Those enter the path of contemplation who " in beholding the passion of Christ sorrow their wickedness... and then lift up their hearts to the love and the goodness of his Godhead, in the which he vouchsafed to meek himself so low in our deadly manhood. " (P.C. 159:19)

Here is obviously stressed the fact that in Christ *the same person* is God and Man: through the physical characteristics of Christ one is led to the Person who is the Word. In another passage, the author shows that he has mastered the theology underlying his spiritual direction. Our Lord, he says, is one Person; by His Manhood He is the door, and by His Godhead He is the porter; in order to reach the porter one must pass through the door—and, moreover, there is no other way in:

> For Our Lord is not only porter himself, but also the door; the porter by his Godhead, and the door by his Manhood. Thus saith he himself in the Gospel: " Ego sum ostium. Per me si quis introierit, salvabitur; et sive egredietur sive ingredietur, pascua inveniet. Qui vero non intrat per ostium sed ascendit aliunde, ille fur est et latro. " That is to thine understanding as if he said thus according to our matter: " I that am almighty by my Godhead and may lawfully as porter let in whom I will, and by that way that I will, yet because I will that there be a common plain way and an open entry to all that will come, so that none may be excused by unknowing of the way, I have clothed me in the common nature of man and made me so open that I am the door by my Manhood, and whoso entereth by me, he shall be safe. (P.C. 159:5)

[10] *De adhaerendo Deo*, c. 2.

The theology, as always, is accurate. The prayer he teaches is devoted completely to Christ, but to Christ as the porter, not to Christ as the door. It is interesting to remember that some of the Fathers refer to the humanity of Christ as " the cloud of unknowing " because it, as it were, conceals the divinity of the Word. With the eyes of faith and love, the contemplative pierces through the physical qualities of Christ and finds the Word of God—and it is here that he remains in Trinitarian rest.

It is precisely what Mary Magdalen does, and the chapter of *The Cloud* devoted to her illustrates this doctrine well. Rapt in deep contemplation, she has forgotten the humanity of Christ, which she has buried beneath the cloud of forgetting; yet she finds God in Christ. Through the humanity of Christ (which is present, though forgotten) she contemplates His divinity. Here is the passage where Mary, kneeling at the feet of Christ, gazes at His human form and sees therein, in faith, His Godhead:

> Yea! and full oftimes I think that she was so deeply disposed to the love of his Godhead that she had but right little special beholding unto the beauty of his precious and blessed body, in the which he sat full lovely, speaking and preaching before her; nor yet to anything else, bodily or ghostly. That this be truth it seemeth by the Gospel. (C. 46:20)

Continuing with his description of Mary's deep absorption in love, he says that " she regarded the sovereignest wisdom of his Godhead lapped in the dark words of his Manhood. " (C. 47:11)

Here the object of her contemplation is the Godhead, the divinity that is the ultimate object of all adoration. But it is important to note that *she finds God in Christ*. Just as anyone with faith finds divine truth hidden in the words of Scripture and the Church, so she finds " the sovereignest wisdom of his Godhead lapped in the dark words of his Manhood. " In the same way, the author goes on, the contemplative should cease from discursive acts and from forming mental pictures of the man Christ (for these, in any case, are of less value than the prayer of Mary since we know little about Christ's personal appearance and such images are, consequently, largely fictitious) to see and love the divinity hidden beneath human appearances in " the dark words " of Christ.

In short, the prayer of Mary is founded on faith by which she sees in the words and actions of Christ the eternal truth that the Word is made flesh; and from this grasp of the truth her heart goes out in love toward that Person who is the Word of God. Her contemplation is that of faith and love.

MANHEAD AND GODHEAD

In the description of Mary Magdalen here quoted, the author states that she is in the cloud of unknowing and that she has forgotten the sacred humanity of Christ; yet the whole context indicates that her forgetting of the humanity of Christ is quite different from the forgetting of other creatures. It would seem that Mary is making no deliberate attempt to forget the sacred humanity; she is not vigorously " treading it down beneath the cloud of forgetting " as is done with other creatures; it is rather that she is so fascinated and absorbed by the Divinity that the beauty of His Humanity falls into the background—" she had but right little special beholding unto the beauty of his precious and blessed body. " Moreover, the humanity of Christ is present to her—which is true of no other creature. It can be presumed, then, that the humanity of Christ still has a special role to play in the English author's contemplation.

One might compare the auther's mysticism with that of St. Teresa of Avila about whose doctrine a word can here be said. The great Spanish Carmelite is by no means as apophatic as the English mystic; she vigorously opposes any effort to put away the sacred humanity, saying that this is like " making the soul, as they say, to walk in the air; for it has nothing to rest on, how full soever of God it may think itself to be. " [11] Yet even she is willing to admit that there are times when the Humanity will be forgotten; but she explains that this forgetfulness is only apparent:

When God suspends all the powers of the soul—as we see He does in the states of prayer already described—it is clear that

[11] *Life*, c. XXII, 12.

whether we wish it or not this presence [i.e., the presence of the humanity of Christ] is withdrawn. Be it so, then. The loss is a blessed one, because it takes place *in order that we may have a deeper fruition* of what we seem to have lost. [12]

In other words, at the very pinnacle of the mystical life the soul is closely united to the humanity of Christ, which it seems to have lost and forgotten. St. Teresa indicates that there is a way of being united to the humanity of Christ without images and without concepts. [13] If so, this would be in keeping with the *Jesu Dulcis* which teaches of a lower form of union in which Jesus is united with the soul imaginatively in the memory and a higher form of union by presence. The first stage is the sweetness of the thought of Jesus: " Eius dulcis memoria "; the higher stage is the savoring of His presence: " Eius dulcis praesentia. " Of this poem Etienne Gilson writes that it " describes the movement by which the soul rises from re-membrance of the Passion of Christ to mystic union. " [14] The *praesentia* seems to be that " sense of presence " of which all the mystics speak, the deep awareness of Another without thought or concept or image. For that the humanity of Christ can be closely united to a soul that has closed its senses to all exterior things, that has shut out all images from its memory, all thoughts from its intellect and all love of creatures from its will—that Christ, God and Man, can enter such a soul, as He entered the upper room to His disciples when the doors were shut, is stated by St. John of the Cross in the following beautiful passage:

> Let the soul, then, remain " enclosed, " without anxieties and troubles, and he that entered in bodily form to His disciples

[12] *Ibid.*

[13] St. Teresa describes deep experiences of the humanity of Christ during which she had no *imaginative* picture of Him and no clear-cut thought. Thus even when the mind is emptied of all images and concepts one can still be with Christ. " I was in prayer one day, it was the feast of the glorious St. Peter, when I saw Christ close by me, or, to speak more correctly, felt Him; for I saw nothing with the eyes of the body, nothing with the eyes of the soul. He seemed to me to be close beside me; and I saw, too, as I believe, that it was He who was speaking to me... Jesus Christ seemed to be by my side continually, and, as the vision was not imaginary, I saw no form; but I had a most distinct feeling that He was always on my right hand, a witness of all I did; and never at any time, if I was slightly recollected, or not too much distracted, could I be ignorant of His near presence. " (*Life*, c. XXVII, 3)

[14] Gilson [1], p. 82.

when the doors were shut, and gave them peace, though they neither knew nor thought that this was possible nor knew how it was possible, will enter spiritually into the soul, without its knowing how He does so, when the doors of its faculties— memory, understanding and will—are enclosed against all apprehensions. And He will fill them with peace, coming down upon the soul, as the prophet says, like a river of peace, and taking from it all the misgivings and suspicions, disturbances and darknesses which caused it to fear that it was lost or was on the way to being so. Let it not grow careless about prayer, and let it wait in detachment and emptiness, for its blessing will not tarry. [15]

It is Christ, God and Man, who enters the soul when its memory, understanding, and will are void of all creatures— though the soul does not know how this is so or how it is possible.

CHRIST WITHIN

There are some indications that the author of *The Cloud* teaches a form of prayer to Christ who is within the soul. This appears in the short prayers that, we have already indicated, rise up in the midst of mystical contemplation; example of these are, he says, " Good Jesu! Fair Jesu! Sweet Jesu! " prayers directed to the Person of Christ, God and Man. Here is one of the passages in which he says that words may be used:

I say not this because I will that thou desist any time, if thou be stirred to pray with thy mouth, or to burst out, for abundance of devotion in thy spirit, for to speak unto God as unto man, and say some good word as thou feelest thyself stirred, as be these: " Good Jesu! Fair Jesu! Sweet Jesu! " and all such other. Nay, God forbid thou take it thus! For truly I mean not thus,

---

[15] *Ascent*, III, III, 6. And yet St. John of the Cross banishes all imaginations of Christ with the same ruthlessness as the author of *The Cloud*: " And to these two faculties (i.e., imagination and fancy) belongs meditation, which is a discursive action wrought by means of images, forms, and figures that are fashioned and imagined by the said senses, as when we imagine Christ crucified, or bound to the column, or at another of the stations... All these imaginings must be cast out from the soul, which will remain in darkness as far as this sense is concerned, that it may attain to Divine union; for they can bear no proportion to proximate means of union with God, any more than can the bodily imaginings, which serve as objects to the five exterior senses. " (*Ascent*, II, XII, 3)

and God forbid that I should separate what God hath coupled, the body and the spirit. (C. 90:12)

These prayers are addressed to Christ, God and Man, who is present in the soul when there is no image in the phantasm nor clear concept in the intellect; they call to mind the words of Ruysbroeck: " The coming of Christ to us is from within outwards, and we go towards Him from without inwards. " [16]

In conclusion, then, it may be said that when the English author speaks of forgetting the humanity of Christ, his primary meaning is that discursive, imaginative meditations on the life of Christ should be abandoned in favor of a dark contemplation of the Divinity concealed in His humanity. The prayer of the cloud is typified by Mary Magdalen who, finding the Divinity hidden in the humanity, is so enthralled thereby as to be no longer conscious of the merely human qualities of the man Christ. [17]

The author's teaching is based on a sound theology which states that in Christ there is one Person who is both man and God. As man, Christ is the door; as God, He is the porter. Through the door (and there is only one door) the contemplative enters to meet the porter who is the Second Person of the Blessed Trinity.

In the highest mystical prayer the humanity of Christ may be somehow present as it was present to Mary Magdalen, but the fascination of the divine may entail a temporary forgetting of the human. There is, however, a species of mystical prayer in which the contemplative is consciously united with the humanity of Christ; but this high union is never brought

---

[16] *Adornment of the Spiritual Marriage*, Bk. II, c. LVI.

[17] When one realizes that Christ can be present without clear-cut images and concepts, it can be understood why at the very summit of the mystical life, when the mind is dark and naked, the author can bring in references to the humanity of Christ, as in the following: " Yea! Jesu help thee then, for then hast thou need. For all the woe that may be without that, is not a point to that. For then art thyself a cross to thyself. And this is true working and the way to our Lord, as he himself saith: ' Let him bear his cross ' first in the painfulness of himself, and after ' follow me ' into bliss, or into the mount of perfection, tasting the softness of my love in godly feeling of myself. " (P.C. 157:14) Here the author is speaking of the cross at the summit of contemplation; namely, the cross of feeling one's own existence. And it is here that he brings in the humanity of Christ and quotes the Gospel.

about by concepts and mental images in the phantasm, rather is it a development of that " sense of presence " of which the mystics speak; it is a union with the man Christ who enters the silent soul as He entered the upper room to meet the disciples. when the doors were shut. [18]

THE BALANCE

In order to understand the mystical love of the English author, one must recall his idea on the harmony that should exist between body and soul in man. As there is to be no sentimentality, so there is to be no angelism. " God forbid that I should separate what God hath coupled, the body and the spirit, " he writes. (C. 90:16) As body and spirit will rise in glory, so must body and spirit adore God. [19] Here we find the key to his attitude toward Christ who is God and Man: he is looking for that Christian balance in which sense is subject to spirit and spirit is subject to God.

---

[18] Quite apart from mysticism, P. de Letter points out that the meeting of the ordinary Christian with Christ is not just built upon images and conceptual knowledge. " The knowledge of a person, such as is involved in and necessary for meeting a person, is not a purely conceptual knowledge. Even apart from direct contact, the idea we form of someone, from past experiences or from an indirect knowledge of his actions, sayings or writings, is not a mere concept or synthesis of concepts; it is rather a sort of general synthetic intuition resulting, not by reasoning but by ' seeing ', from the assemblage of many partial experiences or ideas. It apparently cannot be anything else if it is to be knowledge of the person, of the someone, of the *who* he is and not merely of *what* he is ". He then goes on to explain that the meeting with Christ is principally a question of love. " It should be noted here that the decisive element in our mental picture of Christ is less that of any of the particular features that go to its making and are generally rather blurred and dimmed than that of their synthesizing principle. And this is more a matter of love than of knowledge... No conceptual representation is by itself an adequate means to express the true personality of Christ, His divine Person. It is therefore by another way, that of love, that we are to arrive at a personal contact with Christ. Love is the way to a living encounter with Christ. " (De Letter [1]) From this it is not hard to see how, with the author of *The Cloud*, an intense love for Christ, God and man, can dispense with images and concepts.

[19] In the *Epistle of Prayer* the author reminds us that body and soul will " be oned in undeadliness at the uprising in the last day. " (P. 58:20)

5

THE CLOUD AND THE CHURCH

Before bringing this first part to a conclusion, it may be of some interest to consider the author's attitude to the Church. If, as has been said, the dark knowledge found in the cloud is a deeper penetration into the Christian mysteries, then the mystery of the Church, the Mystical Body of Christ, should be central to contemplative prayer. But here again, doubts have been cast on the orthodoxy of the English author's ecclesiology, in such wise that he has been depicted as a rebel against the authority of an organized Church. This way of thinking is part of a modern tendency to regard the mystic as someone who enters cloudy darkness in an effort to break with sacramental life and communal prayer, flying to a form of worship that is utterly personal. " Mysticism " is thus interpreted as an escape from ritual, the sacraments, and organization into an atmosphere of subjectivism, obscurity, and vagueness.

LIFE WITHIN THE CHURCH

In fact, *The Cloud* and its accompanying treatises speak of mysticism as a way of life within the Church. The mystic is precisely one who lives the life of the Church at its highest level and in all its richness. At the beginning of *The Cloud* the author takes up the objection of the contemplative who, though called to higher things, wishes to cling to the devotions of the ordinary Christian life; and he explains that within the Church there are various vocations or ways of life, so that to enter the cloud, far from being a rejection of the Church, is to unite oneself ever more closely with her, resting silently in her maternal bosom. His doctrine, a faithful transmission of the traditional teaching from the time of St. Augustine and St. Gregory, speaks of two manners of life in " Holy Church " (C. 31:3): the contemplative, which is the higher, and the active, which is the lower. The latter is the life of those who perform good and honest bodily works of mercy and charity, and it develops into the higher stage of the active life, which is also the lower stage of the contemplative life—and here one devotes self to " good ghostly meditations on the Passion and one's wretchedness. " But the highest stage, beginning in this life and lasting without end, " hangeth all wholly in this darkness and in this cloud of unknowing with a loving stirring and a blind beholding unto the naked being of God himself only. "

The lower merges gradually into the higher, there being no clear-cut break between them. There are, so to speak, degrees of membership in the Church, and the mystic rises to the highest. But in order to get to the higher one must to some extent sacrifice the lower; and that is why, when the call comes from the Good Shepherd, one must give up pious meditations and discursive prayer in order to enter the cloud. Here one leads a life like that of the Church triumphant. " For in the other life there shall be no need, as now, to use the works of mercy, nor to weep for our wretchedness, nor for the passion of Christ. For then shall no man hunger or thirst, as now, nor die for cold, nor be sick, nor houseless, nor in prison; nor yet need burial, for then shall no man die. " (C. 54:12) [1]

A somewhat similar view of the Church is given at the beginning of *The Cloud*, where the various ways of life (common, special, singular, and perfect) are described. (C. 3:8) The author goes on to say that the vocation to the highest, or perfect,

---

[1] The modern Church would scarcely approve of this line of argument. Surely Christ is speaking of the highest perfection in this passage from Matthew 25.

form of life comes through the others—one passes through the lower stages in order to reach the higher.

These two ways of life are later exemplified in the Martha-Mary motif already touched on. The author reminds us that "actives" will often criticize contemplatives, failing to understand them; but in fact it is precisely the contemplatives who do the greatest service to the Church.

THE MYSTICAL BODY

An interesting point is that, plunged in the cloud of unknowing and forgetful of all created things, the contemplative is by no means alone. He is united with all the saints in heaven, with all the faithful on earth, with all the souls in purgatory. That contemplation is the most social prayer imaginable is stressed in such words as the following:

> This is the work of the soul that most pleaseth God. All the saints and angels have joy of this work and hasten them to help it with all their might. All fiends be mad when thou dost thus, and try for to defeat it in all that they can. All men living on earth be wonderfully helped by this work, thou knowest not how. Yea, the souls in purgatory are eased of their pains by virtue of this work. Thou thyself art cleansed and made virtuous by no work so much. (C. 16:10)

Here is the Mystical Body, or the Communion of Saints. The mystic holds a special place in this social gathering and by his prayer he helps all who are in need. This does not mean that he is thinking explicitly of the souls in purgatory or of those on earth whom he helps. In the "ghostly work" of the cloud, he has forgotten them all; he has no longer clear-cut conceptual knowledge nor does he have in his phantasm mental images of Our Lady and the saints. Yet he is united with them all. The tone of the author is that of one who would reassure an anxious soul: "Don't worry because you do not think explicitly of the souls in purgatory or of your friends in need; in fact you help them all the more in your dark forgetting of the cloud." Such again is the Pauline strain in the following words:

A soul that is perfectly disposed to this work, and thus oned with God in spirit, doth what in it is to make all men as perfect in this work as itself is. For right as if a limb of our body feeleth sore, all the other limbs be pained and distressed, or if a limb fare well, all the remainder be gladdened therewith— right so is it ghostly with all the limbs of Holy Church. For Christ is our head, and we be the limbs, if we be in charity; and whoso will be a perfect disciple of our Lord's, he must strain up his spirit in this ghostly work, for the salvation of all his brethren and sisters in nature, as our Lord did his body on the cross. And how? Not only for his friends and his kin and his dear lovers, but generally for all mankind, without any special regard more to one than to another. (C. 60:19)

So, far from being a flight from one's fellow-men, the silent and imageless prayer of the cloud is a means to the closest union with them. Indeed, when mystical prayer reaches its highest point, when it is at its existential level, the contemplative saying, " That that I am and how that I am... I offer unto thee "—at this stage the author reminds us that he is no individualist; for all this is done " for the help of all mine even Christians and of me. " (P.C. 141:22) That is to say, the highest mystical prayer is a sacrifice of oneself for all men. The author continues later:

And more charity may no man do than thus to sacrifice himself for all his brethren and sisters in nature and grace. (P.C. 142:23)

It is hardly necessary to labor the social aspect of the author's doctrine: his mysticism is no escape from the world, no flight from one's duties to society, but a service of all men through the Church.

THE VISIBLE CHURCH

Furthermore, just as this silent prayer of the cloud arises out of the lower stages of prayer and is a way of life within the Church, so it never ceases to depend on the prayer of the Church and on her sacraments for its nourishment. The author is clear in his assertion that he is not opposing liturgical prayer; it is only during his " special prayers " that the contemplative remains silent in the cloud, but liturgical prayer is also necessary and should be performed in the traditional way. Having said that the contemplatives' special prayers rise straight to God, he continues:

> I mean their special prayers, not those prayers that be ordained by Holy Church. For they that be true workers in this work, they worship no prayer so much as those of Holy Church and therefore they do them in the form and in the statute that they be ordained by holy fathers before us. (C. 74:1)

The prayers " ordained by Holy Church " are presumably those of the Divine Office recited in choir by the monks of the time: fidelity to these is demanded of the contemplative.

And this is only part of his general tendency to put great stress on the external observances of the Church. Far from trying to escape from the organized Church with its observances, he shows such fidelity to it and such a strong opposition to heresy that many of his broadsides against " the heretics " jar somewhat on our modern ecumenical ears. All the intolerance of the Middle Ages wells up in such passages as the following:

> Some there be that. . . for pride and curiosity of natural wit and letterly knowledge leave the common doctrine and counsel of Holy Church. And these with all their favourers lean over much to their own knowing. And because they were never grounded in this meek blind feeling and virtuous living, therefore they merit to have a false feeling, feigned and wrought by the ghostly enemy. Insomuch that at the last they burst up and blaspheme all the saints, sacraments, statutes, and ordinances of Holy Church. Fleshly living men of the world, the which think the statutes of Holy Church over hard for them to amend their lives by, they lean to these heretics full soon and full lightly, and stalwartly maintain them, and all because they think that they lead them a softer way than is ordained by Holy Church. (C. 104:5)

The English author then proceeds to make a somewhat unpleasant attack on the personal character of these " heretics, " putting them into a dire part of the " inferno ":

> Now I trow that whoso will not go the strait way to heaven they shall go the soft way to hell. Each man prove by himself. For

I trow that all such heretics, and all their favourers, if they might clearly be seen as they shall on the last day, should be seen full soon cumbered in great and horrible sins of the world and their foul flesh secretly, apart from their open presumption in maintaining error. So that they be full properly called Antichrist's disciples. (C. 104:17)

Together with this opposition to all forms of heresy is a meticulous fidelity to the laws of " Holy Church. " It is especially to the sacrament of Penance that he attaches importance, stressing that this gives the fundamental grace on which the life of contemplation is built. It is that sanctifying grace, received in Baptism and restored through Penance, that incorporates one in the Church—living in a society where infant Baptism was the ordinary thing, it is to Penance that he gives the emphasis, reminding his reader that this is the point of departure, incomparably more important than any subjective experience of loving stirrings:

But if thou ask me when they shall work in this work, then I answer thee and say: not till they have cleansed their conscience of all their special deeds of sin done before, according to the common ordinance of Holy Church. (C. 63:8)

This emphasis on confession is indeed remarkable, turning up as it does in the most unexpected places. In the *Epistle of Prayer*, for instance, he has been telling his disciple that he must have great confidence in God for, should he die before the end of his prayer, God will show him mercy; but then he makes the interesting proviso—" I mean thus, provided that thou hast beforehand lawfully amended thee after the common ordinance of Holy Church in confession. " (P. 49:18) Such conditions cannot but give the reader something of a jolt. [2]

And the fasts of the Church are important too. Self-chosen

[2] In *Privy Counsel*, when advocating the darkest prayer in existential darkness, he sternly inculcates the necessity of the sacrament of Penance: " And therefore, I pray thee, do no more now in this case; but think simply that thou art as thou art, be thou never so foul nor so wretched so that thou have beforetimes (as I suppose that thou hast) been lawfully amended of all thy sins in special and in general, after the true counsel of Holy Church. For else shalt thou never, nor any other by my consent, be so bold as to take upon you this work. " (P.C. 138:18)

penance, he states clearly enough, is of little value compared with the blind stirring of love; but it is taken for granted that every Christian will keep the fasts of the Church. [3]

SUBJECTIVISM

Contrary to the common opinion that mystical experience is something subjective, the author insists on the necessity of an objective norm. No man can see himself without a mirror, and the same is true of the things of the spirit:

> And right as thou seest that if a foul spot be in thy bodily visage, the eye of the same visage may not see that spot nor learn where it is, without a mirror or the teaching of another than itself: right so is it ghostly. Without reading or hearing of God's word it is impossible to man's understanding that a soul that is blinded in a habit of sin should see the foul spot in his conscience. (C. 72:6)

He goes on to say that if a man has such a " foul spot on his visage, " he runs to the well to wash himself. " If this spot be any special sin, then is this well Holy Church, and this water confession, with the circumstances thereof. If it be but a blind root and a stirring of sin, then is this well merciful God, and this water prayer, with the circumstances thereof. " (C. 72:15)

It is hardly necessary here to quote at length the passages declaring that those appointed by the Church can judge the conscience of men [4] or those that stress the necessity of " counsel " and obedience to the director appointed by the Church. It is " the perilest purpose that may be, a young man to follow the fierceness of his desire unruled by counsel. " (P.C. 160:17) Those who will not be governed by the advice

---

[3] " And what is more : assuredly I had rather have the reward of him that persevereth in such doing, although he never did bodily penance in this life *but only that enjoined to him of Holy Church,* than of all the penance doers that have been in this life, from the beginning of the world unto this day, without this manner of doing. " (P. 51:13)

[4] " But I pray thee, by whom shall men's deeds be judged? Surely by them that have power and cure of their souls: either given openly by the statute and the ordinance of Holy Church, or else privily in spirit at the special stirring of the Holy Ghost in perfect charity. " (C. 65:10)

of others are in great danger: " I grant that many fall and have fallen... because they would not rule them by true ghostly counsel... have become the devil's servants and his contemplatives; and turned either to hypocrites or heretics... to the slander of Holy Church. " (C. 49:12) True contemplation must be " proved by examination of Scripture and of counsel and of conscience. " (P.C. 170:14)

The conclusion is that the English mystic is depicting what he considers the highest way of life within the Church; it is a life in which the contemplative, united with Our Lord, " Our Lady Saint Mary, " and the saints sacrifices himself for the salvation of all men on earth and in purgatory. Contemplation, built upon obedience to the Church and fidelity to her prayer and sacramental life, is a development of that sanctifying grace received at Baptism and restored through the sacrament of Penance. Though it is a gratuitous gift of God, it can scarcely be called an extraordinary grace insofar as it is the climax of the normal path by which God leads His chosen ones to perfection, calling them from the active life to the contemplative through ways of life that are named " common, " " special, " " singular, " and " perfect. "

6

CONCLUSION

Having touched upon the principal problems of unknowing, it may now be possible to reach some general conclusions about the cloud and about the enigmatic phrase that " the most godly knowledge of God is that which is known by unknowing. "

Two Kinds of Knowledge

From what has been said, it is clear that the English author divides knowledge into two clear-cut, psychological categories.

The first kind of knowledge is that of discursive reasoning and logical thinking central to all scholastic thought. This knowledge takes its origin in the external senses that contact the outside world, conveying to the phantasm images that are spiritualized or " de-materialized " by the so-called *intellectus agens* and thus conceived in the mind. In this way is born discursive reasoning with its successive judgments and conceptual thinking that, ordinarily speaking, is not performed without some image in the phantasm—though the image is distinct from the concept, images being singular while concepts are universal.

Concepts are applicable in a univocal sense to the world around us, since it is precisely from this world that we abstract them; but when man applies these concepts to God he must in part deny them. He continues to use them, of course, but at the risk of falling into an erroneous anthropomorphism he must always keep in mind that no concept can be applied univocally to God—much less can any man have a mental image of what God is.

Provided he keeps this in mind, however, man can think correctly about God in images and concepts; and, indeed, this is the ordinary approach to God used in the Scriptures and in the teaching of the Church. Furthermore, man can reflect discursively on the things of God; he can reason from cause to effect, finding God in the universe—and this is philosophy. Or he can reflect on the Christian message, penetrating into its hidden meaning—and this is theology. But here a new element enters in; namely, supernatural faith that enlightens the mind: this faith in no way destroys conceptual thinking, nor does it hinder it, nor does it give new concepts; but it enables the mind to find in the propositions of Scripture and the Church a hidden truth completely inaccessible to the unaided human powers.

The second kind of knowledge takes place at a deeper level of the personality. This is the knowledge of the cloud: it is dark, supraconceptual, contemplative, mystical. It is that knowledge which fills the mind when, in utter silence and devoid of all images and thoughts, it remains in tranquillity. Phenomenologically speaking, dark and supraconceptual knowledge is in no wise extraordinary or miraculous, nor is it peculiarly Christian, being found from the earliest times in India and being highly developed in the Orient as, for example, in Zen. For the grasping of spiritual reality, whether it be the reality of God, of self, of the hearts of others, or of being, this supraconceptual knowledge is incomparably superior to that of discursive reasoning.

The contemplative knowledge of the English author has, however, in common with all Christian mysticism, one important characteristic: it is grounded on faith filled with love; and its object is the Triune God. In his doctrine, this sublime knowledge is not acquired by any " *kōan*-like " destruction of the reasoning powers but by the upward (or downward) impulse of a blind stirring of love that rises from the darkness of faith. All love (but especially that which is divine) longs for union with an urgency that is impatient of reasoning and intolerant of discourse: it does not deny but transcends reasoning and carries the intelligence to God Himself, where it finds new and deeper wisdom. It cannot be sufficiently stressed that his *via negativa* is meaningless without his *via amoris*.

The dividing line between these two kinds of knowledge, conceptual and supraconceptual, is not made clear by Augustine, the Victorines, and St. Thomas, for whom discursive prayer merges into contemplative prayer; and mysticism, far from being a distinct phenomenon, is the climax of the ordinary life of prayer. But the dividing line *is* clear in Dionysius (for whom dark knowledge is something apart) and later in the Rhineland mystics and St. John of the Cross. The author of *The Cloud* is in this latter company, though he seems to hold, too, that discursive prayer somehow develops into contemplation.

If, after some time spent in discursive prayer, the love of God has burnt deeply into the heart and one finds oneself called to the quiet of supraconceptual prayer, one must abandon the lower form of discursive reasoning for the higher form of spiritual rest; and this is done by voiding the mind of images and concepts, surrounding oneself with a cloud of forgetting. One does so, not because images and concepts are false but because they are inadequate and because one is descending to a deeper level of the psyche at which it is easier to contact God. Now it is that one enters the cloud of unknowing; now it is that one " knows nothing "—that is to say, one abandons the first way of thinking; but, on the other hand, one " knows everything, " being in contact with God in a new and superior way. For the mind is emptied of images and thoughts only in order to be filled with God in love at a deeper level.

SUPERNATURAL FAITH AND LOVE

Obviously, it would be a theological blunder of the first magnitude to identify supraconceptual or mystical with supernatural, as though ordinary reasoning in Christian prayer were a natural process whereas supraconceptual contemplation were supernatural. In fact, the supernatural stands apart from such phenomenological or psychological distinctions in such wise that the discursive prayer of the simplest believer is penetrated with faith, giving him a knowledge that no human endeavor is capable of obtaining; whereas, conversely, the highest supra-conceptual knowledge (the state in which the mind rests in quiet, or even in ecstasy, devoid of thoughts) need not necessarily be penetrated by the supernatural gift of faith. Supraconceptual knowledge may even be illusory as the author indicates when he says in his quaint medieval way that " the devil has his contemplatives as God has his, " (C. 86:19) and in this he is backed up by the tradition of the Church, indicating that there can be all kinds of supraconceptual knowledge that are not filled with supernatural faith and love.

The all-important thing for the author is that knowledge (be it conceptual or supraconceptual) should be penetrated with the grace of God; and that is why he keeps hammering home that the first thing is to receive the sacrament of Penance and to remain loyal to the Church. This is in keeping with the doctrine of St. Thomas who says that the faith of an old woman (his famous *parvula vetula*) is superior to the wisdom of the philosophers—and, he might have added, to the tranquil prayer or the ecstasies of the mystics who lack grace. [1]

In short, for the author of *The Cloud* the tranquillity of the contemplative mind resting silently in supraconceptual knowl-edge is of value only because here that supernatural faith and love which are the basis of the ordinary Christian life, infused at Baptism and restored by Penance, sink deeper and deeper into the human psychology rooting themselves in its very core and (as shall be seen later) removing the scars of sin. Divorced from concepts and reasoning, faith and love grow in strength and reach their perfection; for now they rely on no human prop but are naked, supported by God alone who is their proper object. Contemplative prayer does not change the essence of supernatural faith and charity; the supernatural gifts of the mystic are not fundamentally different from those of the newly baptized—only they are stronger. And the value of contemplation lies in this, and in this alone. The cloud, far

---

[1] I do not mean to imply here that unbaptized people lack grace or that they are incapable of mystical experience in the Christian sense of the word, since it is certain that God gives His grace outside the visible Church. I merely wish to emphasize that grace cannot be measured by psychological phenomena.

from being a rejection of dogma and of faith, is no more than the heroic adherence of the mind to those truths contained in the deposit of revelation and a heroic adherence of the will to God who reveals Himself in Christ and in the Church.

THE UNITY OF TRUTH

From this it can be seen that the object of mystical knowledge and love is precisely the same as that of knowledge and love in the ordinary Christian life which, when it reaches its peak, develops into mysticism. And this is the point made by Augustine Baker who holds that the prayer of *The Cloud* is ordinary, saying: " And I call it ordinary because it is the way by which God usually calleth and guideth those souls whom he would have to attain to his perfect love. " [2] And furthermore it indicates that the mysticism of *The Cloud* is phenomenologically ordinary in the sense that God acts through His ordinary psychological laws that can be reduced to a science.

As for theology, which is discursive reflection on the Christian message in the light of faith, enough has been said to show that the English author holds firmly its validity, though he hates vanity and attacks a *false* theology which might presume to claim that man can know God univocally by means of the discursive intellect: it may also be that he is in reaction against an exaggerated Aristotelianism with its excessively dialectical approach to the things of God. His true esteem for theology, however, is proved conclusively by his approach to his subject; for he writes not primarily as a mystic but as a theologian, and the greater part of his doctrine is built upon traditional theology.

The general conclusion is that his doctrine is an accurate and personal expression of Christian mystical theology, teaching a form of contemplation that is no more than an intense form of the Christian life, deriving all its value not from anything phenomenological but from the fact that it entails a heroic practice of faith and love. His contemplative sees and loves nothing different from the ordinary Christian—he enters, like Moses, with great love into the darkness of that cloud which is faith.

[2] McCann, p. 160.

PART II

Love

7

THE BLIND STIRRING

DESCRIPTION

Two Kinds of Love

It has been said that there are two kinds of knowledge, the ordinary conceptual knowledge accompanied by images and exercised through discursive reasoning, and the dark knowledge of the cloud which is supraconceptual, situated in silence at the lowest level of the personality.

Corresponding to these two psychological divisions of knowledge are two kinds of love: the ordinary love that goes out to what we know and experience through the senses, and to God known through sensible things; and another kind of love that, again, burns at a lower level of the personality in silent tranquillity stretching out toward God whom the contemplative scarcely seems to know—or, more correctly, he knows *that* He is but not *what* He is; for God is surrounded by a cloud of unknowing. This is love founded not upon anything one can think but on naked faith: " I would leave all that thing that I can think, and choose to my love that thing that I cannot think. " (C. 26:2) And this is the author's " blind stirring of love "; it is that love which fills the heart of Mary when, in total forgetfulness of all things, she sits rapt in contemplation of Christ's divinity; it is no different from the " living flame of love " of St. John of the Cross; and it is the characteristic feature of all Christian mysticism.

The work of the English author is largely a eulogy of this blind stirring of love. He refers to it as a " secret little love, " as a " naked intent of the will, " as a " blind outstretching, " as a " meek stirring of love, " as " this working, " or simply as " it. " It should be noted, however, that he uses these expressions for an activity that *includes* knowledge or consciousness of some kind. For purposes of analysis it is possible to speak of knowledge and love in contemplation; but the activity the author speaks of is a blend of both, a completely simple experience arising in the depth of the contemplative's heart: in the last analysis it is indescribable as the author declares when he says that " all that is spoken of it is not it, but of it. " (P.C. 153:20) He has no doubt, however, that its predominant element is love and it is upon this that he puts all the emphasis. The practice of unknowing with its treading down of all distinct knowledge beneath the cloud of forgetting is no more than a preparation for the cultivation of this blind stirring that is the most important thing in life. This is reiterated many times as, for example, in such words as the following:

> And therefore, if thou wilt stand and not fall, cease never in thine intent, but beat evermore on this cloud of unknowing that is betwixt thee and thy God with a sharp dart of longing love. And loathe to think on aught under God. And go not thence for anything that befalleth. (C. 38:11)

This, a typical passage, shows how the business of forgetting is relegated to a secondary place, being no more than means of making room for the " sharp dart of longing love " which, however, is accompanied by a deep consciousness of God.

EXPERIMENTAL NATURE

Evidently, this stirring is different from that love of the ordinary Christian who, possessing grace, keeps the commandments; for the author gives certain tests (already referred to) by which it can be distinguished from any vague interior movements that might perchance masquerade as mysticism. Perhaps its most distinctive feature is its intensely experimental nature, indicated by the very words used to describe it. " For what is stirring but motion? " writes Augustine Baker, " And he calleth it a ' blind stirring ' because it is without use of the understanding which is the eye of the soul. And he calleth such exercise a ' stirring of love ' because the soul thereby heaveth herself up towards him, choosing him and seeking after him for his sake."[1]

The psychological repercussions of this stirring are described in several passages where the author indicates that love has wonderful effects upon the body, suffusing the contemplative's countenance with serenity, making him attractive in the eyes of other men, and giving him insight into the workings of their souls. Even those who are not highly endowed by nature are rendered beautiful by this little love:

> Whoso had this work, it should govern him full seemly, as well in body as in soul; and make him full favourable unto each man or woman that looked upon him. Insomuch, that the worst-favoured man or woman that liveth in this life, if they might come by grace to work in this work, their favour should suddenly and graciously be changed, so that each good man that saw them should be fain and joyful, to have them in company, and full much they should think that they were pleased in spirit and helped by grace unto God in their presence. (C. 100:5)

This stirring will, moreover, govern the contemplative's actions. " His countenance and his words should be full of ghostly wisdom, full of fire and of fruit, spoken in sober certainty without any falsehood, far from any feigning of piping hypocrites. " (C. 100:23) In a passage of remarkable beauty in *Privy Counsel*, the author describes how the contemplative is always longing silently for God with a desire that is even an obstacle to his daily work; this blind stirring rises with him in the morning; it accompanies him all during the day; with him it goes to bed. He would run a thousand miles to converse with someone who had a similar experience

[1] McCann, p. 164.

and can speak about " it, " but usually he prefers to be alone:

> It changeth thy gesture and maketh thy countenance seemly; while it lasteth all things please thee and nothing grieve thee; a thousand miles wouldst thou run to converse mouthly with one that thou knewest verily felt it; and yet, when thou comest there, canst thou nothing say, speak whoso speak will, for thou wouldst not speak but of it. (P.C. 166:19)

From the author's words, one gets the impression that this stirring is sometimes like a beautiful but foreign intrusion into the life of the contemplative, interfering with his life and somehow cutting him off from society in such wise that (not unnaturally) he becomes a target of criticism. Yet, even if he does not quite fit in and is abandoned by friends and acquaintances, the author, with characteristic humanity, advises the contemplative not to be harsh on his critics but to leave them (and himself) to God: Our Lord who works in their hearts will see to it that His friends are finally justified.

Meanwhile this stirring develops, grows in intensity, and comes to possess the whole life of the contemplative. It is his criterion of right and wrong in the affairs of daily life:

> And if they think that there is no manner of thing that they do, bodily or ghostly, that is sufficiently done with witness of their conscience, unless this secret little love set upon the cloud of unknowing be in ghostly manner the chief of all their work; and if they thus feel—then it is a token that they be called by God to this work; and surely else not. (C. 131:12)

From this it can be seen that even outside the time devoted to prayer as such, the secret little love is dominating the life of the contemplative. In time of prayer, it is silently beating against the cloud of unknowing while all the natural faculties are rapt in deep sleep. But sometimes it will rise up violently to God, bringing about the state of ecstasy. The author of *The Cloud* has little of the Victorine emphasis on ecstatic experience, but he does make some reference to *excessus mentis*, one of the traditional words for ecstasy, telling us that by Benjamin is meant " all those that in excess of love be ravished above mind, the prophet saying thus, ' Ibi Benjamin adolescentulus in mentis excessu. ' " ²

Such is the wonderful power of this meek stirring that at first rises quietly and delicately in the heart, but later comes to fill the whole personality, enriching it wonderfully.

PSYCHOLOGICAL IMPORTANCE

I have stressed the deeply experimental nature of the blind stirring of love with its repercussions on the body, because all this points to the author's belief that contemplative love enters deeply into the human psyche, exploring those parts of the mind that we moderns have come to call " subliminal " or " subconscious " and that remain untouched by ordinary reasoning and colloquies in prayer. This will become even clearer when, in the next part, we see his doctrine that contemplation removes the " roots " of sin, entering that part of the psyche where concupiscence takes its origin and exercising what, again, we moderns call " therapeutic " influence upon the human psychology. This alone can explain the serenity of the countenance, the facility of acts of virtue, the unification of the personality that accompany contemplation. That such an intense love of God should have a transforming effect upon the whole man is no more than we should expect; for a love that transformed the soul, leaving the body untouched, would be

---

² St. Thomas writes: " excessus mentis, extasis et raptus, omnia in Scripturis pro eodem accipiuntur; et significant elevationem quandem ab exterioribus sensibilibus... ad aliqua quae sunt super hominem. " (*De Ver.*, XIII, 2 ad 9) Neither St. Thomas nor the author of *The Cloud* are referring to those bodily repercussions that in modern parlance are associated with the word " ecstasy. " Such phenomena are natural. Joseph de Guibert writes of the phenomenon of ecstasy that it is " by no means an essential part or even an integral part of infused contemplation... it is only a consequence arising from the weakness of the human organism which cannot bear the force of the Divine action without becoming incapable of performing the lower psychological actions, or without being compelled to perform these actions incompletely and with difficulty. Therefore where ecstasy is present it does not always and necessarily presuppose that the divine action is more intense than where it is lacking; it is dependent on other factors, both psychological and physiological. In fact, the common opinion is that in the highest degree of infused contemplation, the transforming union, ecstasies either cease altogether or become less frequent and less profound. It seems that this is due to the organism's being indirectly strengthened to bear the weight of the Divine action. " (De Guibert, Part 7, c. 4, p. 354)

Platonically unacceptable to the Christian mind. Prayer transforms the body, as it transformed the body of Christ at the Transfiguration, and the author explains that his contemplation is only a preparation for that time when body and soul will rise in " undeadliness " at the day of judgment.

Such, briefly, is the blind stirring of love around which the work of the English author centers.

THE PROBLEMS

The first problem posed by the above description of the blind stirring concerns its relationship to that charity infused with Baptism to all Christians who are obliged to love God with their whole heart and their whole soul and their whole mind and their whole strength, and their neighbor as self. The traditional, evangelical doctrine, held by the Church against gnostics, Montanists and Messalians, was that Christian perfection consists in charity; and the English author, as ever obstinately loyal to tradition, has no hesitation in following that doctrine:

> At the first I ask of thee what is perfection of man's soul and which be the properties that pertain to this perfection? I answer in thy person and I say that perfection of man's soul is nought else but a onehead made betwixt God and it in perfect charity. (P.C. 153:24)

This is a theologically correct statement, but (and here the problem arises) he seems to identify the blind stirring with perfect charity; as, for example, when he says: " For if it be wisely looked, the ground and strength of this working shall be nought else but the glorious gift of love, in the which by the teaching of the Apostle all the law is fulfilled: ' Plenitudo legis est dilectio, ' ' the fulness of the law is love. ' " (P.C. 146:11) Here the author equates the contemplative love he teaches with the love St. Paul prescribes for the ordinary Christian in the Epistle to the Romans. Does this mean that the blind stirring is no more than a strong expression of that supernatural charity that all in grace possess?

The second problem concerns the relationship of this love to knowledge. He speaks of it as " blind " making it very clear that it does not depend upon discursive reasoning. Does this mean that it is something irrational springing out of the depths of nowhere and beginning to dominate a man's life? Or has it a rational basis of some kind, albeit not the product of discursive reason?

The third problem concerns the knowledge or consciousness of God that accompanies it. It has already been said that this stirring is a blend of knowledge and love; for " a great clerk that men call Richard of St. Victor " has said that " as Rachel and Lya were both wives to Jacob, right so man's soul, *through light of knowing in the reason and sweetness of love in the affection* is spoused unto God, " (S.W. 12:9) and in contemplation the soul is " inflamed with the fire of love in the affection and... illumined with the light of knowing in the reason. " (S.W. 22:3) What is the nature of this knowledge or wisdom that enlightens the mind of the contemplative in darkness when concepts and reasoning are abandoned? The author states that God can be *known* by love. What is the nature of this knowledge?

The pages that follow will attempt to discuss these problems.

8

THE BLIND STIRRING
AND CHRISTIAN PERFECTION

CONTEMPLATIVE LOVE AND EVANGELICAL LOVE

Even a casual reading of the work of the author of *The Cloud* reveals that he makes no distinction between the blind stirring of love and the love taught by Christ in the Gospels. At the beginning of *The Cloud* he states that he is teaching the following of Christ whose chief commandment is to love God and one's neighbor: this " working, " then, is the perfect way of love. If contemplation is not for everyone and strict tests are required to discern the voice of the Good Shepherd, this is because (to quote his own words) " I make a difference betwixt them that be called to salvation and them that be called to perfection. " (P.C. 161:17) Not every Christian is called to *experience* so deeply and so intensely that infused love that he possesses by the grace of his redemption in Christ; but those called to perfect love are also called to contemplation. This doctrine appears in several of his works.

LOVE IN THE *Epistle of Prayer*

The author's teaching about love is clearly set out in his *Epistle of Prayer*, which might equally well be called an *Epistle of Love*, for in fact it deals with the perfect love of God.

Having been asked to give his disciple advice on the subject of prayer, the author in his reply divides prayer into three stages. At the beginning of his prayer, the disciple should reflect that he may die before this prayer comes to an end, and so he will arouse in his heart the feeling of holy dread—" initium sapientiae timor Domini "; but this holy dread must be tempered by hope and trust in the goodness of God who (provided the disciple has repented of his sins in confession according to the laws of Holy Church) will grant him salvation after this prayer even if he should die; and in the third stage he can (like Moses) " climb into the high mount of perfection, that is to say, the perfect love of God. " (P. 50:13) Thus the three stages are fear, hope, and love.

At first, however, this love is imperfect, being directed not to God as He is in Himself but being based on His gifts to us: " It may not be but that thou shalt feel a great stirring of love unto him that is so good and so *merciful unto thee.* " (P. 50:20) Nevertheless, even though something of self is mingled in this love, it is a very good thing.

Fear and love, mingled with hope, go to make up " reverence. " And this reverence, or " reverent affection, " is so wonderfully important that if a man has this and does no penance except that enjoined him by Holy Church, his reward is greater than that of " all the penance doers that have been in this life, from the beginning of this world unto this day, without this manner of doing. " (P. 51:15) This reverence is necessary for salvation: " And it were impossible any soul to have reward of God without this... and all these other things, as is fasting, waking, sharp wearing and all these other, they are of value in as much as they be helpful to get this; so that without this they are nought, and this without them is sometime sufficient at the full by himself. " (P. 51:24)

Yet even this, sufficient though it is for salvation, is not sufficient for perfection, for it contains fear and hope so that an element of self remains. Perfect love is that which goes to God not for His goods but for Himself—" and then thou shalt be called God's own child, loving him with a chaste love for himself and not for his goods. " (P. 53:7) For while it is true that the thought of God's wonderful mercy is sufficient cause to make us love Him with our whole heart and soul and mind and strength, yet if it were possible (and it is not) that there were a soul to whom God had never shown any kindness and love, " yet this soul, seeing the loveliness of God in himself and the abundance thereof, should be ravished over his might for to love God till the heart break, so lovely and so liking, so good and so glorious he is in himself. O what a wonderful thing, and how high a thing is the love of God for to speak of. " (P. 53:17) But it is impossible to speak adequately of this love, for it transcends all understanding.

The author describes the growth of this perfect love in an image used also by St. Thomas; namely, the root, the tree, the branches, and the fruit. [1] The root of the tree, the part within the earth, is fear; the part above the earth, the body and the boughs, is hope—this hope, insofar as it is certain and stable, is the body, and insofar as it stirs to works of love it is the boughs; and the reverent affection is the fruit. But while the fruit is joined to the tree, it has a green smell of the tree, whereas when it is removed from the tree for a while it becomes ripe and delicious so that now it is " king's meat that before was knave's meat. " This ripe fruit is the perfect love of God. No longer joined to the tree, it depends on neither fear nor hope; it is inspired by no thought of the benefits of God. " Therefore shape thee for to depart this fruit from the tree and to offer it up by itself to the high king of heaven. " This is perfect love for which everyone must strive, " for evermore as long as thou offerest him this fruit green and hanging on the tree, thou mayest well be likened to a woman that is not chaste, for she loveth a man more for his goods than for himself. " [2] (P. 54:22) When your love is chaste, you do not ask for release from pain nor for reward in this life nor for sweetness in prayer, " but thou askest of God nought but himself. "

This chaste and perfect love is found in man when his " affection is stirred unto God without mean, that is without

---

[1] II^a-II^{ae}, Q. XIX, art. vii.

[2] St. Bernard speaks frequently of the soul's chaste love. " That its love is chaste is very evident, for we know that ' chaste ' here means *disinterested*. Now Whom the soul loves she loves then for Himself, and for the sake of nothing else whatever, not even for any one of those gifts He has to give. " (Gilson [1], pp. 111, 112)

messenger of any thought in special causing that stirring. "
(P. 55:21) This sentence is of some significance. What is this
" without mean "?

St. Thomas has said that Adam knew God " without mean "
(sine medio), and he explains that this means without
reasoning from sensible things (" Non per medium argumentationis ex creaturis sensibilibus "). The English author, too,
has used this expression frequently and now he adds " without
messenger of any thought in special causing that stirring, " as
if to stress the fact that the love of God reaches its chaste and
perfect state when special thoughts, conceptual thinking and
reasoning are buried beneath the cloud of forgetting. When
the most perfect love of God rises stirringly within the breast
of man, it is not caused by any process of natural thinking but
by God Himself. He it is who brings about that union " that
knitteth man's soul to God and that maketh it one with him
in love and accordance of will " (P. 56:13), a union that
reaches its climax in " the marriage made betwixt God and
the soul. "

An interesting feature of the above is that it is substantially
the ordinary theological doctrine of St. Thomas. [3] The Angelic
Doctor, too, teaches that perfect love is motivated by the
goodness of God in Himself: it is not inspired by any " mean "
or intermediary, nor by holy fear nor yet by remembrance of
the goodness of God but only (as the English author has it)
by " the loveliness of God in himself. " The contribution of the
English author is that he identifies his *contemplative* love with
perfect love, indicating that one cannot love God perfectly
unless the cloud of forgetting has done away with discursive
reasoning and " special " thoughts. In short, he indicates that
the blind stirring of love is that perfect love in which Christian
perfection consists.

---

[3] The " without mean " is the *sine medio* of St. Thomas that also occurs
frequently in Ruysbroeck. In the *Second Book of the Sentences*, St. Thomas
states that Adam saw God without mean *(sine medio)*; but he explains that
this does not mean that Adam had the beatific vision, which is to see God *per
essentiam*, but that he knew God without reasoning from created things: " non
per medium argumentationis ex creaturis sensibilibus... sed mediante effectu
spirituali in intellectum ejus resultante... " (*II Sent.*, d. 23, q. 2, art. 1, ad 1)

IN *The Cloud*

From beginning to end, *The Cloud* is a treatise on divine love; but here it is only necessary to draw attention to one passage where the author identifies the " naked intent " with that love which is enjoined upon all Christians in the Gospel and that has been analyzed by St. Thomas. He is speaking of " this blind little love set on God... beating upon this dark cloud of unknowing, all other things being put down and forgotten, " and he says that it includes all the virtues but especially charity:

> For charity meaneth nought else but love of God for himself above all creatures, and of man for God even as thyself. And that in this work God is loved for himself and above all creatures, it seemeth right well. For, as it is said before, the substance of this work is nought else but a naked intent directed unto God for himself. (C. 58:11)

This definition of charity is similar to that of the *Epistle of Prayer*; now he goes on to say why the naked intent demands *perfect* love, arguing that contemplative love is perfect because centered on God without consideration of any creature whatever; and this is the meaning of " naked ":

> A " naked intent " I call it. Because in this work a perfect prentice asketh neither releasing of pain, nor increasing of reward, nor (shortly to say) *nought but himself.* Insomuch, that he neither recketh nor regardeth whether he be in pain or in bliss, but only that his will be fulfilled whom he loveth. And thus it seemeth that in this work God is perfectly loved for himself, and above all creatures. For in this work a perfect worker may not suffer the thought of the holiest creature that ever God made to share with him. (C. 58:16)

The resemblance to the *Epistle of Prayer* is obvious: the contemplative asks of God " nought but himself " and the way of doing this is by abandoning all thoughts, even " the thought of the holiest creature that ever God made. "

The author then goes on to speak about charity toward the neighbor, the conclusion being that " this work " is nothing else but the fulfillment of the commandment of love in its most perfect form.

IN *Privy Counsel*

As often, *Privy Counsel* strikes a more somber note. This work is the perfect love taught by Christ precisely because of its nakedness and abandonment of all creatures. " This is the work of love that none may know but he that feeleth it. This is the lesson of our Lord when he saith, ' Whoso will love me, let him forsake himself.' " (P.C. 156:20) In order to fulfill Christ's precept of perfect love, one must renounce all things. Just as the mind is naked because it has renounced all conceptual knowledge to remain in the darkness of faith, and just as it suffers because of its craving to know and possess natural learning, so now is the will naked because it renounces love of all creatures to love God for Himself alone. If you wish to be a perfect lover, then you must " strip, spoil, and utterly unclothe thyself of all manner of feeling of thyself, that thou mayest be able to be clothed with the gracious feeling of God himself. " (P.C. 156:13) Here the rejection of " all manner of feeling of thyself " is that forgetfulness of essences and of self which is outlined throughout *Privy Counsel*; and the author seems to be saying that in order to love God perfectly it is *necessary* to put into practice the doctrine he is teaching. Perfect love demands this mystical forgetting of self that is the apex of the cloud of forgetting and forms so central a theme in his work:

> And this is the condition of a *perfect lover*, only and utterly to spoil himself of himself for that thing that he loveth, and not admit or suffer to be clothed but only in that thing that he loveth; and that not only for a time, but endlessly to be en-wrapped therein in *full and final forgetting of himself*. (P.C. 156:16)

Thus it is that this work of contemplation is no more than an intense form of that charity demanded of all Christians by the Gospel.

CONTEMPLATIVE LOVE AND CHRISTIAN LOVE

IT CONTAINS ALL THE VIRTUES

If, then, this " secret little love " is identical with perfect charity, it should contain all the virtues; for the Gospel, and after it traditional theology, taught that charity includes every other virtue. And it is precisely this that the author says, stating that " in this little love set upon the cloud of unknowing be contained all the virtues of man's soul, the which is the ghostly temple of God. " (C. 126:23) In such a way does it penetrate other virtues that they become perfect because the intention is. pure " without any mingling ":

> This by itself is " the best part " of Mary, without these other.
> They without it profit little or nought. It destroyeth not only
> the ground and the root of sin, as it may be here, but also it
> getteth virtues. For if it be truly conceived, all virtues shall be
> subtly and perfectly conceived, felt and comprehended in it,
> without any mingling of thine intent. (C. 39:9)

This point is made so often that it need hardly be labored here. It was this love that more than anything won pardon for Mary whose sins were forgiven " not for her great sorrow, nor for her thought of her sins, nor yet for her meekness that she had in the beholding of her wretchedness only. But why then? Surely, ' because she loved much. ' " (C. 45:1)

One last passage from *Privy Counsel* is remarkable because the author gives his reasons for " declaring of the nobleness of this ghostly exercise before all others " (P.C. 154:4), and he states that everything he has said in his previous works is summed up in this—the ripe fruit of the *Epistle* of *Prayer* that had symbolized perfect love, the hidden wisdom of *Denis Hid Divinity*, the cloud of unknowing and so on. Declaring that he will " touch no virtue here in special, for it needeth not " since " all virtues be clearly and perfectly comprehended in it, " he continues:

> For this same work, if it be verily conceived, is that reverent
> affection and the fruit separated from the tree that I speak of

in the little *Epistle of Prayer*. This is the " cloud of unknowing ";
this is that privy love put in purity of spirit; this is the ark of the
testament. This is Denis' divinity, his wisdom and his treasure,
his lightsome darkness and his unknowing. This it is that
setteth thee in silence, as well from thought as from words.
This maketh thy prayer full short. In this thou art learned to
forsake the world and to despise it. And—that more is—in
this thou art learned to forsake and despise thine own self,
according to the teaching of Christ in the Gospel, saying
thus: " Si quis vult venire post me, abneget semetipsum et tollat
crucem suam et sequatur me. " That is: " Whoso will come
after me, let him forsake himself, let him bear his cross and
follow me. " (P.C. 154:13)

In short, this simple act, this tiny love contains all that is
written in so many treatises from that of Dionysius to his own:
it is that all-embracing charity of the Gospel.

Virtue without " This Working "

Not only is this blind stirring of love a deep expression of
evangelical charity, but the converse is also true: without this
" little love " there can be no perfect virtue. " And have a man
never so many virtues without it, all they be mingled with
some crooked intent, for the which they be imperfect. "
(C. 39:15) In other words, perfection *demands* this contemplative love, a point that is again made clearly enough in the
following words:

> And therefore I pray thee, lean listily to this meek stirring of
> love in thine heart, and follow thereafter... It is the substance
> of all good living, and *without it no good work may be begun
> nor ended*. (C. 92:14)

This seems a strong statement and one might conclude that
the author had momentarily forgotten himself and overstepped
the mark, were it not for many similar sentences indicating
that man *ought* to be contemplative. Adam was so before the
sin; and man, reformed by grace, should try to get back to
that state:

> For this is the work, as thou shalt hear afterward, in the which
> man should have continued if he never had sinned. And to this

working was man made, and all things for man, to help him and further him thereto. And by this working shall man be repaired again. *And for want of this working a man falleth evermore deeper and deeper into sin, and further and further from God.* And by heeding and continual working in this work alone, without more, a man riseth evermore higher and higher from sin, and nearer and nearer unto God. (C. 19:19)

Here the author is clearly identifying the work of contemplation with perfect charity—for this was man made; without it he falls into sin; by means of it he draws nearer and nearer to God.

CONCLUSION

In describing the blind stirring, reference was made to its deep-rootedness in the personality: the flame burns at a lower depth than any love built upon sensible knowledge or discursive reasoning; and the author goes to no small pains to point out that it is not, in fact, produced by any ratiocinative process. Yet one need not deduce from this that it is phenomenologically extraordinary. Just as supraconceptual knowledge can be explained by the laws of psychology, so this profound love seems to demand no appeal to the miraculous intervention of God into the life of man. It *is* an intervention—and a very real one—but an ordinary one. This is indicated by the author's insistence that the exercise he teaches is the normal way to Christian perfection: it is the ripe and luscious fruit of that tree which is the Christian life. And it is hardly likely that God would dispense from His laws to work a miracle every time he calls a soul to perfection.

Burning at a low level of the human personality, the very silent depth and deep-rootedness of this love gives it an intensity and a value that can scarcely be claimed by a love situated at a more superficial plane. Yet, however true this may be, the author nowhere gives an indication of esteeming it for any such psychological or phenomenological reason. Many moderns put the emphasis here, but not he.⁴ For him, as supraconceptual knowledge is only of value insofar as it is penetrated by the dazzling and darkening light of faith, so mystical love is only of value insofar as it is an expression (and, in his opinion, the most perfect expression) of the supernatural gift of charity—that love gratuitously bestowed on every Christian at Baptism and restored by the sacrament of Penance.

His doctrine is that the perfect following of Christ manifests itself in this contemplation—or, more correctly, this love is an answer to God's gratuitous call to perfection, a call that can only be answered with the help of grace. The Christian life is founded on charity of which there are two kinds: one kind (sufficient for salvation), symbolized by the "reverent affection" or the green fruit attached to the tree, is mingled with filial fear, hope of reward, and consideration of God's benefits; the second is divorced from all consideration of self and of God's benefits: it is love of God for Himself. This latter charity, in which perfection consists, can be attained only by those in whom God arouses this blind stirring that, at its highest point, entails a total forgetfulness of all things, even of self and one's being. That is to say, that perfect charity which seeks nought but God can only be attained to by him who is drawn up into the cloud by God in such a way that the other cloud (that of forgetting) has engulfed all creatures, including the being of the contemplative himself. Now he has abandoned the knowledge of all creatures to know God in naked faith, and he has abandoned the love of all creatures to love God in perfect charity. This, he claims, is the summit of love demanded by the Gospel of Christ from those who would be perfect.

---

⁴ In recent times a good deal of research has been done on the therapeutic value of all forms of supraconceptual thinking that aid in resolving complexes and in the unification of the personality. "Modern psychology expects from Zen an enrichment of its therapeutic treatments. While the 'minor therapy' seeks to heal neuroses by resolving complexes suppressed into the subconscious, the 'major therapy' aims at the integration of personality by making use of the wisdom of humanity stored in the 'collective unconscious.' In stirring the subconscious layers of the human psyche, Zen appears to favor these tendencies. Those who practice it are aware that here they are on religious ground...." (Dumoulin [1], p. 281) Christian mysticism also unifies the personality, and its dark supraconceptual silence can undoubtedly have the same effect of solving complexes buried in the subconscious. But it is not for this reason that it is valued by the author of *The Cloud*.

Some of his phrases might indicate that he expects every Christian to attain to contemplation at the risk of falling into sin, but they need not be interpreted in this way in view of the fact that he distinguishes between those called to salvation and those called to perfection (showing himself aware that the latter are not so very numerous) and, moreover, he is clear that the " reverent affection " is sufficient. Yet he may mean that the Christian life should normally become increasingly deep and increasingly experimental, developing into this " secret little love " in some form; and if it does not do so, all virtues are " mingled with some crooked intent, for the which they be imperfect. "

The conclusion is that perfect love (and consequently Christian perfection) cannot be had without the gift of contemplation. [5]

---

[5] This is one of the points, however, on which I beg to differ with the good author, as I explain in the General Conclusion, pp. 257 ff.

9

KNOWLEDGE AND LOVE (I)

It is now time to consider the second problem posed, namely, the relationship between knowledge and love. In his enthusiasm for the blind stirring, the author not infrequently disparages knowledge, strongly emphasizing the superiority of love. " And therefore, I pray thee, seek more after feeling than after knowing, for knowing oftentimes deceiveth with pride; but meek, lovely feeling may not beguile: Scientia inflat, caritas aedificat. In knowing is travail, in feeling rest. " (P.C.171:26)

THE SUPERIORITY OF LOVE

The reasoning of the English author is similar to that of St. Thomas who holds that the will is superior to the intellect by reason of its end *(ratione finis)*—that is to say, that while conceptual knowledge brings God down, as it were, to our level, imposing on him the concepts we take from the surrounding world, love goes out to its object: it goes to the essence of God Himself, as He is in Himself. " For why, love may reach to God in this life, but not knowing. " (C. 33:11) The same idea is put forward with strange realism in the *Epistle of Stirrings* where the author, after telling the reader that love can go to God when reason lags behind, proceeds to say that by love we can " hit " God and " wound " Him even as He is in Himself:

> For by love we may find him, feel him and hit him even in himself. It is a wonderful eye love, for of a loving soul it is said of our Lord: " Thou hast wounded mine heart in one of thine eyes "; that is to say, in love that is blind to many things and seeth only that one thing that it seeketh, and therefore it findeth and feeleth, hitteth and woundeth the point and the prick that it shooteth at much sooner than it should, if the sight were distracted in beholding of many things, as it is when the reason ransacketh and seeketh among all such things. " (St. 72:22)

This is a good expression of the scholastic dictum: " Cognitum est in cognoscente per modum cognoscentis: amans est in amato per modum amati. " It is because love goes out to its object that scholastics speak of it as " ecstatic. "

Generally the author's intention is to stress the superiority of love over discursive reasoning, that form of knowledge which, incapable of bringing man to God as He is in Himself, is to be buried beneath the cloud of forgetting; but he also regards it as superior to the dark knowledge of faith, which is not vision and does not pierce the cloud, even though it enables man to see God in an obscure way. Mary " learned to love a thing the which she might not see clearly in this life by light of understanding in her reason, nor yet verily feel in sweetness of love in her affection. " (C. 46:16) She did not see clearly and she did not feel sweetness—yet she loved. Indeed, the author may be hinting at the Pauline doctrine that faith and hope pass away when he writes:

> For that perfect stirring of love that beginneth here is even in number with that that shall last without end in the bliss of heaven; for it is all one. (C. 52:21)

Perfect love on earth is identical with that of everlasting life.

THE PART PLAYED BY REASON

But what about the part played by discursive reasoning? Enough has been said to show that he admits its validity and that he is not the declared enemy of this function of man. The problem now is as to its role in the mystical life. Does the contemplative, after entering the sheepfold, quietly put aside anything discursive to remain in silent abandonment of conceptual knowledge; or has it some role to play still?

Some passages from the author might give the impression that the discursive work of the intellect is simply jettisoned. There is, for instance, the passage in *Privy Counsel* (re-echoing a similar passage in the *Study of Wisdom* where he says that when contemplation is born reason dies:

> How oft have ye read and heard, and of how many both holy, wise, and true, that as soon as Benjamin was born his mother Rachel died? By Benjamin contemplation, and by Rachel we understand reason. And as soon as a soul is touched with very contemplation—as it is in this noble noughting of itself and this high alling of God—surely and verily then dieth all man's reason. (P.C. 150:10)

This is a strong way of speaking; and the author goes on with an even bolder metaphor, declaring that the contemplative who continues to make meditations ends up by killing contemplation like the mother who strangles her child at birth:

> Look therefore that ye be not like to those wretched women in body that kill their own children when they be new born. It is good ye beware. (P.C. 150:23)

Yet all this is no attack on reason as such but only a strong application of the doctrine of the cloud of forgetting: discursive reasoning may smother the tiny flame that is the essence of contemplation and therefore it must be allowed " to die. "

But that reason still has something to say (even though its role is secondary) is indicated in the *Epistle of Stirrings*.

THE *Epistle of Stirrings*

In this short work the author teaches how the blind stirring of love can be a norm or criterion for the direction of daily life. A disciple has asked for advice for the making of the decisions of ordinary life—" of silence and of speaking, of common dieting and of singular fasting, of dwelling in company and of remaining alone. " (St. 62:2) How is one to make decisions about such matters and to what extent can one be governed by those interior promptings or stirrings that rise in the heart?

In an answer conspicuous for its prudence and discretion, the author first points to the extreme delicacy and difficulty of this matter. It is dangerous to strain nature in fasting and watching and devotion: these things are good and holy " if grace only be the cause of that silence, of that singular fasting, and of that only dwelling... And if it be otherwise then there is but peril on all sides. " (St. 62:14) But how is one to discern the motion of grace? Any blind or irrational stirring arising in the heart is not to be followed but only the true working of grace— in the discernment of which reason plays an important part.

In order to judge reasonably of the motions of grace in the soul one must, first of all, have much experience. The grace of discretion (for it is this he is teaching) does not come easily to a man but only when he has been exercised in many tribulations and the little ship of his soul has passed through many storms— only then does he come to the haven of peace " the which is the clear and true knowing of himself and all his inward dispositions. " (St. 64:19). Moreover, he must on no account trust his own judgment alone; counsel from a spiritual guide should be sought, for it is perilous to follow one's own stirrings indiscriminately. Experience and counsel will, however, help him to form a reasonable judgment.

Together with this, however, comes an insistence that true discretion in things spritual is found in a judgment that arises from within the heart, not from outside. This point (insisted upon quite often by the author in other places) is now stated with a certain ironic humor:

> And touching these stirrings, of the which thou askest my opinion and my counsel: I say to thee that I conceive of them suspiciously; that is that they should be conceived on ape manner. Men say commonly that the ape doth as other seeth. Forgive me if I err in my suspicion, I pray thee. (St. 68:6)

Imitation of others is not the following of the inspiration of God, as the author knows well from direction of a spiritual man who was stirred to penance and silence not from within but from desire to imitate another. " And therefore beware, and prove well thy stirrings and whence they come. For howso thou art stirred, whether from within by grace or from without on ape manner, God wot and I not. " (St. 68:24)

The true stirring of God does not come through any of the sense, nor does it come from reasoning but from abundance of love welling up in the heart:

> Look that thy stirrings to silence or to speaking, to fasting or to eating, to onliness or to company, *whether they come from within of abundance of love* and devotion in spirit and not from without by windows of thy bodily wits, thy ears and thine eyes. (St. 69:1)

The genuine stirring comes from the love of God, not from any reasoning process; but the mode of proceeding is eminently reasonable. That is to say, reason tests the stirrings to ensure that they really come from love: it gets advice, it weighs experience and so on. Thus is prepared the way for a love that enlightens the intelligence. This way of thinking becomes clearer as the epistle proceeds.

The Guidance of Love

Granted that the stirring is not " on ape manner " but arises from abundance of love, the author gives his disciple advice demanding an activity of the intelligence enlightened and guided by interior love alone. Choose God, he tells him, in all things, since only God is the aim and end of man's life while silence, fasting, and watching are in themselves indifferent. In fact, no one should choose either silence or speaking—" choose thee a thing the which is hid betwixt them. " And what is this thing? It is nothing else but God Himself:

> It is God for whom thou shouldst be still, if thou shouldst be still; and for whom thou shouldst speak if thou shouldst speak; and for whom thou shouldst fast, if thou shouldst fast; and for whom thou shouldst be alone, if thou shouldst be alone; and for whom thou shouldst be in company, if thou shouldst be in company; and so for all the remnant, whatso they be. (St. 71:13)

Here is the loving soul seeking God alone, fixing its love on nothing else however good and holy. This is an application of that perfect love which seeks God for Himself and not for any of His goods. " Lift up thine heart unto God with a meek stirring of love, " he has written in *The Cloud*, "and mean himself and none of his goods. " (C. 16:3) And now this attitude, cultivated in prayer, is carried into daily life. " And therefore look that thou loathe to think on aught but himself, so that nought work in thy mind nor in thy will but only himself, " he has again said in *The Cloud* (C. 16:4); and now nothing is working in the mind and will but God. This is put in a striking way:

> For silence is not God, nor speaking is not God; fasting is not God, nor eating is not God; being alone is not God nor company is not God; nor yet any of all the other such two contraries. He is hid betwixt them, and may not be found by any work of thy soul but only by love of thine heart. He may not be known by reason. He may not be thought, gotten nor traced by understanding. But he may be loved and chosen with the true, lovely will of thine heart. Choose thou him; and thou art silently speaking and speakingly silent, fastingly eating and eatingly fasting; and so forth of all the remnant. (St. 71:19)

Love is now guiding the contemplative, teaching him to choose God who cannot be thought nor understood nor found by any rational activity. As it grows stronger, it comes to take possession of him in such a way that it dominates every action. It *orders* him to choose God, and if he does not follow its command it wounds him and gives him no peace until he does its bidding:

> Then that same that thou feelest shall well know how to tell thee when thou shalt speak and when thou shalt be still. And it shall govern thee discreetly in all thy living without any error, and teach thee mystically how thou shalt begin and cease in all such doings of nature with a great and sovereign discretion. For if thou mayest by grace keep it in custom and in continual working, then if it be needful to thee for to speak, for to eat in the common way, or for to bide in company, or for to do any such other thing that belongeth to the common true custom of Christian men and of nature, it shall first stir thee softly to speak or to do that other common thing of nature, whatso it

be; and then, if thou do it not, it shall smite as sore as a prick on thine heart and pain thee full sore, and let thee have no peace but if thou do it. And in the same manner, if thou be speaking or in any such other work that is common to the course of nature, if it be needful and speedful to thee to be still and to set thee to the contrary, as is fasting to eating, being alone to company, and all such other, the which be works of singular holiness, it will stir thee to them. (St. 75:15)

Now the blind stirring of love has become a bright flame, guiding the contemplative's every choice. It stirs him softly and sweetly to act; but it also impels him to do God's will with a certain inevitability against which it is useless to struggle: he seems to be in the grip of something more powerful than himself that he must obey at the risk of losing interior peace when it smites upon his heart. That this is the guidance of God Himself is indicated in *The Cloud* where the author speaks of the guiding action of God in the very depths of the soul to which no evil spirit can penetrate and on which no reasoning can make impact:

Trust then steadfastly that it is only God that stirreth thy will and thy desire, plainly by himself, without means either on his part or on thine. And be not afraid of the devil, for he may not come so near. He may never come to stir a man's will, except occasionally and by means from afar, be he never so subtle a devil. For sufficiently and without means may no good angel stir thy will; nor, shortly to say, anything but only God. (C. 70:55)

And this guidance of God Himself, says the author, is the true discretion and the true wisdom. It is for this great gift that one must strive; it is to arrive at this truest of all wisdoms that discursive reasoning and conceptual knowledge are abandoned; in comparison with this wisdom, available to the simplest Christian who really loves God, the wisdom of the philosophers and theologians looks like ignorance. " It seems to the soul, " writes St. John of the Cross, " that its former knowledge, and even the knowledge of the whole world, is pure ignorance by comparison with that knowledge. " [1] And

[1] *Canticle*, Stanza XVII .11

the attacks of the English author on the theologians must be viewed in the light of this. He means that no theologian, however learned, really knows God unless he also loves Him.

Yet this grace, he warns, comes only to him who has loved and longed for God for a long time in complete detachment from, and forgetting of, creatures. You must have desired God " with all the love of thine heart, utterly voiding from thy ghostly beholding all manner of sight of anything beneath him. " (St. 75:4)

In this way is the wisdom of man, found by reasoning, put aside for the infusion of the wisdom of God in darkness. [2]

KNOWLEDGE THROUGH LOVE

Now it is possible to understand the doctrine of the author that God can be known by love. He has said that in man there is a knowing power and a loving power, and that God is comprehensible to the latter but not to the former:

> But since all reasonable creatures, angel and man, have in them, each one by himself, one principal working power, the which is called a knowing power, and another principal working power, the which is called a loving power. Of the which two powers, to the first, the which is a knowing power, God who is the maker of them is evermore incomprehensible; but to the second, the which is the loving power, he is, in every man diversely, all comprehensible to the full. Insomuch, that one loving soul alone in itself, by virtue of love, may comprehend in itself him who is sufficient to the full — and more without comparison — to fill all the souls and angels that ever may be. (C. 18:22)

The author, grounded as he is in scholasticism, knows that strictly speaking the loving power does not know; when he says that love " knows " he means that in its intensity it enlightens the intelligence which is then filled with a wisdom not coming " from without " through the senses but from within from " abundance of love. " St. John of the Cross, too, speaks of this " mystical theology, which theologians call secret

---

[2] See also C. 80:23.

wisdom, and which, as St. Thomas says, is communicated and infused into the soul through love. " [3] The parallel is indeed interesting. For the Spanish mystic says that this wisdom comes from love; he says it is secret (" this secret little love "); he says it is mystical theology (" hid divinity ")—and he appeals to the authority of St. Thomas.

CONCLUSION

Love is superior to knowledge because it goes straight to the essence of God even in this life, whereas discursive reasoning cannot know God as He is in Himself and faith sees God only from afar in darkness. Faith, however, is the " ground " of the contemplative life; and reasoning has an important part to play.

The contemplative path may now be divided into three stages. The first stage is that of reasoning and conceptual thinking: it is the time of meditations on the Passion of Christ and one's own wretchedness in the light of faith; here one learns from experience and earnestly looks for counsel in the government of one's life and the discernment of the work of grace. In the second stage, love becomes experimental—a " stirring. " Discursive prayer becomes difficult and the soul finds its faculties hindered as though it were in a cloud of unknowing. Now meditation must be abandoned for the silent emptiness of naked faith; but reason still has its work to do, sifting and interpreting the stirrings, asking for counsel, avoiding illusion. In the third stage love (having abandoned discursive knowledge) finds a higher knowledge that is the true wisdom infused by God Himself. Yet even here reason must do its work of discerning the origin of the stirrings and taking counsel, thus protecting the soul from the pitfalls of this dangerous, if glorious, path.

---

[3] *Dark Night,* II, VII, 1.

10

KNOWLEDGE AND LOVE (II)

The doctrine, outlined in the last chapter, that love leads to a higher wisdom is again stated by the author in his *Study of Wisdom*. Here, following Richard of St. Victor, but liberally adding his own ideas, the author describes the interplay of knowledge and love in the mystical life from its very origin in discursive prayer made in faith. Much of what he says is a repetition of the doctrine of the *Epistle of Stirrings*, but the slant is sometimes different.

THE *Study of Wisdom*

The *Benjamin Minor* of Richard of St. Victor is a somewhat complicated allegory in which Jacob stands for God, Rachel for reason, Joseph for discretion, Benjamin for contemplation, and so on. Lest one become lost in this entanglement of names, the English author kindly appends a table that makes things considerably easier and which is worth reproducing here:

Husband
Jacob—God

Wife	*Wife*
Lya—Affection	Rachel—Reason

Maiden	*Maiden*
Zelfa—Sensuality	Bala—Imagination

The sons of Jacob of Zelfa	*The sons of Jacob of Lya*	*The sons of Jacob of Rachel*	*The sons of Jacob of Bala*
Gan—Obstinence	Ruben—Dread of God	Joseph—Discretion	Dan—Sight of pains to come
Asser—Patience	Simeon—Sorrow of sin	Benjamin—Contemplation	Neptalys—Sight of joys to come

(S.W. 15:3).

In the above scheme, perhaps the most significant thing for the present problem is the importance attributed to reason and discretion in the mystical life. Benjamin (Contemplation) is not the child of Lya (Affection) but of Rachel who stands for Reason. Moreover, the brother of Benjamin is Joseph (who stands for Discretion); and the author later tells us that long after Joseph is Benjamin born, as if to say that contemplation is granted only to those who have long exercised themselves in discretion. Thus is the reasonable basis of contemplation firmly established.

RACHEL AND JOSEPH (REASON AND DISCRETION)

As in the *Epistle of Stirrings*, the importance of discretion is heavily underlined:

> Thus it seemeth that the virtue of discretion needeth to be had, with the which all others may be governed. For without it, all virtues be turned to vices. This is he, that Joseph, that is the late-born child. But yet the father loveth him more than them all, for why truly without discretion may never goodness be gotten nor kept. And therefore no wonder if that virtue be singularly loved without which no virtue be had nor governed. (S.W. 39:6)

Discretion, however, comes only as a result of long experience and much suffering; and one must learn to look for counsel and to follow it. After many falls, failings, and mistakes " a man learneth by the proof that there is nothing better than to be ruled after counsel, the which is the readiest getting of discretion. " (S. W. 40:17)

Moreover (and this is a point less in evidence in the *Epistle of Stirrings*), love alone cannot give this virtue, but only reason:

> And here is the open reason that neither Lya nor Zelfa, nor Bala can bear such a child, but only Rachel. For, as it is said before, that of reason springeth right counsels, the which is very discretion, understood by Joseph the first son of Rachel. (S.W. 41:6)

When he speaks of the reasonable foundation of discretion and contemplation, he probably has two things in mind. One is the meditation on the Passion that must precede contemplative prayer. " And I would think, " he writes in *Privy Counsel,* "that it were impossible to man's understanding—although God may do what he will—that a sinner should come to be restful in the ghostly feeling of himself and of God, unless he first saw and felt by imagination and meditation the bodily doings of himself and of God, and thereto sorrowed for that that were to sorrow, and made joy for that that were to joy. " (P.C. 158:19) And the second reasonable basis is the reliance upon counsel, or the advice of an experienced guide. Be that as it may, contemplation is the child of reason:

> And therefore it is that after Joseph is Benjamin born, for as by Joseph discretion, so by Benjamin we understand contemplation. And both are born of one mother and begotten of one father. (S.W. 42:4)

Thus is contemplation born from the union of reason with God.

BENJAMIN (CONTEMPLATION)

At last Benjamin is born. The soul has exercised itself for a long time in discretion; it has meditated on the Passion of Christ and on its own wretchedness; it knows its own weakness; and now (and only now) can it come to know God—for it is unthinkable that anyone could know God who does not know himself.

But now at the climax, when reason has done its work, when Rachel has suffered the bitter pangs of bringing forth her beloved child—now she dies.

Yet in his description of the birth pangs of Rachel and her death, the author shows that he does not sever reason from the other workings of the human psychology—he does not indicate that Benjamin is born of only reason. Rachel, though she stands for reason, is no cold abstraction but a woman of flesh and blood, an expectant mother longing for the birth of her child. " And therefore she multiplied her study, and whetted her desires, each desire on desire, so that at last, in great abundance of burning desires and sorrow of the delaying of

her desires, Benjamin is born, and his mother Rachel dieth. "
(S.W. 45:3) And in the same way, the contemplative relies on
reason, meditation, and discretion, but he is also filled with a
great love, sighing for God with yearning—and it is then that
the tiny flame of contemplation is born in his heart. " And
yet no man may take such grace without study and burning
desires coming before. And that knew Rachel full well. "
(S.W. 45:1)

In this way, contemplation is preceded by much study and
meditation and counsel, all dominated by a great love of God.
But just as Rachel dies after her travail, so discursive reasoning
comes to an end with the birth of contemplation:

> For why in what time that a soul is ravished above himself by
> abundance of desires and a great multitude of love, so that it
> is inflamed with the light of the Godhead, surely then dieth all
> man's reason. (S.W. 45:6)

Reason dies because intelligence is " inflamed with the light
of the Godhead. " This is a cornerstone of the English author's
thought. For this light is that which comes from within " from
abundance of love, " not from without " on ape manner ": this
is the gift of wisdom.

THE LIGHT OF LOVE

As a burning candle enlightens both itself and the objects
around, so the light of love enables us to see both our own
wretchedness and the great goodness of God:

> As when the candel burneth, thou mayest see the candel itself
> by the light thereof, and other things also; right so when
> thy soul burneth in the love of God, that is when thou feelest
> continuously thine heart desire after the love of God, then by
> the light of his grace which he sendeth in thy reason, thou
> mayest both see thine unworthiness, and his great goodness.
> And therefore... profer thy candel to the fire. (S.W. 43:8)

This enlightening of the intelligence through love is not
unlike the doctrine of St. Thomas who holds that the highest
wisdom comes from love and from a certain " connaturality. "

Love, he argues, unites us to God, making us one with Him in spirit and enabling us to judge about divine things with an intuitive accuracy; it penetrates into divine things and finds there a knowledge the discursive intellect can never discover. [1] Indeed, such knowledge is apparent even in human relationships when love can discover in the loved one things that the intellect alone cannot find. This knowledge in things divine St. Thomas here attributes to the Holy Spirit whose greatest gift is wisdom. [2]

Later, John of St. Thomas has an interesting description of how love goes beyond faith, finding a certain relish in the truths that faith darkly and distantly proposes to the intellect:

> In its darkness faith attains God yet as He remains at a distance, inasmuch as faith is of things not seen. But charity attains God in Himself immediately, intimately uniting us to that which is hidden in faith. And so, even though faith rules love and the union with God, inasmuch as it is faith that proposes their object, yet, *in virtue of this union in which love clings to God immediately, the intellect is, through a certain affective experience, so elevated as to judge of divine things in a way higher than the darkness of faith would permit.* [3]

Here is doctrine similar to that of *The Cloud*—the intellect, grounded in faith, sees from afar: the will goes directly to God; and touching God it enables the mind to judge of divine things in a superior way.

The idea of " touching " God appears often in *Privy Counsel*. To touch is an act of the will, an act of love that puts aside all creatures and goes to the very heart of God. But touching is obviously also something experimental or sapiential: when we touch God we know Him, not in concepts but in darkness:

---

[1] See II^a-II^{ae}, q. 45, a. 2.

[2] It has been described how true wisdom is a gift of the Holy Spirit transcending logic and conceptual reasoning. This guidance of the Holy Spirit, however, has a natural foundation, as St. Thomas points out when he writes: " Even the Philosopher [i.e., Aristotle] says in the chapter on Good Fortune that for those who are moved by divine instinct, there is no need to take counsel according to human reason, but only to follow their inner promptings, since they are moved by a principle higher than human reason. " (*Summa*, I^a-II^{ae}, q. 68, a. 1)

[3] Quoted by Maritain, p. 262.

> Bear up thy sick self as thou art and try for to *touch by desire*
> good, gracious God as he is, the touching of whom is endless
> health, by witness of the woman in the Gospel, saying thus:
> " Si tetigero vel fimbriam vestimenti ejus, salva ero. " " If I
> touch but the hem of his clothing, I shall be safe. " Much more
> shalt thou then be made whole of thy sickness by this high
> heavenly touching of his own being. (P.C. 139:1)

From the darkness and emptiness of a mind void of distinct
knowledge, the " naked intent " of love goes to the very
essence of God and " touching " Him finds relish and wisdom.

WISDOM AND LOVE

Toward the end of *Privy Counsel* the author asserts that love
or " desire " is blind—" for right so is desire of the soul as
groping and stepping are of the body; and both groping and
stepping be blind works of the body, thou knowest well
thyself. " (P.C. 165:6) Yet, he goes on to say, however blind it
be, there accompanies it a certain " ghostly sight ":

> But though that the work of this desire be never so blind, yet
> nevertheless there commoneth and followeth with it a manner
> of ghostly sight, the which is part cause and a mean furthering
> this desire. (P.C. 165:8)

It would seem that wisdom, or " ghostly sight, " is not only
the fruit of love but also the *cause* of love—it furthers the
desire. Love finds wisdom; and this wisdom; in turn, urges
the soul to love even more. So there is a circular movement
in which love begets wisdom and wisdom begets more love:
the more one knows God the more one wants to love Him;
and the more one loves the more one thirsts for even more
knowledge.

The conclusion is that the contemplative, after long exercise
in meditation and discretion, abandons clear and distinct
knowledge to be guided by a love that, rising out of the darkness
of faith, finds a new and superior knowledge. This is nothing
else but that wisdom which is the principal gift of the Holy
Spirit. As love finds wisdom, so wisdom leads to a deeper love.
This is the ordinary apophatic doctrine of the darkness of faith

and the light of love, described well by Maritain when he says that " the proper light of infused contemplation only comes from the ardour of a love which burns in the night. " [4]

Yet apophatic mysticism never finds, in this life, pure and untramelled brightness; and this light of sapiential love, when it burns at white heat giving discretion and intuitive certainty about the things of God, blinds even more the faculties of the soul, which continues to walk in an ever-deepening night of pure darkness. " Although as it [the soul] journeys, " writes St. John of the Cross, " it is supported by no particular interior light of understanding, nor by any exterior guide, that it may receive satisfaction therefrom on this lofty road—it is completely deprived of all this by this thick darkness—yet its love alone, which burns at this time, and makes its heart to long for the Beloved, is that which now moves and guides it, and makes it to soar upward to God along the road of solitude, without its knowing how or in what manner. " [5]

The next chapter will briefly examine the nature of this dark wisdom that is the gift of the Holy Spirit.

[4] Maritain, p. 264.
[5] *Dark Night*, II, XXV, 4.

11

CONCLUSION:
" HIGH GHOSTLY WISDOM "

That the gift of wisdom plays a special role in the contemplative life had been taught by Peter the Lombard when treating of the gifts of the Holy Spirit in *The Third Book of the Sentences*; and medieval theology tended to follow this line of thought. St. Thomas held that a great love of God calls down the Holy Spirit, according to the promise of Our Lord at the Last Supper that if anyone loved Him he would be loved of the Father who would send another Paraclete: [1] progress in charity, then, meant progress in wisdom. Ruysbroeck has this doctrine, too; and for him, wisdom is characteristically dark. " When we turn within ourselves in contemplation, " he writes, " the fruitive unity of God is like darkness, a somewhat which is unconditioned and incomprehensible. And the spirit turns inward through love... In this loving introversion, there arises the seventh gift, which is the spirit of Savouring Wisdom; and it saturates the simplicity of our spirit, soul and body, with wisdom and with ghostly savours. " [2]

THE GIFT OF WISDOM

Once again, then, the author of *The Cloud* is loyal to tradition in holding that the " fruit " of contemplation is " high ghostly

---

[1] *Commentarium in Evangelium Joannis*, V.
[2] *The Adornment of the Spiritual Marriage*, C. LXIII.

wisdom. " (P.C. 145:27) Analyzing the text from the *Book of Proverbs*, " Worship thy Lord with thy substance... and thy presses shall run over with wine, " he makes this interpretation:

> By the which wine in Holy Scripture is verily and mistily understood ghostly wisdom in very contemplation and high savour of the Godhead. (P.C. 144:24)

The above is from *Privy Counsel* in which, a few pages later, he proceeds to interpret yet another text in a similar way. " Beatus homo qui invenit sapientiam, " he quotes; and then proceeds to give his own interesting commentary:

> He is a blissful man that may find this oneing wisdom and that may abound in this ghostly working... in offering up of his own blind feeling of his own being, all curious knowledge of learning and of nature far put back. (P.C. 145:15)

He goes on to explain how this wisdom is of much more value than " all other bodily and ghostly knowing " found through the activity of one's " natural wits. " In other words, he equates this scriptural wisdom with the work of contemplation he is teaching. It is the blind stirring of love, the cloud of unknowing, hid divinity, and the rest; for, as has been pointed out already, all these phrases are used to express an interior stirring that is not love alone nor yet knowledge, but is a blend of the two, so simple and yet so profound that it defies definition. Later, St. John of the Cross will refer to it as " faith "—" pure faith " he calls it; but his terminology is a little different. " What St. John of the Cross calls pure faith in nakedness of spirit, " writes Maritain, " is theological faith, indeed, dogmatic faith, but it is not theological faith isolated by ontological analysis according to its species from the other energies of our supernatural organism; it is living faith, one with the charity which informs it and the gifts which illumine it, the loving, wise and fertile faith which acts concretely in the life of a holy soul. " [3]

I quote this because the contemplation of the author of *The Cloud* contains these three elements that Maritain attributes to

[3] Maritain, p. 329.

the pure faith of St. John of the Cross: faith, charity, and the gift of wisdom. Faith is the " ground " (but for him faith seems to mean dogmatic, not the all-embracing faith of the Spanish mystic); from faith springs love—" the naked intent "; and the fruit is the gift of wisdom. All three are present, but this is an analytic description of something completely simple.

DARK WISDOM

Wisdom, then, is dark, supraconceptual, silent. It is far superior to any sensible knowledge—" full far from fantasy "—nor does it " fall under the working of natural wit, " being a gratuitous gift of God. (P.C. 145:29) It is " nothing " because no clear and distinct ideas are present in the mind; it is " all " because it is " the high wisdom of the Godhead graciously descending into man's soul. " (P.C. 145:4) The play on the " alling " and " noughting " is an interesting anticipation of the *todo y nada* of St. John of the Cross:

> What is he that calleth it nought? Surely it is our outer man and not our inner. Our inner man calleth it All; for by it he is well taught to understand all things bodily and ghostly, without any special beholding to any one thing by itself. (C. 122:13)

The inner man calls it all: the outer man calls it nothing. The inner man calls it light: the outer man calls it darkness. The inner man calls it wisdom: the outer man calls it ignorance. The highest human wisdom is put aside in order that God may infuse His heavenly wisdom in mystic silence. " But in things contemplative, the highest wisdom that may be in man, as man, is far put under, so that God be the principal in working, and man but only consenter and sufferer. " (P.C. 163:9) The soul, in forgetfulness of all things, is passive while God infuses His grace. And this grace and light enable man " to understand all things bodily and ghostly " without clear and distinct ideas.

Thus, the " cloud of unknowing " might equally well be called " the cloud of knowing " or " the cloud of wisdom. " It is " unknowing " because of the abandonment of conceptual knowledge; it is " knowing " because of that infused wisdom in the obscurity of which the soul meets God.

TRANSCENDENCE OF CONTEMPLATIVE WISDOM

It can be seen that the author greatly emphasizes the absolute transcendence of contemplative wisdom: man's utter inability to come to it by his unaided faculties is heavily underlined. The same point has been stressed in *The Cloud* where he strikingly says that " without this work a soul is as it were dead, and cannot covet it or desire it. " (C. 70:5) Whence comes this remarkable transcendence?

One might be tempted to think that transcendence comes from the fact that this wisdom is dark, supraconceptual, found in silence at the uttermost depth of one's personality. But the difficulty to this interpretation is that phenomenologically speaking some such psychological condition can be induced by the unaided human powers. We know this, for example, from Zen that lays considerable stress on the fact that man can attain to supraconceptual enlightenment by his own determination. Describing the inner disposition of the Zen contemplative, one specialist on the subject writes: " The will to succeed, regardless of cost, constitutes his basic disposition. Many, however, are agitated beyond this, often because of the thought that they are about to face a decisive change in their lives. The Zen masters encourage this mood of excitement with such remarks as: ' If a man only wills to obtain enlightenment, he can obtain it, ' or: ' This is the opportunity which will not return a second or a third time in life. Heaven and earth be thanked... Proceed, and practice with determination! ' " [4] In this way, by his own efforts, does the Zen contemplative bring himself to a psychological state somewhat similar to that outlined by the author of *The Cloud*, entering into that lower region of the personality designated as " the sovereign point of the spirit " by the English author.

Obviously, the English writer knew nothing about Zen; but he may have been aware of similar phenomena in neoplatonism

---

[4] Dumoulin [2].

and in Greek mystical trends and realized that such mystics reduced themselves to a state which, phenomenologically speaking, was not unlike that to which he leads. Why, then, does he speak of the special transcendence of the particular wisdom he himself is teaching?

THE SUPERNATURAL

Once again we moderns, transporting ourselves to the fourteenth century, must recall that for the author of *The Cloud* the psychological state as such was of very secondary importance. In itself silent emptiness (or even ecstasy) and the holding of oneself in existential nakedness at the sovereign point of the spirit—all this was of little significance unless the whole operation was begun, terminated, and penetrated by that transcendental element that is divine grace. It is true that technique can induce a similar psychological condition of silent supraconceptuality, leading a person vertically down toward the center or core of his being; but the all-important thing for the author (as for every Christian mystic) is not the psychological condition itself but the motive that has induced it and the object toward which it tends. If the motive, or driving power, behind the whole action is divine love for God (that blind stirring about which there is no mention in Zen), then the process is of tremendous significance. If supernatural faith and love (these divine gifts that also act in a mind filled with concepts and discursive reasoning) reach such an intensity that they abandon images and concepts in their naked search for God, then this psychological state is a symptom of something immensely valuable; it is a symptom of deep charity. Otherwise (however great its cultural value) it is just one more technique, no more capable of bringing the mind to God as He is in Himself than any other activity of the " natural wits. " And the wisdom he is speaking about is nothing but an outcome of that supernatural love that is an answer to a gratuitous call of God.

What is completely transcendent and gratuitous, then, is not any psychological state as such but the faith, the love, and the wisdom that may lead to it and that (Christian tradition has always taught) can never be obtained by any effort of man. That the blind stirring of love is not something which human endeavor arouses within the heart but is an answer to a gratuitous intervention of God is driven home strongly from the first pages of *The Cloud* where the author, in words that recall the Joannine " Let us love God because God has first loved us, " reminds us that the whole initiative in the contemplative life (which is only a stage of the Christian life) comes from God. It is " the everlasting love of His Godhead " that has called you, he reminds the disciple; He it is who has " kindled thy desire full graciously "; this desire must always be wrought in thy will by the hand of Almighty God and thy consent. " In the call to the Christian life and in every stage in its development (however small) there is a gratuitous call of God transcending all technique and all human endeavor. Whether this call comes through God's ordinary psychological laws or whether it is an extraordinary intervention is a question that, perhaps, the author never clearly formulated to himself; but the answer implicit in his writing is that God is acting in an ordinary way, working through those laws that operate in Zen and neoplatonism and the rest, to give to man a supernatural gift beyond the reach of his natural powers.

CONCLUSION

Consequently, we come to the same conclusion as was reached in the first part of this work. Just as " belief, " the ground of contemplation, is no different from the belief of the ordinary Christian—except that it is deep and " naked "; just as the blind stirring of love is no different from that Christian charity incumbent upon all who hold allegiance to the Gospel—except that it is more intense; so this dark wisdom is no more than an increase of the gift of wisdom bestowed by the Holy Spirit at Baptism and restored by the sacrament of Penance. That this gift of wisdom is not the prerogative of contemplatives but is possessed by all who are in charity is clearly enough taught by St. Thomas. " The gifts of the Holy Spirit, " he writes, " are connected with each other in charity in such a way that he who has charity has all the gifts of the Holy Spirit, none of which can be possessed without charity. "⁵ And this, the common doctrine of theologians of the day, is not likely to be denied by the author of *The Cloud*.

In short, the mysticism of the author of *The Cloud* is ordinary; it is no more than a normal development of the Christian life; it is a path to perfection for those who believe more strongly, love more deeply, and are consequently more highly endowed with a rich outpouring of the gift of wisdom.

Iᵃ-IIᵃᵉ, q. 68, a. 3.

PART III

Purification

12

NECESSITY OF PURIFICATION

The mystics unanimously assert that no one comes to union with God in love without suffering; and the author of *The Cloud*, for all his humor, common sense, and lack of morbidity, is adamant in his teaching that the path he outlines demands a total renunciation and is accompanied by bitter trials.

It might be asked, however, why man must suffer in order to love God since he was made precisely for this end. What is the connection between mystical love and mystical suffering? And the author, as though anticipating this difficulty, gives a sound theological basis to his work.

SCATTERED BY ADAM

The Pauline drama of our death in Adam and life in Christ left its imprint on Christian theology from the earliest times, and it is hardly surprising that the author of *The Cloud* should use this scriptural motif as a foundation stone for his doctrine of Redemption. Adam, in the state of innocence, was contemplative; he was preoccupied with this silent exercise; he loved God with the meek stirring of love. Moreover, thanks to this operation, he was unified within himself since all his faculties were concentrated on God alone. In this way he had a twofold unity: union within himself and union with God.

But Adam fell from this loving union—from this " oneing affection "—and was " scattered " over creatures so that to love God became difficult and burdensome. Or, rather than difficult and burdensome, it became utterly impossible for him to love God were it not for the blood of Christ that redeemed all mankind.

And we too, the children of Adam, though redeemed by Christ, are still sadly scattered over creatures; for we bear the wound of Adam's sin, irritated by our personal transgressions. That is why we need purification, the aim of which is not to destroy anything but to restore to us that unity in ourselves and with God that is our rightful heritage by grace. And, the author claims, this work of contemplation is purificatory. " And therefore, whoso coveteth to come to the cleanness that he lost through sin... he must bidingly travail in this work, and suffer the pain thereof. " (C. 64:10) Let us examine this doctrine in his own words.

The Pauline doctrine is stated in unequivocal terms:

> For as all men were lost in Adam because he fell from this oneing affection, and as all, that with work according to their calling will witness their will of salvation, be saved and shall be by virtue of the Passion of only Christ, offering himself up in veriest sacrifice, all that he was in general and not in special, without special beholding to any one man in this life, but generally and in common for all. (P.C. 142:14)

In an interesting addition to St. Paul, the author here indicates that Adam was a contemplative, united within himself, and that he fell from this " oneing affection " to be scattered over creatures; and Christ was completely unified within Himself " in general " and " without special beholding of any one man in this life "; that is, without the clear and distinct ideas that accompany discursive reasoning. The same idea is expressed a little later:

> For since all sickness and corruption did fall to the flesh when the soul fell from this work, therefore shall all health come to the flesh when the soul by the grace of Jesu—the which is the chief worker—riseth to this same work again. (P.C. 148:5)

Here again Adam is contemplative: he falls from " this work " by his sin.

And just as Adam fell and was scattered, so we his children, dissipated and scattered through his sin and our own, must try to return to that contemplative unity that Christ has won back for us by His blood. Hence, when the call to contemplation comes one must fix all one's attention on the meek stirring of love, emptying the mind of all other thoughts so that (the author tells his disciple) " thy sight may not be scattered nor thy feeling defouled. " (P.C. 140:22) The whole work of contemplation is a " oneing " exercise, the author constantly telling his disciple to hold all his faculties in complete simplicity and unity. " And therefore, " he writes, " hold thee whole and unscattered, as far as thou mayest by grace. " (P.C. 147:15) This will lead to union in self and union with God: " so that thy thought be not scattered nor separated, but oned in him that is all. " (P.C. 136:14)

The aim of contemplation, then, is to return to that state of original justice in which, before sin, all the faculties of man were united and fixed on God in perfect union with Him.

THE RAVAGES OF SIN

When he speaks of this " scattering " called sin, the tranquil English contemplative adopts a surprisingly realistic attitude: man is terribly damaged by sin, and this is a truth never to be forgotten. The way of life he teaches presupposes long meditations on one's wretchedness leading to the conviction that of oneself one has nothing but sin, that one is " less than nothing " because of sin. When the time for contemplation arrives, discursive meditation about one's sinfulness is abandoned; but the deep conviction of one's sinfulness remains:

And this [i.e., discursive meditation] hast thou done now many a day with help of grace, so that thou knowest now in part, and as I suppose it is profitable to thee for the time, what thou art: a man by nature, and a foul stinking wretch by sin, thou knowest well how. And peradventure thou thinkest sometimes too well all the filths that follow and fall to a wretch. Fie on them! Let them go, I pray thee! Stir no further in them for fear of stink. (P.C. 138:9)

The realism may seem surprising; but it is the tone generally adopted by the author when he speaks about sin. In *The Cloud*, while telling the contemplative to avoid discursive meditations, he yet encourages him to hold in his consciousness a general notion of his own awful sinfulness; even when considerations about sin are gone, the feeling of one's own unworthiness remains:

> Do thou, in the same manner, fill thy spirit with the ghostly meaning of this word SIN, and without any special regard unto any kind of sin, whether it be venial or mortal: pride, anger, or envy, covetousness, sloth, gluttony, or lust. What recks it in contemplatives what sin it be, or how great a sin it be? For all sins they think—I mean for the time of this work—alike great in themselves, when the least sin separateth them from God, and hindereth them from their ghostly peace. (C. 78:25)

In this way is the soul filled with the consciousness of its own sinfulness. And in the depths of the most truly contemplative prayer, when the mind is void of clear and distinct ideas remaining in mystic silence—even then, " without special thought " the consciousness of sin may fill the contemplative so that he cries out, " Sin, sin, sin! " from his anguished heart. The author writes:

> And feel sin a lump, thou knowest never what, but none other thing than thyself. And cry then ghostly ever this one cry: " Sin, sin, sin! Out, out, out! " (C. 78:17)

Sometimes it is as if there were in his contemplative prayer two poles: sin and God; and his play on these two words recalls the " noverim me noverim Te " of St. Augustine:

> And therefore lift up thine heart with a blind stirring of love; and mean now sin, and now God. God wouldst thou have, and sin wouldst thou lack. God is wanting to thee; and sin art thou sure of. Now good God help thee, for now hast thou need. (C. 81:16)

And the same idea is again put forward with stark realism:

> And because that ever whiles thou livest in this wretched life, thou must always feel in some part this foul stinking lump of

sin, as it were oned and congealed with the substance of thy
being: therefore shalt thou alternatively mean these two words
—Sin and God. With this general understanding: that if thou
hadst God, then shouldst thou lack sin; and mightest thou
lack sin, then shouldst thou have God. (C. 79:13)

And so are emphasized the glory of God and the sinfulness
of man.

We can conclude, then, that the general consciousness and
deep realization of one's sinfulness play a fundamental role in
the mystical life; the contemplative must never forget that
he is " a lump " of sin while he stretches out in love to the
infinite purity of God.

But what is the nature of this sin?

THE NATURE OF SIN

In his theology of sin, the author stresses two points. The
first is that sin causes disorder in man: it brings about disunity;
it " scatters " man so that his higher faculties, intellect and
will, are no longer in control. The second point is that this
disorder cannot be remedied by any effort of man unless aided
by divine grace.

In contemplation, reason, dethroned by sin, is reinstated as
mistress of the faculties (so free is the author from any taint
of real anti-intellectualism), but this is not brought about
without great suffering and effort, for man is grievously
wounded by the fall of Adam and his own sins. Thus it is that
suffering is something inevitably bound up with the work of
contemplation.

In a somewhat scholastic description of the wounds of
original sin, the author points to its deleterious effects upon
the soul of man, which has four principal powers: reason, will,
imagination, sensuality. It is interesting to note that before
him St. Thomas had already written of the four wounds
inflicted upon the soul by original sin according to these four
faculties mentioned by the English author:

But there are four of the soul's powers that can be the subject of
virtue, namely, the reason, where prudence resides, the will

where justice is, the irascible, the subject of fortitude, and the concupiscible, the subject of temperance. Hence so far as the reason is deprived of its order to the true there is the wound of ignorance; so far as the will is deprived of its order to the good, there is the wound of malice; so far as the irascible is deprived of its order to the delectable, moderated by reason, there is the wound of concupiscence. [1]

In this way St. Thomas points to the loss of right order (the " scattering " of the English mystic) as the wounding effect of original sin. [2]

Like St. Thomas, then, the author of *The Cloud* takes the faculties one by one, showing how they have been weakened. First of all, reason. This is the faculty by which we distinguish good and evil, worse and worst, better and best. The author goes on:

Before man sinned, might reason have done all this by nature. But now it is so blinded with the original sin that it cannot work this work unless it be illumined by grace. (C. 116:12)

That is to say, before the fall reason was naturally mistress of the faculties, guiding even the will; but now it can only do so with the help of grace.

As for the will, it is " a power through the which we choose good, after that it be determined by reason; and through the which we love God, desire God, and rest with full liking and consent finally in God. " (C. 116:17) But this too has been weakened:

---

[1] I^a-II^{ae}, q. 85, a. 3.

[2] I point out here that the doctrine of the English author is in conformity with that of St. Thomas; Justin McCann points out the similarity to Richard of St. Victor, asserting that the ultimate source is probably St. Augustine (see McCann, p. 85). It is very difficult to state with certainty from whom the author of *The Cloud* is borrowing in view of the fact that his ideas and terminology are found in so many medieval authors. It is well known that St. Thomas owes a considerable debt to Richard of St. Victor and (needless to say) to St. Augustine. Whether the English author got his ideas directly from Richard or whether he read Richard with a Thomistic slant is difficult to say. The fact that he uses the Augustinian division of " memory, understanding, and will " might argue that he is less Thomistic, were it not for the fact that almost all mystical writers (including the deeply Thomistic St. John of the Cross) use this terminology as being more practically suited to the activity of the contemplative life.

Before man sinned, will might not be deceived in his choosing, in his loving, nor in none of his words; because it could then by nature savour each thing as it was. But now this may not be, unless it be anointed with grace. For ofttimes, because of infection of the original sin, it savoureth a thing for good that is full evil, and that hath but the likeness of good. (C. 116:20)

In this way the will that formerly " might not be deceived " because subject to reason now needs the healing or anointing power of grace.

The next faculty is the imagination; and this too must be brought under the control of reason through the guidance of grace. It is " a power through the which we portray all images of all absent and present things "; but it has gone wild because of original sin:

Before man sinned, was imagination obedient unto reason—to the which it is as it were a servant—that it ministered never to it any disordered image of any bodily creature, or any fantasy of any ghostly creature; but now it is not so. For unless it be restrained by the light of grace in the reason, it will never cease, sleeping or waking, to portray diverse disordered images of bodily creatures; or else some fantasy, the which is nought else but a bodily conceit of a ghostly thing, or else a ghostly conceit of a bodily thing. And this is evermore feigned and false and next to error. (C. 117:8)

The author proceeds to show how the imagination is what St. Teresa calls " the fool of the house, " presenting wild phantasies to the mind; and he concludes with the same refrain: " All this disobedience is the pain of original sin. " (C. 118:6)

Once again he has emphasized two things: reason must command the faculties of man, and reason alone cannot do this unless aided by divine grace.

The same principles appear in his analysis of the fourth faculty that, he says, must be subjected to the will. Sensuality " is a power of our soul, reaching and reigning in the bodily wits, through the which we have bodily knowing and feeling of all bodily creatures, whether they be pleasing or unpleasing. " This faculty " grumbleth in the lack of pleasing creatures, and lustily is delighted in their presence. " (C. 118:7) But the will has lost control of this faculty nor can it regain its power without the help of grace:

> Before man sinned was the sensuality so obedient unto the will—unto the which it is as it were a servant—that it ministered never unto it any disordered delight or dislike made by any ghostly enemy in the bodily wits. But now it is not so; for unless it be ruled by grace in the will, so as to suffer meekly and in measure the pain of the original sin — the which it feeleth in the absence of needful delights and in the presence of speedful dislikes—and to restrain itself from lust in the presence of needful delights, and from lusty pleasure in the absence of speedful dislikes: it will wretchedly and wantonly welter, as a swine in the mire, in the wealths of this world and the foul flesh so much, that all our living shall be more beastly and fleshly, than either manly or ghostly. (C. 118:19)

In this way does the author wish to establish the rule of reason, once dethroned by sin—but this work can only be done under the gentle guidance of grace. Once, however, reason is in command, there will be order in the soul; man will be unified so that his faculties are centered upon God. This doctrine is like that of St. Thomas who writes:

> As a result of original justice, *the reason had perfect control over the lower parts of the soul*, while reason itself was perfected by God and was subject to Him. Now this same original justice was lost through the sin of our first parents, as already stated; so that all the powers of the soul are left, as it were, *destitute of their proper order*, whereby they are naturally directed to virtue; which destitution is called a wounding of nature (*vulneratio naturae*). [3]

Such are the wounds of sin: reason is blinded and the will is weakened. The English author clinches the matter with the exclamation:

> Lo, ghostly friend! to such wretchedness as thou here mayest see be we fallen through sin. (C. 119:11)

So deep in us are the roots of original sin that evil thoughts arise spontaneously in the mind. " If they be fastened to the

---

[3] I^a-II^{ae}, q. 85, a. 3.

ghostly heart [that is to say, the will] with a full consent, " they result in deadly sin; and the roots of sin are analyzed according to the seven deadly sins—wrath, envy, sloth, pride, avarice, gluttony, and lust. Again, a similar analysis is found in St. Thomas who, telling us that he is following St. Gregory, speaks of these deadly sins—not deadly in the sense that they are the most grave but that they are those to which man is most easily inclined and that most easily lead to other sins.

Any man, then, who would be purified and come to God must undergo the suffering that accompanies contemplation in order that the scars of original sin may be blotted out. But these very scars are irritated and inflamed by personal sin:

> All men have travail in this work: both sinners and innocents that have never sinned greatly. But far greater travail have those that have been sinners than they that have been none; and that with reason. (C. 64:14)

The reason for the greater travail is that personal sins have weakened the character, rendering more acute the necessity of purification and demanding greater effort; but it must never be forgotten that the chief agent in all this is Our Lord who can do as He wishes. While under normal circumstances the innocent person comes more quickly to this grace, " nevertheless, ofttimes it befalleth that some, that have been horrible and customary sinners, come sooner to the perfection of this work than those that have been none. And this is the merciful miracle of Our Lord, that so specially giveth his grace, to the wondering of all this world. " (C. 64:17)

It would seem that the sin which is " as it were oned and congealed with the substance of thy being " is original sin; this is " the foul stinking lump of sin " that is overlayed with the ugliness of personal transgression.

CONCUPISCENCE AND CONTEMPLATION

The " roots of sin " about which the author often speaks, translated in Latin as " *fomes peccati,* " refer to what the theologians called " *concupiscentia.* " This is the deep-rooted *inclination* to evil, the " pain " or penalty of original sin later analyzed with devastatingly accurate psychological insight by St. John of the Cross in the opening chapters of the first book of *The Dark Night* where, following once again the lead of Aquinas and the author of *The Cloud*, the Spanish mystic shows how deeply these seven wounds enter into the psychology of even well-intentioned people. The English author, too, is emphasizing the inherent weakness of man, " the filth, the wretchedness, and the frailty of man, into the which he is fallen by sin, and the which he must always feel in some degree the whiles he liveth in this life, be he never so holy. " (C. 40:12) While a man may remove some of the penalty of personal sin, that of original sin remains until death:

> Then it is no doubt to me that thou art cleansed not only from sin, but also from the pain of sin. I mean from the pain of thy former special sins, and not from the pain of original sin. For that pain shall always last on thee to thy death day, be thou never so busy. Nevertheless it shall but little trouble thee, in comparison of the pain of thy special sins; and yet shalt thou not be without great travail. For out of this original sin will every day spring new and fresh stirrings of sin; the which thou must every day smite down, and be busy to shear away with a sharp double-edged sword of discretion. And hereby mayest thou see and learn that there is no certain security, nor yet rest in this life. (C. 68.1)

And yet all this sinfulness or inclination to sin is not to be confused with sin itself; it is no more than the condition of man, and it becomes sin only when the thoughts arising therefrom be " fastened to the ghostly heart [that is to say, the will] with a full consent. " (C. 36:18)

This doctrine, however, though accurately orthodox is not just a repetition of current theology but contains a personal contribution of great significance. Contemplation, he insists, enters deeply into the human psychology, removing the very roots of sins, purifying man from concupiscence itself—not, it is true, completely removing the scars of original sin (for these remain until death, be we never so busy), but weakening their power and removing concupiscence insofar as it is caused by personal sin. Thus it does a work that confession and ordinary prayer can never do:

For in this work a soul drieth up in itself all the root and the ground of sin that will always remain in it after confession, be it never so busy. (C. 63:12)

In this way does the author insist that contemplation does a work that is totally beyond the power of any other kind of prayer, of any kind of penance—fasting, watching, or whatever it may be. This is emphasized in such words as the following:

Fast thou never so much, watch thou never so long, rise thou never so early, lie thou never so hard, wear thou never so sharp; yea, and if it were lawful to do—as it is not—though thou put out thine eyes, cut thy tongue out of thy mouth, stop up thine ears and thy nose never so fast, shear away thy privy members, and do all the pain to thy body that thou couldst think; all this would help thee right nought. Yet will stirring and rising of sin be in thee. (C. 38:16)

This is the context in which he is insisting that only contemplation will remove the roots of sin. Not only are fasting and watching of no avail but sorrow for sin, tears for the Passion of Christ, joyful reflection on the joys of heaven—all these are good in themselves, but they never explore that part of the human psychology purified and beautified by the blind stirring of love that is contemplative prayer. " It destroyeth not only the ground and root of sin, as it may be here, but also it getteth virtues. " (C. 39:11) So deeply does contemplative prayer transform the inmost heart of man—not completely purifying it (for he has the saving little phrase, " as it may be here ") but bringing man to a freedom from the penalty of sin remotely akin to that which he will have in glory.

And a similar doctrine is again taught by St. John of the Cross two centuries later. He, too, insists that one must make great efforts at self-purification; but he adds that there is a perfection that can be attained only by the dark purification of passive prayer:

But neither from these perfections nor from those others can the soul be perfectly purified until God brings it into the passive purgation of that dark night whereof we shall presently speak. It befits the soul, however, in so far as it can, to contrive to labour on its own account to purge and perfect itself, so that it may merit being taken by God into that Divine care wherein it becomes healed of all things that it was unable to cure. Because, however greatly the soul itself labours it cannot actively purify itself so as to be in the least degree prepared for the Divine union of perfection of love, if God takes not it in hand and purges it not in that dark fire, in the way and manner that we have described. [4]

In this way do the " dark fire " of St. John of the Cross and the " blind stirring of love " of the English mystic perform a purificatory work that all the fasting and watching and " sharp wearing " in the world cannot achieve.

CONCLUSION

The aim of life, to know and love God, cannot be achieved without a twofold unity: union in oneself in such wise that all the faculties are in harmony, and union with God in such wise that they are all directed toward Him. Such union, however, cannot now be realized by the unaided effort of man because of the sin of Adam who fell from the unifying grace of contemplation to be scattered over creatures. Because of this sin, the wounds of which are irritated by personal sin, man is so deeply injured that he may well be called a " lump " of sin. Concretely, the disunity in man consists in the dethronement of reason from her honored position as queen of the soul. In the resulting disorder or scattering, reason is blinded, the will is fascinated by evil, imagination and sensuality are no longer in subjection to the higher powers. Order or unity can be restored only when the rule of reason is once more established; that is to say, man is unified or " oned " when reason, subject to God, is in tranquil command of all the other faculties.

And the restoration of order in man has been made possible, not by his own efforts (which are totally incapable of lifting him out of the welter of his sin) but only by that grace won through the Passion of Christ. Thanks to this, man may purify his soul in the sacrament of Penance which, like a well of pure water, will remove the guilt of his special sins.

[4] *Dark Night*, I, III, 3.

But confession alone does not remove concupiscence; it does not tear up the roots of sin. These roots, manifesting themselves in seven deadly inclinations, remain in the soul until death; but their malicious power can be checked and their influence weakened—and this is done effectively not by any discursive prayer, not by fasting and watching, not by any self-inflicted penance but only by the blind stirring of contemplative love. This is the flame that burns out the very roots of concupiscence insofar as that is possible in this life, penetrating to a level of the personality upon which those other activities make no impact.

In short, the author asserts that the work of contemplation is the best and most efficacious way of removing the scars of original sin and achieving that unification of the personality which is an integral part of the Christian life, being a necessary prelude to union with God in eternity.

13

THE PATH OF PURIFICATION

ACTIVE PURIFICATION

Having considered the necessity of purification, it is now necessary to examine how, concretely, this cleansing work is performed.

THE FOLLOWING OF CHRIST

In common with all Christian mystics, the English author teaches that the path he describes is that trodden by Christ. " For Christ went before by nature, and we come after by grace. " (P.C. 154:28) The mystical life is, once again, an intensive practice of that abnegation enjoined upon all Christians by Him who told His followers to take up their cross.

To behave as Christ would have behaved is, for the author of *The Cloud*, to be a contemplative; for he insists that Christ, like Adam, engaged in this " oneing exercise "—He was the perfect contemplative, raising up His blind being to the being of the Father in total forgetfulness of any particular man, offering Himself for all men in general and for the salvation of the world. Thus was the sacrifice of Christ a complete renunciation in self-forgetfulness; and this sacrifice is demanded of His generous follower. " And whoso will be a perfect disciple of our Lord's, he must strain up his spirit in this ghostly work, for the salvation of all his brethren and sisters in nature, as our Lord did his body on the cross. And how? Not only for his friends and his kin and his dear lovers, but generally for all mankind, *without any special regard more to one than to another*. For all they that will leave sin and ask mercy shall be saved through the virtue of his passion. " (C. 61:1) In having no special regard to one than to another, Christ had abandoned clear and distinct knowledge in favor of the blind wisdom that accompanies love of God and men.

And, moreover, such forgetfulness is the most perfect practice of the abnegation He asks for. " ' Whoso will come after me (in the manner aforesaid) let him forsake himself. ' I pray thee, how may a man more foresake himself and the world, than for to disdain for to think of any qualities of their being? " (P.C. 155:22) In this way does the cloud of forgetting demand the most thorough forsaking of self.

THE CLOUD OF FORGETTING: PURIFICATORY ASPECT

Something has already been said about the cloud of forgetting in its function as a path to God by negation, and some reference was made to the suffering it inevitably entails. When one examines closely this aspect of the author's teaching, it becomes clear that it is nothing more than a rigourous program of detachment from all the creatures that God ever made.

The author often refers to the " travail " demanded of the contemplative:

> And therefore travail fast awhile, and beat upon this high cloud of unknowing, and rest afterwards. Nevertheless a travail shall he have, whoso shall use him in this work; yea, surely! and that a full great travail, unless he have a more special grace, or else he have for a long time used him therein. (C. 61:11)

He then proceeds to ask wherein this travail consists. Surely it is not in the devout stirring of love, since this is a great gift of Almighty God. No, the travail is in the human effort made to forget creatures:

But wherein is this travail, I pray thee? Surely this travail is all in treading down of the thought of all creatures that ever God made, and in holding of them under the cloud of forgetting named before. In this is all the travail; for this is man's travail, with the help of grace. And the other above—that is to say, the stirring of love—that is the work of only God. And therefore do on thy work, and surely I promise thee he shall not fail in his. (C. 61:16)

In this way is the cloud of forgetting a real ascesis, a work of great renunciation.

If it be asked why forgetting of creatures should cause suffering and why it should bring the soul into desolation and darkness, it is only necessary to recall the author's appeal to Aristotle and his assertion (following the Stagirite) that all men naturally desire to know. The craving for knowledge being one of the most fundamental urges of the human heart, if it is frustrated the soul suffers greatly; for our faculties are ordained to knowledge and they naturally want to know; they clamor to be fed with that knowledge for the attainment of which they were made. Deny them this knowledge and they cry out in acute pain. So says the author. Telling his disciple to offer up his *naked* being to God in abandonment of all quidditive knowledge, of all consideration of the qualities of creatures and of all love toward them, he warns that this is painful to man:

But look, as I oft said, that it be naked, for fear of deceit. If it be naked, then will it be full painful to thee in the beginning to abide therein any while. And that is, as I before said, because thy wits find no meat therein unto them. But no matter thereof, for I would love it the better. Let them fast awhile, I pray thee, from their natural delight in their knowledge. For as it is well said, " A man naturally desireth to know. " (P.C. 171:18)[1]

This "natural delight in their knowledge" is that pleasure which Aristotle and St. Thomas taught accompanies the use of man's faculties, the pleasure of knowing being among the highest accessible to man. Consequently the contemplative who has the cloud of unknowing above his head and the cloud of forgetting beneath his feet, cut off from knowledge of God

[1] See also P.C. 152:10.

and man, is suspended in the anguish of darkness. He has, it
is true, the knowledge of faith; but its blinding brightness
only intensifies his agony, causing suffering of another kind.
Thus suspended between heaven and earth the soul, clamoring
for God and for creatures, is unable to know either. Hence
its extreme discomfiture.

Crying out for their proper object, the faculties will grumble,
but they must not be heeded. " And although thy wanton
seeking wits can find no meat unto them in this manner of
doing, and therefore grumblingly they will bid thee always to
leave off that work and do some good on their curious manner—
for it seemeth to them that it is nothing worth what thou
dost, and all is because they have no skill therein—yet I would
love it the better. " (P.C. 139:15) Sometimes, in their starvation,
the cry of the natural wits is like madness, but they must be
mastered:

> And, therefore, although thy wits can find no meat unto them
> in this work, and therefore they would have thee away: yet look
> that thou leave not for them, but be thou their master and go
> not back in feeding of them, be they never so mad. Then
> goest thou back in feeding of thy wits when thou sufferest them
> to seek in the diverse curious meditations of the qualities of thy
> being. (P.C. 139:26)

The problem is that these natural faculties are leading to
that dispersion and scattering which is the very antithesis of
the works he is teaching. If you give them meat, he says, they
have power " to draw thee to many things and to be scattered
thou knowest not how. " (P.C. 152:16) Therefore they must be
ignored, even though their anguished clamor makes for
suffering; for in the abandonment of scattering conceptual
knowledge, one returns in love to that unity lost by Adam at
the fall.

THE ASCESIS OF UNKNOWING

More or less similar teaching, with its Aristotelian-Thomist
foundation appears in St. John of the Cross:

> In order to arrive at knowing everything,
> Desire to know nothing.

This is part of the Spanish mystic's constant rejection of any kind of " desire " or " attachment "—and especially of attachment to that most delectable of created things which is knowledge. And the thought of the English author is the same when he writes: " Be blind in this time, and shear away desire of knowing, for it will more hinder thee than help thee. " (C. 70:17) But when one shears away desire of knowing all things, when one forgets friends and relatives, forgets the consolations of prayer, forgets all things—then one is really detached, able to love God with that chaste and perfect love outlined in the *Epistle of Prayer*. And it is at this forgetting that the author aims, telling his disciple to be detached from even the holiest things that are not God. " And in all other sweetness and comforts, bodily and ghostly, be they never so pleasing nor so holy (if it be courteous and seemly to say), we should have a manner of recklessness. " (C. 93:12)

In time devoted to prayer as such, this forgetfulness takes the form of emptying the mind of all images and concepts: in the affairs of daily life, it is clear that one cannot walk around in a state of oblivion, but even here the cloud of forgetting has its part to play, for it demands a *detachment* from creatures. And that is why he has told his disciple to shear off the *desire* of knowledge; and that is why St. John of the Cross has said " *Desire* to know nothing. " The contemplative " forgets " creatures in the sense that he forgets their creaturehood to see in them God who is (as he says in another context) their very being. " Forgetfulness " is used also by St. John of the Cross in this meaning when he writes the following " Caution ":

The first caution is that for all persons thou shalt have equal love and *equal forgetfulness*, whether they be relatives or no, withdrawing thy heart from these as much as from those... If thou art *equally forgetful* of them all, as befits thee for holy recollection, thou shalt free thyself from going astray as regards the greater or lesser degree of love due to each.[2]

This forgetfulness is detachment; for the saint wishes that the mind never dwell long upon the creature as creature, but

---

[2] *Cautions, Against the World,* Caution the First.

go straight to God who is its center according to his words spoken elsewhere:

> When thy mind dwells upon anything,
> Thou art ceasing to cast thyself upon the All. [3]

In order, then, to remain naked (which is another way of saying to remain in the cloud of forgetting), the soul must make great efforts to check the mind from its eager search for clear and distinct knowledge.

Such is the *todo y nada* of St. John of the Cross. " Nothing, nothing, nothing, " he is reported to have said, " even to leaving one's skin and all else for Christ "; [4] and the " alling and noughting " of the English author demands the same terrible reunciation:

> So that for this noble noughting of itself in very meekness, and this high alling of God in perfect charity, it deserveth to have God. (P.C. 149:13)

The meekness, which is the emptying of oneself of everything to become nothing, is of no value whatever without that " perfect charity " which finds expression in the " alling " work of contemplation. [5] In order to have God who is All, one must renounce creatures (and oneself) that, considered apart from God, are nothing. In this way is prepared the path for the historic words of St. John of the Cross:

> In order to arrive at having pleasure in everything,
> Desire to have pleasure in nothing.
> In order to arrive at possessing everything,
> Desire to possess nothing.

[3] *Ascent*, I, XIII, 12. This doctrine is similar to that of the English author:
   " When thy mind dwells upon anything,
   Thou art ceasing to cast thyself upon the All.
   For, in order to pass from the all to the All,
   Thou hast to deny thyself wholly in all.
   And when you come to possess it wholly
   Thou must possess it without desiring anything.
   For, if thou wilt have anything in having all,
   Thou hast not thy treasure purely in God. "
[4] See Maritain, p. 332.
[5] See P.C. 149:6.

> In order to arrive at being everything,
> Desire to be nothing.
> In order to arrive at knowing everything,
> Desire to know nothing. [6]

Thus all desire is renounced for love of Him who is the source of all pleasure, all knowledge, and all being.

FROM PAIN TO JOY

Lest the disciple lose courage in his effort to keep the mind in silent and loving emptiness, the author constantly reminds him that the pain will pass away giving place to joy, as the work of forgetting is performed with increasing facility. Toward the end of *Privy Counsel* when the disciple is complaining that he finds no rest in this work but " pain and battle on all sides " because he cannot follow his natural " wits " nor yet feel God in total self-forgetfulness, the author reminds him that the travail will pass away:

> To this I answer and say: that thou art not yet used in this work, and therefore it is more painful to thee. But if thou wert wont thereto and knewest by experience what profit were therein, thou wouldst not willingly come out thereof to have all the bodily rest and jóy of this world. And yet it is great pain and travail also. (P.C. 172:11)

The same idea is put forward in *The Cloud* where the author is even more explicit in his statement that the work will become easier with the passage of time:

> Travail fast but awhile, and thou shalt soon be eased of the greatness and of the hardness of this travail. For although it be

---

[6] *Ascent*, I, XIII, 11. This is echoed by T. S. Eliot in *Four Quartets*:
" In order to arrive at what you do not know
    You must go by a way which is the way of ignorance.
In order to possess what you do not possess
    You must go by the way of dispossession.
In order to arrive at what you are not
    You must go through the way in which you are not.
And what you do not know is the only thing you know
And what you own is what you do not own
And where you are is where you are not. "
                                                    (" East Coker, " III)

hard and strait in the beginning, when thou hast no devotion, nevertheless afterwards, when thou hast devotion, it shall be made full restful and full light unto thee, that before was full hard. And thou shalt have either little travail or none. (C. 62:5)

And so the pain decreases and the coming of Our Lord is more and more " merry " as the soul, in growing joy and love, unites its faculties in one. All this stress and hardship and lack of comfort that you feel, he writes in the *Epistle of Prayer*, simply means that the fruit of your charity is still green, hanging on the tree—" the greenness of the fruit hanging on the tree, or else newly pulled, eggen thy teeth. " (P. 57:21) If you want perfect love, however, you must travail and suffer: you cannot expect to eat the sweet kernel unless " thou crack first the hard shell and bite of the bitter bark. " (P. 57:23)

To sum up: the mystical life demands a total sacrifice; it asks for the renunciation of all desires, since affection for creatures causes disunity and scattering while their rejection allow the faculties to unify tranquilly in the love of God. The author of *The Cloud* delineates this inescapable ascesis by his figure of the cloud of forgetting, which is nothing else but the complete abnegation of man's most fundamental craving: his desire for knowledge. When this is mortified, all other desires are automatically mortified; for it is the root of them all.

This ascesis is likewise expressed in the notion of " nakedness, " the offering of one's naked being to the naked being of God in the rejection of all distinct knowledge that might scatter the powers of the soul; it is expressed in the " alling and noughting, " the foreunner of the immortal " *todo y nada* "; it is expressed in the following of Christ, the perfect contemplative who, upon the Cross, made a total sacrifice of self in the offering of His blind being to the blind being of God.

Yet, as one perseveres, the effort to keep the soul in the void of detachment becomes less and less burdensome, the faculties are less and less allured by the seductive fascination of creatures, the clamor of the natural wits for their proper meat becomes less and less imperative. Union becomes automatic as the faculties are completely absorbed in God.

The pain and effort of the ascent of the mountain with Moses, however, are but little in comparison with the passive, searing suffering of the night of the soul.

PASSIVE PURIFICATION

CONTEMPLATION AND PURGATORY

That man, injured by Adam's sin and his personal transgressions, must pass through a purification of fire in order to be united with God in eternity was the ordinary theological explanation of the doctrine of purgatory. And the author of *The Cloud* teaches that his path of contemplation is simply a purgatory in this life: it performs that "oneing" function wholly necessary if " scattered " man is to find union with himself and with God in everlasting life. Urging the contemplative to remain at his task despite its desolatory darkness and burning pain, he goes on: " For truly it is thy purgatory. " (C. 67:22)

The blind stirring of love is purgatorial precisely because it burns out the very roots of sin, performing a function that, he has insisted, cannot be done by endless fasting and watching and vocal prayer—nor yet by the sacrament of Penance. And the very love of God that inflames the heart of the contemplative is that which cauterizes the soul, wiping out the aftermath of sin in a way that nothing else can. For St. John of the Cross again reminds us that " even as spirits are purged in the next life with dark material fire, so in this life they are purged and cleansed with the dark spiritual fire of love. " [7] But how, precisely, does love cause this purgatorial suffering?

[7] *Dark Night*, II, XII, 1. The same theology is put forward by T. S. Eliot, who tells us that the tormenting fire of love redeems us from the pyre of eternal suffering:

" The only hope, or else despair
Lies in the choice of pyre or pyre—
To be redeemed from fire by fire.

" Who then devised the torment? Love.
Love is the unfamiliar Name
Behind the hands that wove
The intolerable shirt of flame
Which human power cannot remove.
We only live, only suspire
Consumed by either fire or fire. "
(" Little Gidding, " IV)

The Light of Love

The light of love reveals not only the beauty of God but also the ugliness of self. In the *Study of Wisdom* the author has compared love to a candle that, burning brightly, casts its light upon everything around—upon self and upon God. In its light, he has written, " thou mayest see thine unworthiness and his great goodness. " (S.W. 43:13) And now he describes how terrible it is to see self in the light of love; for this same self is wounded by sin, is a " lump " of wretchedness. The anguished view of one's sinfulness echoes in the following words:

> For it [i.e., the soul] shall find all the special deeds of sin that ever he did since he was born, bodily or ghostly, privily or darkly, painted thereupon. And howsoever he turneth it about, evermore they will appear before his eyes; until the time be that with much hard travail, many sore sighings, and many bitter weepings, he have in great part rubbed them away. (C. 122:20)

The agony of seeing one's own wretchedness can be likened to the pain of Hell itself. Later, St. John of the Cross is to say that the agony is so great " that the soul seems to be seeing hell and perdition opened "; [8] and a similar way of speaking is used by the English author:

> Sometimes in this travail he thinketh to look thereupon is to look as on hell; for he thinketh that he despaireth to win to perfection of ghostly rest out of that pain. Thus far inwards come many; but for greatness of pain that they feel and for lacking of comfort they go back to the consideration of bodily things, seeking fleshly comforts without, for the lacking of ghostly which they have not yet deserved, as they should if they had abided (C. 123:3)

In this way, the suffering of contemplation is caused by the impurity of the soul; but as the meek stirring of love is permitted to do its work, it gradually burns away the stains of sin and becomes less and less painful; for the soul is in process of purification and the painful torment is due not to the nature

---

[8] *Dark Night,* II, VI, 6.

of the stirring but to the sinfulness of the soul that, in its weakness, cannot endure the intense love of God. Just as the positive striving for loving and forgetful emptiness becomes increasingly effortless; so the passive suffering grows less harrowing. If one perseveres, consolation will come; the flame will not always be painful. " For he that abideth, " he writes, " feeleth sometimes some comfort, and hath some hope of perfection; for he feeleth and seeth that many of his former special sins be in great part by help of grace rubbed away. " (C. 123:10) Thus he finds some alleviation, but still he has much to suffer. " Nevertheless, " continues the author, " ever he feeleth pain; but he thinketh that it shall have an end, for it waxeth ever less and less. And therefore he calleth it not hell but purgatory. " (C. 123:13) But when the " special " sins are rubbed away, there still remains the original sin, the root of all:

Sometimes he can find no special sin written thereupon, but he thinketh that sin is a lump, he knoweth never what, none other thing but himself; and then it may be called the root and the pain of original sin. (C. 123:15)

The penalty of original sin remains; for it is " oned " and " congealed " with the very substance of his being. Yet even in this life there are times when the blind stirring has almost done its work and the soul, inflamed with love, finds only joy and consolation in God:

Sometimes he thinketh it paradise or heaven, for diverse wonderful sweetnesses and comforts, joy and blessed virtues that he findeth therein. Sometimes he thinketh it God, for peace and rest that he findeth therein. (C. 123:18)

In this way the same blind stirring that causes pain also causes intense joy; the flame that tortures with intolerable torment also ravishes with ecstatic joy. Hence the paradoxes of joy and pain filling the pages of the mystics and expressed with characteristic passion by St. John of the Cross: " Oh, sweet burn! Oh delectable wound! Oh, soft hand! Oh delicate touch! " [9]

---

[9] *Living Flame*, Stanza II.

This is the joyful pain of purgatory; for " the souls in Purgatory
see the darkness of sin in the light of God, or, in other words,
in that infused knowledge which he pours into their minds.
The whole work of purgatorial suffering is based on the
knowledge and horror of sin. " [10]

In this way does the contemplative soul pass through
Purgatory in its journey to eternal life. " For the same fire of
love that afterward is united with the soul and glorifies it is that
which aforetime assailed it in order to purge it even as the fire
that penetrates the log of wood is the same that first of all
attacked and wounded it with its flame, cleansing and stripping
it of its accidents of ugliness, until, by means of its heat, it had
prepared it to such a degree that it could enter it and transform
it into itself. " [11] When, in beatific joy, the soul is transformed
into God in knowledge and love, there is no longer pain and
resistence to the blind stirring that is now a brightly burning
flame; but such a state does not come about perfectly in this
life where the ugly root of original sin remains, be we never
so busy. In the passage where he speaks of the comfort that
rewards the contemplative's perseverance, he concludes with
the warning that the contemplation of this world is always
imperfect: his words sound like an appendage or afterthought,
for he simply exclaims: " Yea! think what he think will; for
evermore he shall find it a cloud of unknowing that is betwixt
him and his God. " (C. 123:22)

SUFFERING AT THE SUMMIT

And yet, the author indicates, the sight of one's wretchedness,
harrowing though it be, is not the greatest suffering of the
mystical life, nor does it pertain to the summit. Telling us that
there are two kinds of meekness, one caused by the sight of
one's sins and another arising from the realization of God's
infinite beauty and purity, he assures us that the second alone
is perfect virtue. When one reaches the peak, all preoccupation
with self vanishes, the soul being absorbed wholly in the
immaculate holiness of God. " Two things there be, " he writes,

---

[10] Mother Mary of St. Austin, p. 59.
[11] *Living Flame*, Stanza I, 16.

" that be causes of this meekness, the which be these: One is the filth, the wretchedness and the frailty of man, into the which he is fallen by sin, and the which he must always feel in some degree the whiles he liveth in this life, be he never so holy. Another is the over-abundant love and the worthiness of God in himself; in beholding of which all nature quaketh, all clerks be fools, and all saints and angels be blind. " (C. 40:10)

After all, he reminds us, Our Lord and Our Lady were the meekest of persons, yet they had no wretchedness to humble them:

> For if it so were that there were no perfect cause to be meeked under, except the seeing and feeling of wretchedness: then would I know of them that say so what cause they be meeked under that never see nor feel—nor never shall be in them—wretchedness nor stirring of sin: as our Lord Jesu Christ, our Lady Saint Mary, and all the saints and angels in heaven. (C. 44:7)

And, he continues, we are all called by grace to that perfection which Christ had by nature; so we are invited to a higher degree of meekness than that arising from the view of our " filth " and frailty; and this will be when we are drawn out of ourselves in ecstasy by the overabundant love of God.

All this is, indeed, characteristic of this author whose constant insistence that there can only be true love of God in total forgetfulness of self has constantly been noted. When one is conscious of self (even of one's wretchedness), then there is some imperfection or " crookedness " in one's intention; and so he asserts that meekness " is imperfect when it is caused by any other thing mingled with God, although he be the chief... and is perfect when it is caused of God by himself. " (C. 40:1)

Consequently, he declares that in her sublime mystical love Mary Magdalen had forgotten about her sins:

> Came she therefore down from the height of desire into the depth of her sinful life, and searched in the foul stinking fen and dunghill of her sins, searching them one by one, with all the circumstances of them, and sorrowed and wept so upon them each one by himself? Nay, surely she did not. (C. 46:5)

Mary made no meditations about her sinfulness nor was her greatest sorrow that she had sinned. Her greatest suffering and grief was that she could not love enough:

> Nevertheless it may be said and confirmed by Scripture that she had a more hearty sorrow, a more doleful desire, and a more deep sighing, and more she languished—yea! almost to death —for lacking of love, although she had full much love—and have no wonder thereat, for it is the condition of a true lover that the more he loveth, the more he longeth to love—than she had for any thought of her sins. (C. 45:16)

The mystics agree that the supreme suffering is to long for God with a love that can be sated only by vision—and yet to find oneself still in exile. Love itself then becomes a torture while, says St. John of the Cross, the desires and energies of the soul, inflamed with passionate love yet plunged in darkness, are ravenously hungry " like the dogs of which David speaks as running about the city; finding no satisfaction in this love, they keep howling and groaning. "

Such is the final state of purification when, like Magdalen, forgetful of sin the contemplative longs for God whom he cannot love enough.

In short: passive purification, purgatory upon earth, is caused by the blind stirring of love enlightening the contemplative to his wretched sinfulness hideously contrasted with the infinite purity of God. The flame of love burns out the very roots of sin, removing concupiscence itself, as does the fire of Purgatory: thus it allows the scattered faculties to be " oned " in God. But even when unified as far as can be in this life, the soul still suffers from an intense longing for God that can never be sated but by vision.

PSYCHOLOGICAL REPERCUSSIONS

Striving to annihilate all desire of creatures, working to void the mind of all distinct thoughts, directing the will silently and lovingly to the cloud of unknowing, anguished by the appalling sight of his own sinfulness, wounded by his longing for love—through all this the contemplative finds that his faculties are slowly unified and his soul is " oned " with God. Yet this unification is never effected without the severest shocks to the human personality. Such is the testimony of all the mystics; such is the testimony of the author of *The Cloud.*

For one thing, this prayerful union of the faculties in God entails a degree of concentration asked of no philosopher, no mathematician, no scientist. For what scholar or thinker becomes so absorbed as to forget totally his own being or as to be in ecstasy? This is a terrible marshalling of all the human forces; and it makes its inevitable impact upon a nervous system sometimes already weakened from natural debility, from excessive penance, or simply from neglect.

Again, it has been pointed out that contemplative prayer does its work at a lower depth of the personality than that touched by reasoning; and we have seen that the same " little love " that makes the countenance serene and lovingly guides the soul also tears out the roots of sin and implants virtues. But there is an inexorable law that when roots are torn out the earth trembles; so that when the roots of the seven deadly sins, this deeply embedded concupiscence, are wrenched out of the soil, it is not surprising that the ground of the soul should shake. Resistence and rebellion rise to the surface. Unconscious forces and basic passions, normally submerged in that mysterious part of the personality we call unconscious, may be suddenly unleashed and, surging into the conscious mind, they may threaten to engulf the whole personality with uncontrollable fury.

Toward the end of *Privy Counsel* the author describes the breaking of the storm:

Many great storms and temptations, peradventure, shall rise in this time, and thou knowest never whither to run for sorrow. All is away from thy feeling, common grace and special. Be not overmuch afraid, then, although thou have matter, as thou thinkest; but have a lovely trust in our Lord, so little as thou mayest get for the time, for he is not far. He shall look up, peradventure, right soon and touch thee again with a more fervent stirring of that same grace than ever thou feltest any before. Then art thou all whole and all is good enough, as thou thinkest, last while it last may. For suddenly, or ever thou knowest, all is away and thou left barren in the boat, blow with blundering blasts now hither and now thither, thou knowest never where nor whither. Yet be not abashed; for he shall come, I promise thee, full soon, when he liketh, to relieve thee and doughtily deliver thee of all thy dole, far more worthily than ever he did before. Yea! and if he after go, after will he come again; and each time, if thou wilt bear thee by meek suffering, will he come more worthlier and merrylier than other. (P.C. 167:17)

Here is a period of desolation in which the contemplative is deprived not only of mystical tranquillity but of all consolation —" common grace and special. " But in the midst of the storm he must retain his inward peace, never losing that " lovely trust in our Lord " who will come to deliver him.

Somewhat similar to this is a passage describing the assaults of the fiend on the outer walls of that house within which the contemplative sits rapt in silent prayer. The outer walls are the five senses; the inner sanctuary is the sovereign point of the spirit—and the author writes as follows:

And be not affrighted with any unrestful dread, though the fiend (as he will) come with a sudden fearsomeness, pushing and beating on the walls of thy house where thou sittest; or though he stir any of his mighty limbs to rise and run in upon thee suddenly as it is without warning. Thus shall it be, know thou right well, that whatsoever thou be that settest thee to work truly in this work, thou shalt verily see and feel, or else smell, taste or hear, some affrightening made by the fiend in some of thy five wits without. And all is done to draw thee down from the height of this precious working. (P.C. 148:13)

This passage sharply depicts the dramatic contrast between outer sensible turmoil and inner spiritual peace. It is in the exterior senses that the " fiend " rages and rants, but at a deep center of the soul there reigns unruffled calm; for the author has said that there is a still point of the spirit to which no man, no devil, no angel can penetrate: it is the preserve of God alone. And at this point of delicate repose contemplative prayer goes on, even when the five senses are buffeted by the turbulent waves of temptation. [12]

The author is insistent that this delicate peace be maintained. " And therefore take good care of thine heart in the time of this torment, and lean with a trusty listiness to the love of our Lord. " (P.C. 148:22) Once again he reassures his disciple that Our Lord, who never deserts His friends, is not far: He will come again with gentle consolation. " Lo! friend, thus shall our Lord and our Love, mightily wisely, and goodly succour, keep, and defend all those that for lovely trust that they feel in him will utterly forsake the keeping of themselves. " (P.C. 149:2)

The passages quoted from the English author have sometimes been compared to the night of the senses of St. John of the Cross—and rightly so. The Spanish saint speaks of similar violent uprising of nature; he is more explicit in his description of their content, speaking of blasphemy, impurity, and scrupulosity arising in the mind and heart. He always exhorts the mystic to patient trust in God.

Identical exhortations to passivity are found in the English author, though his choice of words and of figures is significantly different. Here is some of the advice given in *The Cloud:*

And... let that thing do with thee and lead thee wheresoever it willeth. Let it be the worker, and thou but the sufferer; do but look upon it and let it alone. Meddle thee not therewith as though thou wouldst help it, for dread lest thou spill all. Be thou the tree, and let it be the carpenter; be thou but the house, and let it be the husband dwelling therein... It sufficeth enough unto thee that thou feelest thyself stirred sweetly with a thing thou knowest never what, except that in thy stirring thou hast no special thought of anything under God, and that thine intent be nakedly directed unto God. (C. 70:12)

---

[12] See also P.C. 151:23. T. S. Eliot, too, describes the stillness at the center of one's being in darkness, a stillness that is without thought or any activity:

" I said to my soul, be still, and wait without hope
For hope would be hope for the wrong thing; wait without love
For love would be love of the wrong thing; there is yet faith
But the faith and the love and the hope are all in the waiting
Wait without thought, for you are not ready for thought:
So the darkness shall be the light, and the stillness the dancing. "
(" East Coker, " III)

The meaning is the same as that of *The Cloud:* hope in, and love for, creatures must be abandoned for the darkness of a faith enlightened by supernatural love.

In this way, by utterly abandoning itself to God in passive trust, does the soul wait silently in its inner sanctuary of peace until the outside storm has passed and " Jesu " lovingly comes walking across the waters to give succor and consolation.

PSYCHOLOGY AND THEOLOGY

Numerous psychological explanations of these violent up-surgings have been tentatively proposed. It has been suggested that the human organism is, as it were, in rebellion against the excessive starvation or frustration of one section of its psychic life. For that the body can, and does, take compensatory revenge with pitiless inevitability is an ordinary finding of psychology. It is not, therefore, altogether abnormal that the same flame that unifies the scattered faculties should, paradoxically, tear apart in order to unite.

Yet the author of *The Cloud* does not use this way of speaking. For him, the cause of the storm is simply that " Jesu " withdraws His sweet presence, just as He left the disciples in the tempest-tossed boat on the Sea of Galilee. But neither does he exclude a psychological explanation nor is he ignorant of psychology: it is simply that he, according to the spirit of his age, prefers to assign things to their First Cause, while we, according to the spirit of our age, generally tend to stress secondary causes. But the net result is the same.

For this same " Jesu " usually comes and goes according to His own psychological laws. That is to say, His action manifests itself in the ordinary functioning of man's physiological life, in the anguished reactions of his nervous system, in the normal working of his Jungian archetypes. And we are permitted (nay, we are encouraged) to study His ways and His laws with reverent psychological insight.

Nor is this to deny, on the other hand, that God in dealing with His mystics may work miracles transcending His ordinary laws. God can, of course, work miracles; but usually He does not. Consequently, the ordinary must always be presupposed until the extraordinary is proved. And in his description of mystical temptation there is nothing to make us deviate from the view of Augustine Baker that the English author's contemplation is ordinary, accessible to those who devote themselves wholeheartedly to the service of God.

THE TWO NIGHTS

The English author's notable resemblance to St. John of the Cross has given rise to the question as to the role in his work of the two nights—of sense and of spirit—made classical by the great Spaniard. The latter traces the soul's path from the stage of beginners' consolation to the silent, helpless prayer of darkness in which erupt the turbulent temptations of sense. After this comes a period of calm prior to the other, more terrible night of spirit that is the prelude to union. Yet St. John of the Cross had no intention of schematizing the spiritual life into " nights " and categories through which the soul must pass with mechanical inevitability. What is at the root of his thought is the theological principle that sense and spirit must be purified from the injuries of sin if the soul is to be united with God in love. That is why he insists that the purification must be performed either here on earth or in Purgatory.

Now the author of *The Cloud*, too, was aware of this principle, and he built his edifice upon it. Following Dionysius, *Hid Divinity* has stressed that God is totally unlike anything we know, either sensible or spiritual, and the conclusion reached is that sense and spirit must be purified in order to come to God. On this point the Dionysian doctrine was quite widespread, influencing even St. Thomas who speaks of how the soul's " twofold lack of uniformity " must be removed preparatory to the divine union. [13] Hence the author's doctrine that man " is a mixture of two substances, a bodily and a ghostly " and that both of these are " to be oned in undeadliness at the uprising in the last day. " (P. 58:20)

At the same time, the English author does not separate chronologically the two stages as does the Spanish saint; and much of what he says can be applied to the purification of both

[13] See II^a-II^{ae}, q. 180, a. 6, ad 2.

sense and spirit. The cloud of forgetting, if interpreted as the rejection of attachment to all creatures, however spiritual—to all consolation, all visions, all revelations, all sweetness—covers the whole rigorous program of asceticism outlined in the *Ascent of Mount Carmel*. And that the English author did intend it in this sense is abundantly clear from his attitude to consolations, reiterated in not a few passages of his work. [14] Again, the nakedness on which he insists—nakedness of the mind that knows nothing and of the will that loves nothing, but only God—covers the same radical detachment of the two nights. Furthermore, the " alling and noughting " leads to the " *todo y nada* "; so that it can safely be said that the principles laid down by the English author, if applied with logical rigor, lead to the same conclusions as St. John of the Cross. Indeed, the *Ascent of Mount Carmel* is little more than a detailed analysis of all the things, sensible and spiritual, that must be " forgotten " (that is, from which the soul must be detached) in the path to God in naked faith.

When it comes to the passive purification of the *Dark Night*, the same telescoping of the two nights is apparent. The violent temptations mentioned above correspond obviously enough to the tempestuous night of the senses. But they are described in such vigorous terms that one concludes the author is thinking of higher stages in the spiritual ascent. " As a rule these storms and trials, " writes St. John of the Cross, " are sent by God in this night and purgation of sense to those whom afterwards He purposes to lead into the other night (though not all reach it), to the end that, when they have been chastened and buffeted, they may in this way continually exercise and prepare themselves, and continually accustom their senses and faculties to the union of wisdom which is to be bestowed upon them in that other night. " [15] In other words, the very intensity and violence of these temptations is a token of the coming of the second night. Moreover, the English author's descriptions of the horrible view of one's sinfulness, the feeling of something like despair, the notion that one is looking on Hell itself—all

---

[14] See, for example, C. 93:11.

[15] *Dark Night*, I, XIV, 4.

this seems more in keeping with the second night of the Carmelite mystic.

The theology of the English author (and particularly his analysis of the powers of the soul) is much more simple than that of St. John of the Cross and scarcely calls for a detailed analysis of the twofold purification. The Spanish mystic, having mastered the scholastic theology of his day with all its intricacies, penetratingly analyzes the " spiritual organism " to outline in detail its union with God: God is united with the intellect through faith, with the memory through hope, with the will through charity—and corresponding to this union, the purification of these faculties brings in its train temptations against the three theological virtues. Furthermore, he has mastered the Thomistic teaching on the gifts of the Holy Spirit and applies it in great detail to the mystical life. All this makes his work more acute, difficult, and theological than that of the author of *The Cloud* who is primarily a spiritual director and secondarily a theologian.

The Englishman does not attack his subject with the same ruthless logic. He is not systematic; and his Teresian touches of humor together with his sporadic outbursts against the theologians are symptomatic of a tendency to go off at tangents. His theology, while scrupulously accurate and orthodox, puts all the stress on essentials that then stand out in bold relief. Yet the fundamentals are always present in his teaching; the second night, albeit in embryonic form, is there; and his work is a safe guide for those who would climb to the very summit of Mt. Carmel.

The general conclusion to this chapter is that man, scattered by sin, must pass through a purification of both sense and spirit in order that, unified in self, he may come to union with God. Active purification means the rejection of attachment to creatures, desire of which causes dispersion. Passive purification is that purgatorial suffering, caused by an intense love of God, which burns out concupiscence or the roots of sin.

In the passage from dispersion to unity, violent temptations may arise in the depths of the soul; and these are overcome not by positive efforts but by utter passivity, tranquil trust in God, and abandonment of self to the cauterizing, therapeutic working of the blind stirring of love. In this way, under the guidance of grace, is recovered that unity lost by Adam.

And this is no more than that purification which every man must pass through, either here on earth or in Purgatory, on his journey to eternal salvation. That is to say, it is an intense form of the purification that forms an integral part of every Christian life.

14

CONCLUSION

CREATION

Any modern reader of *The Cloud* must sooner or later find himself confronted with the following difficulty: What man has the right to close his eyes to the beauty of the world, to reject the exquisite creatures God has given him, to abandon the splendor of science, and to surround himself with a cloud of forgetting? Who has the right to enclose himself in silent oblivion when God's creation is so good? Is not the doctrine of *The Cloud* somehow un-christian? This objection has all the more force in view of the modern theological trend toward a Teilhardian vision of the universe resplendent with the glory of the Incarnate Word and " divinized " by the gift of His Body and Blood. What man has a right to forget such a world? [1]

From what has been said the answer to this objection may already be apparent.

Keeping in mind that the English author never questions the validity of sensible knowledge, it should also be recalled that the cloud of forgetting is not calculated to annihilate knowledge but *inordinate desire* of knowledge. The whole stress is on

---

[1] This is perhaps the strongest objection the young Japanese have against Zen: they feel that it is escapist.

detachment; and it is precisely the wrenching of self from inordinate love of creatures that causes the pain of contemplation.

Injured and terribly dissipated by sin, man has a blindingly inordinate desire for creatures to which (since he fails to estimate them at their true value as gifts of God) he has become the slave when he should be the master. The author keeps insisting that it is only true and proper that man be above all creatures: he should be in regal command. " All manner of bodily thing is without thy soul and beneath it in nature. Yea! the sun and the moon and all the stars, although they be above thy body, nevertheless they be beneath thy soul. " (C. 114:17) Man, then, should never be subject to any material thing; for all matter is beneath him. Nor should he be subject to any spiritual thing except God. " All angels and all souls, although they be confirmed and adorned with grace and with virtues, for the which they be above thee in cleanness, nevertheless they be but even with thee in nature. " (C. 114:20) Man is subject only to God: " Above thyself in nature is no manner of thing, but only God. " (C. 115:3)

After the sin, however, man has become a slave; creatures, instead of reminding him of, make him forget, his God. That is why the author asserts that they proudly press above him " betwixt him and his God ":

And this is the just judgment of God, because man, when he had sovereignty and lordship of all other creatures, wilfully submitted himself to the stirring of his subjects, leaving the bidding of God and his Maker: that he should therefore afterwards, when he would fulfill the bidding of God, see and feel all the creatures that should be beneath him proudly pressing above him, betwixt him and his God. (C. 64:3)

In short, man when he was in command wilfully sinned, thus making himself a servant.

And now man must try to remedy this situation. To do so he must forget (that is, be detached from) all creatures. But why *forget* them? Because knowledge, in our present plight, is accompanied by inordinate desire; and " a naked thought of anything under God, pressing against thy will and thy witting, putteth thee further from God than thou shouldst be if it were not. " (C. 34:23) For knowledge is the root of all desire (" ignoti nulla cupido " said the scholastics) and when knowledge has gone, desire goes too.

The all-important thing, however, is that when inordinate desire has been vanquished, so that man can see creatures as they really are, then he may know again. For then (and only then) is he capable of true knowledge. Strangely enough, when the cloud of forgetting has done its work perfectly, man is permitted to remember; and now for the first time he really *knows*: no longer is he warped by the ignorance of concupiscence. He looks out on the created world and he sees there only God for (writes St. John of the Cross) " even as all the trees and plants have their life and root in the grove, so the creatures, celestial and terrestrial alike, have their roots and their life in God "; [2] and the English author puts the same idea even more forcefully when he says (and reiterates several times) that God *is* the being of all things—not in the sense of a pantheistic identity but because we share analogously in what He has by right. To look on the world and see only God is truth (for he who sees the creature divorced from its Creator is in abysmal ignorance), and it is to this God-filled vision of the world that the author leads.

And not only is God the being of all things; He is also our being. " He is thy being, and in Him thou art what thou art, " he has said; so that at the summit of divine union the contemplative looks, as it were, through the eyes of God at a world filled with God. This again is what St. John of the Cross means when he speaks of the great delight one has " to know the creatures through God and not God through the creatures; to know the effects through the cause and not the cause through the effects; for the latter is secondary and this other is essential. " [3] So in the final stage nothing is rejected: science, music, poetry, and the beauty of nature are not rejected but seen and loved and relished in God who is their being. It is simply that when the cloud of forgetting has purified the soul, it is free to love in liberty of spirit.

[2] *Canticle*, Stanza XXXVIII, 8.
[3] *Living Flame*, Stanza IV, 5.

At the summit of the mystical life, the soul is so closely united to God that it is He who knows and acts and loves within it; it truly knows creatures, but it knows them as He knows them. This seems to have been hinted at in the *Epistle of Stirrings* where the author has spoken of a state in which the blind stirring of love so takes possession of the contemplative, acting within him, that it tells him when to speak and when to be silent and when to fast—and it smites " as sore as a prick " on his heart when he does not do its bidding. (St. 75:25) This is the high state of union when all that was abandoned is received back, when all that was forgotten is remembered, when naked of creatures the contemplative is clothed in God. This is the " alling " to which the " noughting " was but a prelude: it is ludicrous to concentrate on the *nada* and forget the *todo*.

The author, far from teaching a doctrine of destruction, aims at nothing less than the perfection of the human personality under the gentle guidance of divine grace. That he never falls into what Teilhard de Chardin calls " the mistaken notion that God grows in us by destruction or substitution rather than by transformation " [4] is evident from the type of person his doctrine is calculated to produce, a person balanced in body and soul, a person perfected in sense and intelligence, a person truly *transformed* in God. This can be illustrated by consideration of a typical phrase of his; the passage from " bodilyness " to " ghostliness. " " Suffer meekly and bide patiently the will of our Lord, " he writes to the disciple tossed on the sea of temptation, " for now art thou in the ghostly sea (to my likeness) shipping over from bodilyness to ghostliness. " (P.C. 167:13) What is the ghostly man? A consideration of this will help clarify the fruits of dark purification.

TOWARD THE SUMMIT

Harmony restored by purification, the personality is ready for the delicate action of God at its deepest center. This richly spiritual communication is hidden in the very depth of man's

---

[4] Teilhard de Chardin, p. 75.

being at a point where no creature can enter. " I would...
bring thee out of the boisterousness of bodily feeling, " he
writes, " into the purity and depth of ghostly feeling " (C. 88:14),
as if to say that the contemplative is leaving everything exterior
to meet God in the finest point of spirituality. Words seem
inadequate to describe this " purity and depth of ghostly
feeling, " so deeply embedded in the psyche that the author,
once again using a word steeped in mystical overtones, speaks
of it as " secret. " The " ghostly knot of burning love " between
God and the soul is knitted at a level that is " secret " because
unaffected by the clamorous petulance of the wild wits and
inaccessible to the noisy interference of the fiend. (C. 88:17)
So deep, so secret, so gentle, so far from sense is the flame of
contemplation that the author bids his disciple to keep it
" hidden " not only from self but even from God; but then,
lest his quip be taken literally, he explains that this is a childish
mode of expression, no more than an emphatic way of saying
that contemplative love is so deeply spiritual and removed
from sense that the faculties cannot grasp it. In a masterly
phrase he exclaims of this stirring, " I would that thou shouldst
cast it into the depth of spirit " (C. 89:16); and this " depth of
spirit " is one of the key concepts of his spiritual doctrine. Here
is what he says:

> And here mayest thou see somewhat and in part the reason why
> that I bid thee so childishly cover and hide the stirring of thy
> desire from God. And yet I bid thee not plainly hide it; for that
> were the bidding of a fool, to bid thee plainly do that which
> in nowise may be done. But I bid thee do what in thee is to hide
> it. And why bid I thus? Surely because I would that thou
> shouldst cast it into the depth of spirit, far from any rude
> mingling of any bodilyness, the which would make it less
> ghostly and insomuch farther from God... (C. 89:11)

This secrecy and this " hiding " from God express something
that will be dealt with more at length in treating of " the
sovereign point of the spirit. "

It is in " darkness and concealment, " writes St. John of the
Cross, that the soul goes forth " unobserved " on its journey to
God. He, too, writes of the secrecy:

In the happy night, In secret, when none saw me,
Nor I beheld aught. Without light or guide, save that which
burned in my heart.⁵

This is the silent secrecy experienced in the depth of the spirit
when " the house " is at rest; that is to say, when the faculties
have been harmoniously tranquillized in the night of purification. No longer clamorous, they have been lulled to rest
in spiritual sleep; and the spirit goes forth in concealment.
And, as intimacy with God becomes more intense, the secrecy
becomes more deep, until in the end, at the very zenith of
spirit, the Spanish saint describes this union in words that
sound paradoxically sensual:

How gently and lovingly thou awakenest in my bosom, Where
thou dwellest secretly and alone! ⁶

It is to this same apex of " ghostliness " where God resides
" secretly and alone, " far from the boisterous clamor of
bodilyness, that the English author plots his purificatory path.

And so in the purified tranquillity of darkness, guided by the
blind stirring, the soul goes down, down to the very center of
its own being, nakedly to encounter God who secretly dwells
in silent love at the sovereign point of the spirit.

---

⁵ *Dark Night*, Stanza III. The notion of secrecy or concealment occurs
constantly in St. John of the Cross. " The soul is in concealment and in hiding,
in the which hiding-place, as we have now said, it continues to be strengthened
in union with God through love, wherefore it sings this in the same phrase,
saying, ' In darkness and in concealment. ' " (*Dark Night*, II, XXIV, 13)

⁶ *Living Flame*, Stanza IV. Commenting on these words, St. John of the
Cross writes: " The soul says that He dwells secretly in its breast, because,
as we have said, this sweet embrace is made in the depth of the substance of
the soul. " (*Living Flame*, Stanza IV, 14)

PART IV

Union

15

THE SUMMIT

THE CLIMAX

FEELING OF ONE'S OWN EXISTENCE

Throughout his work the English author insists that what he is teaching is a " oneing exercise "; it is a path to union with God. Moreover, this union is progressive, growing deeper and deeper as with Moses one ascends the mountain with eyes fixed upon that summit which is nothing else but the state of total forgetting of one's own being in absorption in God. This state will reach its perfection only in the next life, but it is accessible to God's friends in some anticipatory form here below.

Even when describing the lower forms of mysticism, the author clearly has in mind this final stage. This is the point at which the cloud of forgetting has done its work perfectly and God " acts all by himself " in the tranquilly expectant soul. As long as a person has not reached this summit point, his prayer is still weak, his union imperfect—and he has reason for sorrow. Indeed, the greatest sorrow imaginable is that of the contemplative who, failing to arrive at the peak, still remains conscious of his own being, is still overwhelmed with the grief of knowing and feeling that he *is*:

All men have matter of sorrow; but most especially he feeleth matter of sorrow that knoweth and feeleth that he *is*. All other sorrows in comparison with this be but as it were game to earnest. For he may make sorrow earnestly that knoweth and feeleth not only what he is but that he is. And whoso felt never this sorrow, let him make sorrow; for he hath never felt perfect sorrow. (C. 83:20)

The sorrow here is that of the person whose purification is almost complete, who is on the verge of the summit, no longer thinking of *what* he is (even that he is a lump of sin) but filled with sorrow from the very realization *that* he is. For the author insists in unmistakably clear terms that he who would climb to the summit must utterly destroy all sight and feeling of self:

And therefore break down all knowing and feeling of all manner of creatures, but most busily of thyself. For on the knowing and the feeling of thyself hangeth the knowing and the feeling of all other creatures; for in regard of it, all other creatures be lightly forgotten. For, if thou wilt busily set thee to the proof, thou shalt find, when thou hast forgotten all other creatures and their works—yea! and also thine own works—that there shall remain yet after, betwixt thee and thy God, a naked knowing and a feeling of thine own being: the which knowing and feeling must always be destroyed, ere the time be that thou mayest feel verily the perfection of this work. (C. 82:19)

The message is clear. The knowledge and feeling of self is an osbtacle to perfect union with God and must, in consequence, be destroyed. Yet, he goes on to remind us, the state of full union in which all is forgotten can in no wise be obtained by human effort—" without a full special grace full freely given by God, and also a full according ableness on thy part to receive this grace, this naked knowing and feeling of thy being may in nowise be destroyed. " (C. 83:10) This special grace by which the naked knowing and feeling of one's being is utterly destroyed shall now briefly claim our attention.

THE BEAM OF GHOSTLY LIGHT

In the twenty-sixth chapter of *The Cloud* the author describes that point at which the mystical life reaches its perfection. This

is a climax somewhat different from the silent prayer of darkness
in which the contemplative beats at the cloud of unknowing
with the dart of love or from the mystical sleep, that prayer in
which the wild and wanton wits are ignored, or reduced to
passivity, in order that the soul may quietly love God like
Mary Magdalen as she sat at the feet of Christ. Now this silent
concentration reaches a peak-point in an intense, even violent,
experience in which the action of God penetrates to the very
core of the contemplative's being. This is a seemingly instantaneous flash of light, a rending dart of love. Psychologically
speaking, it has much in common with intuitions of the great
philosophers and bears interesting resemblances to the enlightenment of Zen. Its distinctive feature, however, is love. For in
this moment the soul is not only flooded with light; it is also
wounded with love.

In this chapter of *The Cloud*, the author has been expanding
on the effort and suffering demanded of the contemplative if
he is to persevere. Urging him to work hard, for rest will come in
eternity, the author goes on to say that there may be times when
the anguishing travail of forgetting becomes easy and effortless;
these are the times when God gives " a more special grace " and
when the contemplative will have " either little travail or none "
because sometimes " will God work ...all by himself ". Such
moments are, of course, gratuitous gifts of God; they are given
" not always, nor yet for a long time together, but when he
liketh and as he liketh; and then wilt thou think it merry to let
him alone. " There follows a description of this privileged
moment of special grace when the beam of ghostly light pierces
the cloud to impart the most profound secrets to the loving soul:

> Then will he sometimes peradventure send out a beam of
> ghostly light, piercing this cloud of unknowing that is betwixt
> thee and him, and show thee some of his secrets, the which
> man may not and cannot speak. Then shalt thou feel thine
> affection inflamed with the fire of his love, far more than I can
> tell thee, or may or will at this time. For of that work that
> pertaineth only to God dare I not take upon me to speak with
> my blabbering fleshly tongue; and, shortly to say, although I
> durst I would not. But of that work that pertaineth to man,
> when he feeleth himself stirred and helped by grace, I like well
> to tell thee; for therein is the less peril of the two. (C. 62:14)

Here there is not too much detail to work on. The author obstinately refuses, here as elsewhere, to speak of God's part in the mystical life; all he wants to teach is the attitude to be adopted by man and the co-operation demanded of him—to speak of this is less perilous. Therefore all he tells us is that the soul is completely passive; action is on the part of God alone, and God grants this to whom He likes and when He likes. As for its content, he says no more than that it is a flash of light, a kindling of love, a revelation of the secrets of God. As to what these secrets are, he gives no hint.

Elsewhere, too, he gives like indications of a shattering experience of love; but, again, they are little more than hints about something the details of which he refuses to disclose. At the beginning of *The Cloud*, for instance, he alludes to a moment in which the cloud of forgetting has done its work so perfectly that the soul is filled only with God:

> And yet, in one stirring of all these, it may have suddenly and perfectly forgotten all created things. (C. 22:10)

But such moments, he reminds us again, are rare because " through the corruption of the flesh " the soul falls back to its ordinary way of action.

Somewhat similar, again, is that passage in *The Cloud* which treats of perfect meekness (that virtue entailing the annihilation of the thought of self in favor of absorption in God) and describes the overwhelming moment in which the contemplative is in actual possession of this perfect virtue:

> ...for full oft it may befall that a soul in this deadly body—for abundance of grace in multiplying of his desire, as oft and as long as God vouchsafeth to work it—shall have suddenly and perfectly lost and forgotten all knowing and feeling of his being, not considering whether he has been holy or wretched. But whether this fall oft or seldom to a soul that is thus disposed, I trow that it lasteth but a full short while. (C. 41:2)

Here the same points are emphasized as before. There is the total forgetfulness of self even of one's sinfulness upon which the author puts so much store; next is stressed the freedom of

God to do as He will; then he tells us that it is a brief experience
—but there is the added indication that it may not, after all,
be so infrequent.

TOTAL SELF-FORGETFULNESS

The doctrine of *Privy Counsel* is remarkably similar to the
above. At the beginning of his letter, the author has instructed
his disciple to forget everything except the fact of his own being
and the being of God. All other thoughts are abandoned; and
in the complete absence of essences, or quiddities, no longer
thinking of *what* God is but only *that* he is, the contemplative
rests in existential silence. His prayer consists only in the
offering of the blind being of self to the blind being of God—
" All I am as I am unto Thee as Thou art. " This is the first stage
of contemplative prayer.

As the letter continues, however, the author explains that
he has allowed the contemplative to retain the consciousness of
his own being only as a concession to weak human nature.
In fact, the climax of contemplation is reached only when the
consciousness of self is annihilated and one feels God alone.
Since, however, such a sublime state is the reward of much
labor and can be attained to only gradually, he has permitted
the consciousness of one's own being to play a part in the
contemplative's prayer. Here is what he says:

> For know thou for certain, that although I bid thee forget all
> things but the blind feeling of thy naked being, yet nevertheless
> my will is—and that was mine intent in the beginning—that
> thou forget the feeling of the being of thyself as for the feeling
> on the being of God. And for this reason I proved thee in the
> beginning that God is thy being. But for me thought that thou
> wert not yet able suddenly to be lifted up to the ghostly feeling
> of the being of God, for rudeness in thy ghostly feeling, there-
> fore, to let thee climb thereto by degrees, I bade thee first gnaw
> on the naked feeling of thine own being unto the time that thou
> mightest be made able to the high feeling of God by ghostly
> continuance in this privy work. (P.C. 155:27)

From this it is clear that any consciousness of self indicates
that prayer is still at a low stage and that love is yet imperfect.

For complete absorption in God in total self-oblivion is that highest act of love:

> For thine own intent and thy desire shall be ever to feel God in this working. For although I bid thee in the beginning, because of thy boisterousness and thy ghostly rudeness, lap and clothe the feeling of thy God in the feeling of thyself, yet shall thou after, when thou art made by continuance more subtle in cleanness of spirit, strip, spoil, and utterly unclothe thyself of all manner of feeling of thyself, that thou mayest be able to be clothed with the gracious feeling of God himself. And this is the true condition of a perfect lover, only and utterly to spoil himself of himself for that thing that he loveth, and not admit nor suffer to be clothed but only in that thing that he loveth; and that not only for a time, but endlessly to be enwrapped in full and final forgetting of himself. (P.C. 156:8)

This is a remarkable passage. Just as the cloud of forgetting has done its work perfectly when all creatures are annihilated and the beam of ghostly light pierces the cloud, so now nakedness reaches its utmost peak when the soul is clothed in God. This is the " alling " and the " noughting "—when the " naked " contemplative is beautifully " clothed " in the gracious feeling of God Himself. And the author leads us to the threshold of eternity—to the " full and final forgetting " of self in the beatific vision.

Moreover, as in *The Cloud*, this is the work of the " perfect lover. " It is for love that the contemplative, utterly naked, clothes and enwraps himself in " that thing that he loveth " which is, in this case, God Himself. And the author goes on in detail about the nakedness of the lover who is clothed in the " garment of love ":

> This is the work of love that none may know but he that feeleth it. This is the lesson of our Lord when he saith: " Whoso will love me, let him forsake himself. " As who should say: Let him spoil himself of himself, if he will be verily clothed in me that am the full garment of love and of lasting that never shall have end. (P.C. 156:20)

So Christ *is* the garment of love. And in this high moment of ecstatic union the naked contemplative puts on the " full garment " that is Christ.

And again as in *The Cloud* the author proceeds poignantly to write of the sorrow of him who feels that he is:

> And therefore, ever when thou beholdest to thy working, and seest and feelest that it is thyself that thou feelest and not God, then shalt thou make sorrow earnestly and heartily long after the feeling of God, evermore desiring without ceasing for to forgo woeful witting and the foul feeling of thy blind being; and covet to flee from thyself as from venom. (P.C. 156:26)

This is the same sorrow as that of *The Cloud*: the deep sorrow of the contemplative who longs to be clothed in only God yet remains conscious of the garment of self—this is " a full heavy and a full painful burthen. " (P.C. 157:14) With an exclamation that, interestingly enough, introduces a deeply human note into the metaphysical or existential atmosphere, he cries:

> Yea, Jesu help thee then, for then hast thou need. For all the woe that may be without that, is not a point to that. For then art thyself a cross to thyself. And this is true working and the way to our Lord, as he himself saith, " Let him bear his cross, " first in the painfulness of himself, and after " follow me " into bliss, or into the mount of perfection, tasting the softness of my love in godly feeling of myself. (P.C. 157:14)

This is to say, the cross of Our Lord is the painful consciousness of one's own being, a cross one carries until entering glory that is " the tasting " of the eternal love of God.

In all this it can be seen how faithfully the author fulfills his promise to speak only of the role of man, refusing to allow his blabbering, fleshly tongue to dwell in detail upon the ineffably beautiful work of God in the soul. No phenomenological description of God's part is in evidence. What does the contemplative see in this rapturous moment? What does he feel? What does he love? Obviously there is some content to the experience: it is not just emptiness, for his nakedness is clothed in God, his darkness is penetrated with light, his nothingness is filled with the All. Beyond the simple process of forgetting is something gigantic, some wonderful enlightenment. Yet the author maintains the same stubborn silence that excites our curiosity even when we admire its wisdom: he will not (or cannot) speak. One thing, however, he does emphasize: this "tasting of the softness" of Our Lord's love, this "godly feeling" of "Jesu" culminates in a tremendous inundation of the overwhelming and abundant love of God. It is love that is stressed as, for example, in that passage where, saying that mortal man must always be burdened with the naked and blind feeling of self, he speaks of exceptional moments of love— "except it be some seldom time when God will let thee feel himself in abundance of love." (P.C. 157:9) This is the love of God Himself that suddenly pours into the soul inducing utter forgetfulness of self in the nakedness of contemplative union.

Love rather than light occupies the center of the picture. Or, more correctly, love is the dominant element in an indivisible experience where abundance of love bathes the soul in blinding and exquisite light.

The same emphasis on love is found in yet another passage that treats of ecstasy. Not of ecstasy in the phenomenological sense of violent bodily repercussions, stiffening of the joints, or trances (the English author eschews such things), but of literal *ecstasis*, or the "going out" of self in extreme love of one who is enthralled by the beauty of God. This "excess of love" of those who are "ravished above mind" is comparable to that love which made the martyrs joyfully run to a cruel death:

> For since the first beginning of Holy Church, in time of persecution, divers souls and many were so marvellously touched in suddenness of grace that suddenly, without means of other works coming before, men of crafts did cast down their instruments from their hands, and children their tables in the school, and did run without ransacking of reason to the martyrdom with saints: why shall not men trow now, in the time of peace, that God may, can, will, and doth—yea! touch divers souls so suddenly with the grace of contemplation. (P.C. 151:1)

"Marvelously touched in suddenness of grace" the martyrs made no lengthy discourse, they weighed no pros and cons, they ransacked no rational powers—they simply threw away their instruments and ran to death; and so does the contemplative throw away the slow instrument of meditation with its meandering indirectness, hastening to God "without mean."

Or, more exactly, rather than his running to God, God comes to him in grace, drawing him to the love of Himself and to the sweet feeling of His essence.

IN OTHER WORKS OF THE ENGLISH AUTHOR

A careful reading of the other works of the author also reveals that he is always pointing toward the same climax. In *Hid Divinity* this ecstatic love is personified in the traditional figure of Moses who, at the peakpoint of mysticism, is forgetful of his own being. Moses, he tells us, is " made... to feel in experience the presence of Him that is above all things, *not having feeling nor thinking of no being nor yet of himself.* " (H.D. 5:19) Again, there is the *Epistle of Prayer*. It is not necessary to repeat here how the summit of prayer is reached in an ecstatic love of God demanding an utter forgetfulness of, and detachment from, all creatures. Only in this state can the Christian be said to love God for Himself alone; only then is his love like the rich and ripe fruit " departed from the tree "; only then does he love like the chaste woman who looks only to her husband and not to any of his goods. This high point of love is the beam of ghostly light; it is the nakedness of him who is clothed in God; it is the moment at which the cloud of forgetting has perfectly done its work. In this moment is found true ecstasy of mind; for the contemplative asks for nought but God Himself.

And the *Study of Wisdom* propounds the same doctrine. As this work reaches a climax, the author, comparing the love of the contemplative soul to the candle that enlightens the night, describes the moment in which this flame opens up to the mind the wonderful glory of God. Like the beam of ghostly light of *The Cloud*, this is a " manner of sunbeam " that enables the soul to see " God and godly things, heaven and heavenly things and all manner of ghostly things. " (S.W. 44:2) But, again like the beam of ghostly light, it is a rare experience and a brief one; for " this sight is but betimes whiles God will vouchsafe to give it to a working soul, the whiles it is in the battle of this deadly life. But after this life it shall be everlasting. " (S.W. 44:3)

Here again, the author has brought us to the threshold of the beatific vision, indicating some anticipatory touch of that glory which shall be everlasting.

Yet the same reticent absence of detail is here too: the *object* of contemplation is not clearly delineated nor is the nature of the union accurately described. A little more knowledge on this point, however, may be gleaned from a consideration of yet another phrase frequently employed by the author; this is "the sovereign point of the spirit" to which reference has already been made.

THE SOVEREIGN POINT OF THE SPIRIT

TERMINOLOGY

In speaking of "the sovereign point of the spirit," the English author has recourse to a phrase canonized by long mystical usage. This is the *apex mentis*, the *scintilla animae*, the *principalis affectio*, "the substance of the soul," "the center of the soul," the *Seelenfünklein*, the "core" of one's being, and so on. [1] These expressions have a wide variety of meanings; with some mystics they indicate an activity coming into operation only at the zenith of the mystical life: others use such phrases in a wider sense. For the English author, this faculty (I call it faculty for want of a better word) is operative at all stages of the contemplative life, the disciple being told from the beginning to hold himself at this point. "And therefore hold thee before in the first point of thy spirit which is thy being." (P.C. 140:6) Or he is told to come down into "the lowest point" of his "wit"—another expression for the same idea. "And therefore

---

[1] St. John of the Cross often speaks of "the centre of the soul": "And it is to be observed, if one would learn how to find this Spouse (so far as may be in this life), that the Word, together with the Father and the Holy Spirit, is hidden essentially in *the inmost centre* of the soul. Wherefore the soul that would find Him through union of love must go forth and hide itself from all created things according to the will, and enter within itself in deepest recollection, communing there with God in loving and affectionate fellowship, esteeming all that is in the world as though it were not. Hence, St. Augustine, speaking with God in the *Soliloquies*, said: ' I found Thee not, O Lord, without, because I erred in seeking Thee without that wert within.' He is, then, hidden within the soul, and there the good contemplative must seek Him, saying, ' Whither hast Thou hidden Thyself?' " (*Canticle*, Stanza I, 4)

come down into the lowest point of thy wit, " writes the author, " the which some men holdeth by very proof that it is the highest, and think on the simplest manner, but by some men the wisest, not what thyself is, but that thyself is. " (P.C. 138:4) Here is this center of the soul that, though buried deeply in the psychic life, is very high—according to the testimony of those who know; and though very simple, it is wonderfully wise. It is precisely here that one makes existential prayer, reflecting not on *what* one is but on *that* one is. This is the very substance of the soul; it is the naked being of the soul. For, he tells his disciple, " the first point and the prick of thy beholding, whatever it be, is thy naked being. " (P.C. 141:11) The activity of various faculties is complicated, dissipated, dispersed; beneath discourse and diversity there is a point of utter simplicity; and it is at this point that the contemplative must aim. Here one offers oneself completely to God, finding total union with Him.

The constant use of this expression in mystical writing has given rise to considerable speculation. What is this sovereign point of the spirit? In the contemplative life does a new faculty, normally dormant, rise up in the spirit? Or again, what is the relation of this faculty to the intellect, will, imagination, and sense to that scholastic framework the English author has outlined with such detailed accuracy elsewhere? For sometimes he speaks of the activity of the will with its " naked intent, " while at other times he appeals to this mysterious faculty that underlies all superficial activity at the very deepest point of the soul. How reconcile these two ways of speaking?

THE NEW DIMENSION

It is just possible that this mystical term is better explained by depth psychology than by Aristotelian philosophy.

In a stimulatingly interesting analysis of Zen, made by way of introduction to one of the works of Suzuki, C. G. Jung departs momentarily from his principal subject to make some reflections on the mystical experience of St. Paul. [2] Mystical

---

[2] Jung, pp. 17 ff.

knowledge, Jung claims, differs from ordinary knowledge in that it effects a *transformation*. Moreover, it is found not in that succession of images which pass across the imagination and from which we abstract our concepts, but by a penetration of the mind into the center of its own being. " The erasing of one picture and its substitution by another, " he writes, " is quite an everyday occurrence which has none of the attributes of a transforming experience. " Mystical experience, then, that transforms cannot be explained in this way; for in it, Jung tells us, " it is not that something different is seen, but that one sees differently. It is as though the spatial act of seeing were changed by a new dimension. " [3]

This " new dimension " is of vital interest for one who would sympathetically study the mystics. They do not see different things: they see differently. A new mode of mental activity is brought into play. Whereas ordinarily we think horizontally, one image or concept being replaced by another, the language of the contemplatives indicates that mystical thought is vertical: it does not entail the acquisition of new ideas and concepts (which, we have seen, are vigorously trodden down beneath the cloud of forgetting), but is a descent into the darkness of one's own mind, void of images and conceptual thinking. God, in short, is encountered not with new thoughts but at a new level of the psyche. This notion of " depth " so prominent in the author of *The Cloud* is found throughout apophatic mysticism; it is well expressed by T. S. Eliot when he writes:

> Descend lower, descend only
> Into the world of perpetual solitude
> World not world, but that which is not world. [4]

---

[3] *Ibid.* See also De Guibert: " Thus in ecstasy the consciousness of the effects of grace becomes so profound that God is seen therein in an altogether new way. " (p. 333)

[4] *Four Quartets*, " Burnt Norton, " III. Eliot goes on to describe the same utter renunciation as the author of *The Cloud*. One descends to the depths of the soul in darkness, in poverty, in renunciation of the things of sense and of spirit, thus reaching a point of no movement:
> " Internal darkness, deprivation
> And destitution of all property,
> Desiccation of the world of sense,
> Evacuation of the world of fancy,
> Inoperancy of the world of spirit;
> This is the one way, and the other

This " world of perpetual solitude, " found by the descent into oneself, is the sovereign point of the spirit, the center of one's being: it is the world in which there reigns silence and union. It is (to continue with T. S. Eliot) the " still point " transferred to the cosmos of the soul; for it is the point at which there is no movement because all is still, all is silent, all is simple, all is one. [5] In short, mystical knowledge does not move in successive images but spirals down into the depth of the soul to encounter God in the obscurity of supraconceptual silence. That is why this high wisdom does not enrich one's store of knowledge (that is to say, one's store of conceptual knowledge); and that is why all attempts to express it conceptually are doomed to failure. To the end, the universe of the mystic remains wrapped in secret silence.

But how reconcile all this with the author's scholastic analysis of the faculties of the soul in *The Cloud*? What part do intellect and will play in this drama?

To answer this it must be recalled that the English author is using two distinct terminologies. Educated in the scholasticism popular in the universities of his day, he automatically employs the terminology of a psychology which is scarcely adequate to express satisfactorily the deeper experience of the mystical mind. In his way of thinking, the mind, at birth is a *tabula rasa*, receives all its knowledge through the external senses and the phantasm; thus its dependence on matter is greatly stressed, and this is expressed in the scholastic dictum that there is nothing in the intellect that was not first in the senses (" Nihil est in intellectu quod non fuit prius in sensu "). Grounded in this psychology, the English author, when he comes to examine professionally the various faculties of the soul, makes use of the ordinary learning he has acquired in his studies; but when it comes to the more delicate and deep realm of contemplation,

Is the same, not in movement
But abstention from movement; while the world moves
In appetency, on its metalled ways
Of time past and time future. "
(" Burnt Norton, " III)
[5] " At the still point of the turning world. Neither flesh nor fleshless;
Neither from nor towards; at the still point, there the dance is,
But neither arrest nor movement. "
(" Burnt Norton, " II)

when he is giving advice to the disciple who finds himself filled
with silent love, then he unconsciously feels the inadequacy of
this terminology and turns to another psychological trend.
Now he uses a way of speaking employed by numerous mystics
from Augustine to Ruysbroeck—a way of speaking reminiscent
of depth psychology—that views mental activity not horizontally but vertically, not in space but in silence, not in motion
but in rest, not in time but in timelessness.

It is therefore unnecessary (indeed it is scarcely possible) to
translate " the sovereign point of the spirit " into terms of
intellect and will; for the English author has abandoned this
latter terminology precisely because of its inadequacy—and in
this he is at one with many other mystics. Here is an interesting
example from his German contemporary Tauler who, in the
same way, begins with the scholastic terms but then passes on
to the vocabulary of traditional mysticism. Speaking of the
gift of the Holy Spirit, he writes:

> Some receive it in the sensible faculties, under forms and images.
> Others intellectually, and therefore in a more perfect manner,
> in the higher faculties, that is to say, far above the senses. Others,
> finally, receive it also in that secret abyss, in that hidden king-
> dom, in those delicious depths that are the noblest part of the
> soul and the likeness of the most Blessed Trinity. It is there
> that the Holy Spirit has his true abode, and that man receives
> His gifts in a wholly divine manner. [6]

Tauler's ascent (or, more literally, his descent) is interesting:
it passes from sense to intellect, and then (when Aristotelianism
has reached its peak) he finds a " secret abyss " and a " hidden
kingdom " in a section of the psyche far below the diversity
of faculties. Now " in those delicious depths " he has entered
a realm that might have puzzled Aristotle; but it does not
puzzle the English mystic who speaks of " tasting " the " soft
love of Jesu, " thus pointing to a delicate point at which the
love of God is mystically savored in the depths of the spirit
like the gentle manna that the Jews ate in the wilderness or
like that even more delicious Bread of Life that the Son of Man
came to give.

[6] Quoted by Poulain, Chapter IX, *Extracts*, 30.

DIVERSITY AND UNITY

Aristotelian psychology is scarcely equipped to express mystical experience for one more reason; namely, its tendency to stress the diversity of human action, whereas mysticism is primarily an experience of union. For Aristotelianism is highly analytical, emphasizing the *diversity* in human activity—which is precisely what the mystic wants to avoid. This point is of some importance. It is a well-known fact that as the mystical life advances, a certain simplification of the personality takes place, in such wise that the faculties quietly unite in concentration on God; then the contemplative feels that he is not performing many activities with a multitude of faculties—his prayer is not a succession of knowing and loving acts, but one deep activity at the very center of his being, an activity that can scarcely be called either love or knowledge since it is an ineffable blend of both, an exquisite savoring of God. That is why Thomas Merton can write that the divine action " touches the depths of the soul, where mind and will are one. " [7] Being a good theologian and a Thomist, Merton does not hold that mind and will are identical; what he means is that in the psychological situation of contemplative prayer, knowledge and love seem to be one in a completely simple action. Better than " knowing " or " loving, " it is perhaps best described as a " stirring. "

Consequently, when the author of *The Cloud* speaks of holding oneself at the lowest point of one's wit, or at the sovereign point of the spirit, or when he tells the disciple to raise his blind being to the being of God—in all this he has no intention of taking back what he has said about distinction of faculties. It is just that he is now speaking descriptively as a director, emphasizing the necessity of unified action; and, looking for a terminology to depict unity rather than diversity, he says: " And therefore hold thee before in the first point of thy spirit *which is thy being.* " (P.C. 140:6) Contemplative prayer is not the activity of one part of man; it is not thinking nor is it loving nor is it feeling; it is the total offering of one's all to God in utter simplicity. Hence the author insists that one offer one's " blind being " (for " being " is all-embracing) to

[7] Merton[1], p. 275.

God in the utmost rejection of dissipation and diversity. It is difficult to see how the same idea could be satisfactorily expressed in terms of intellect and will.

PLACE AND TIME

There is a second point in this description of the " inmost substance of the soul " to which I would like to draw attention; namely, the assertion that " it is above place and time. " This again is a favorite theme of the author of *The Cloud*. " For time, place, and body, these three, should be forgotten in all ghostly working, " he has said (C. 111:4); and time especially has aroused his interest and inspired his pen:

> This work asketh no long time ere it be once truly done, as men ween; for it is the shortest work of all that man may imagine. It is neither longer nor shorter than is an atom; the which atom, by the definition of true philosophers in the science of astronomy, is the least part of time. And it is so little that, for the littleness of it, it is indivisible and nearly incomprehensible. This is that time of the which it is written: " All the time that is given to thee, it shall be asked of thee how thou hast spent it! " And a right thing it is that thou shouldst give account of it. For it is neither longer nor shorter, but exactly equal to one single stirring, that is within in the principal working power of thy soul, the which is thy will. For even so many willings or desires—no more nor no fewer—may be and are in one hour in thy will, as are atoms in one hour. (C. 17:14)

In this passage where, as can be seen, the author reverts to the Aristotelian " principal working power of thy soul, the which is thy will, " we find an interesting medieval mingling of astronomy and mysticism. The astronomical element is explained by Justin McCann. " A Latin note in Cambridge University MS.Kk.vl.26, " he writes, " gives the following subdivisions of an hour: A point is the fourth part of an hour; a moment is the tenth part of a point; an ounce is the twelfth part of a moment; and an atom is the forty-seventh part of an ounce. So that in one hour there are 4 points, 40 moments, 480 ounces, and 22,560 atoms. " [8]

[8] McCann, p. 9.

What, then, is the English author trying to say in all this? All he means is that mystical experience seems incredibly short— for it is outside time.

And this is altogether logical. If, as has been said, mystical experience does not move in a succession of images but goes down to the center of the soul in silence, it follows that it is not conscious of motion nor of change. And time is intimately connected with change. Aristotle defined it as the measure of change; and the scholastics followed him with their definition— " *numerus motus secundum prius et posterius.* " Where there is no change, no succession of images, no replacement of one mental picture by another, then there is no time. So deep, so silent, so ineffably timeless is the contemplative experience.

What the author really means, then, is not that mystical experience is very brief in our sense of the word, but that it is outside time. Just as it is outside space so that " the highest point of the wit " can be called " the lowest, " so it is neither long nor short but timeless. St. John of the Cross makes this point very clearly, asserting that the peak-point of mystical prayer " seems " brief, but it may last a long time:

> This prayer, therefore, seems to the soul extremely brief, although, as we may say, it may last for a long period; for the soul has been united in pure intelligence, which belongs not to time; and this is the brief prayer which is said to pierce the heavens, because it is brief and because it belongs not to time. [9]

So on the one hand this prayer seems extremely brief; it pierces the heavens like a flash of light; yet it may take much time because it is without forms, without images, without successivity. And this is why T. S. Eliot can say that " the still point " is not connected with place and time:

> I can only say, *there* we have been; but I cannot say where.
> And I cannot say, how long, for that is to place it in time. [10]

And the summit prayer of *The Cloud* is the same; we cannot ask " How long? " for this is to place it in time; and the author

[9] *Ascent,* II, XIV, 11.
[10] " Burnt Norton, " II.

has said that place and time play no part here. That is why I wrote earlier that it is a *seemingly* instantaneous flash of light; for in fact this " beam of ghostly light " may describe something more lengthy. Indeed, that the experience is of some duration is suggested by the Mary Magdalen motif; for Mary (who is clearly at the highest point of prayer since she has forgotten even the physical appearance of Christ, has forgotten her sins, has forgotten our own being) is described as sitting at the feet of Christ for some time.

So much for time and change at the summit of the mystical life. But what about the lower stages? What about the role of time in that mystical sleep in which, though the soul is silently united with God at the lowest level of its psychic life, the wild wits are still working, still clamoring, still full of distraction? In such prayer the contemplative is still conscious of his own being; the cloud of forgetting has not done its work perfectly; and while the contemplative may ignore the wild activity of his faculties to pay attention to the blind stirring of love, he cannot be ignorant of, nor indifferent to, their action.

In such prayer it is obvious that there will be consciousness of change and, consequently, of time. Yet even here the sense of change and of time seems somehow different. This is indicated by the author's opposition to the use of words in such prayer. He has insisted, it will be remembered, that the disciple use only the tiniest words, giving as his reason:

> Since a ghostly worker in this work should evermore be in the highest and sovereignest point of the spirit. (C. 74:11)

In these words (in which, it is interesting to note, the " sovereign point of the spirit " which is usually " low " becomes " high ") the author is trying as much as possible to bring the contemplative outside time and space. When one is at this " highest and sovereignest point, " it seems that words interrupt the flow of prayer, as pebbles thrown into a stream cause jarring ripples on its surface—unless, of course, these words come " from within, " in which case they do no more than promote the tranquil motion of the gently flowing stream of prayer. For words are successive things; they *move*, causing images and concepts to flit across the mind. Hence they intensify the sense of time. Contemplative prayer gets away from matter, away from change, away from time, and " it is best when it is in pure spirit, without special thought or any pronouncing of word. " (C. 78:20)

In short, the forgetting of all things and the emptying of the mind of all concepts in order to meet God in existential nakedness demands, or results in, a progressive entry into a world of no change, of no time, and of no body. It is world that reaches perfection only in eternity.

THE WORLD OF SUPRACONCEPTUALITY

Since the above analysis has borrowed much from Jung's appreciation of Zen, the conclusion might be reached that I now propound a theory previously denied, that all forms of mysticism are the same: that Zen and Hinduism and Christianity are no different at the top insofar as all teach a timeless, spaceless rest in supraconceptual silence. That this is not my meaning I would now like to explain.

First of all, however, it would be futile to deny that as a psychological process there are many elements common to all forms of mysticism—Platonic, neoplatonic, Buddhist, and Christian. Somewhat similar to *The Cloud*, for example, is the following description of enlightenment by a Chinese Buddhist:

> All the bonds that had hitherto bound my mind and body were dissolved at once together with every piece of my bones and their marrow. *It was like the sun suddenly bursting through the snow-laden clouds and brightly shining.* [11]

[11] See Suzuki [2], p. 96. Zen mystics generally refuse to describe (or even to attempt to describe) their experience: one exception, however, is Hakuin who speaks of the enlightenment as follows: " It was like the smashing of a layer of ice, or the pulling down of a crystal tower. As I suddenly awakened and came to my senses, I felt myself to be like Master Yen-t'ou, who all through the three times (past, present, and future) encountered no suffering. All former doubts were fully dissolved like ice which melted away. With a loud voice I called out, ' How glorious, how glorious! ' We need no escape from the cycle of life and death, nor need we strive after enlightenment. The seventeen hundred ' kōan ' exercises are not worthy of being posed. My pride rose up like a mountain and my exaltation welled up like a flood. To myself I thought that for two or three hundred years there had been no sudden breakthrough like mine, with such great ecstasy. With this vision I immediately set out on the road to Shinano. " (In Dumoulin [1], p. 249)

The ray of sunlight breaking through the clouds is a rather obvious metaphor in which to describe a great enlightenment; so it is not surprising that it should be employed by all kinds of mystics. What is clearly common to Zen and the mysticism of *The Cloud* and *Privy Counsel* is the abandonment of discursive thinking with its quidditive, or essential, thinking in favor of existential rest in silence. Indeed, not only Zen but other kinds of Oriental mysticism, and even Yoga, speak of tranquil states of metal calm when the mind, emptied of concepts, is serenely undisturbed, wrapped in a " mystical sleep " like that outlined in *Privy Counsel*. [12] All this points to a similarity of psychological process—the same apparatus of " vertical think-ing " seems to be at work.

But just as in the essential or horizontal activity of the mind there is an infinite variety of ways of thinking, so the vertical, or supraconceptual, working of the mind contains a large number of categories. I believe that the fundamental error of those who claim that all forms of mysticism are essentially one and the same stems from the oversimplified assumption that there can be no species within the genus of supraconcep-tuality. That there *can* be such species is evident from the fact that a mind supraconceptually and silently filled with love is different from a mind supraconceptually silent and lacking in love. And it is precisely supernatural love, based on faith, that forms the whole center essence of the mysticism of *The Cloud*; love is both the point of departure and the goal; take away love and the whole thing crumbles. And it is here that the difference from Zen (and, indeed, from all forms of pantheism) is most in evidence.

---

[12] Sri Aurobindo in *Bases of Yoga*: " In the calm mind, it is the substance of the mental being that is still, so still that nothing disturbs it. If thoughts or activities come, they do not arise at all out of the mind, but they come from outside and cross the mind as a flight of birds crosses the sky in a windless air. It passes, disturbs nothing, leaving no trace. Even if a thousand images, or the most violent events pass across it, the calm stillness remains as if the very texture of the mind were a substance of eternal and indestructible peace. A mind that has achieved this calmness can begin to act, even intensely and powerfully, but it will keep its fundamental stillness—originating nothing from itself, but receiving from Above and giving it a mental form without adding anything of its own, calmly, dispassionately, though with the joy of the Truth and the happy power and light of its passage. " (In Conze [1], p. 109)

Psychologically speaking, the hallmark of Christian mysticism is a dynamic love that leads the intelligence to those lower depths of the being where one encounters God. If the theory of Jung is correct, then Zen penetrates to a similar psychic center—not by love but by the abandonment of discourse and the emptying of the mind, or by smashing the discursive intellect with the illogicality of the *kōan*. This accounts for a certain similarity of process; but it does not make the two things identical. An example of how love performs a work that, as a psychological process, is somewhat similar to the *kōan* can be taken from a Dominican mystic:

> During the time of our union with God we must drive far from us all images, even such as are good in themselves, for they introduce something between Him and us. Hence he who, impelled thereto by grace, aims at this ascension towards God, when he feels himself taken possession of by a violent love and drawn upwards, should at once retrench all kinds of images; let him run without delay to the holy of holies, toward the interior silence in which the operation is no more human but divine. [13]

The above is typical of Christian mysticism; it is substantially the same as the doctrine of *The Cloud*. Whereas the *kōan* is a denial of discursive reasoning, the above is an *ignoring* of reasoning under the impulse of a violent love that abandons images and concepts to go to the heart of that reality they inadequately represent. The English author expresses the same thought when he compares the mystic to the martyrs who threw away their tools and ran to death. Zen, on the other hand, while it may induce similar physical and psychical reactions, involving similar processes, never claims to be an act of the love of God.

And for the author of *The Cloud* the whole value of this " oneing exercise " is that it is love—it is an expression of the chief commandment of the Gospel. His favorite theme is that love alone attains to God—and nothing else. If one were to describe to him a psychological state that has the same silence,

---

[13] Ven. Bartholomew of the Martyrs, O.P. (In Poulain, Chapter IX, *Extracts*, 31)

the same darkness, the same absence of concepts, the cloud of forgetting, and the holding of self at the sovereign point of the spirit—if one were to describe to him such a state devoid of love and attained to by any means other than love, he would immediately disown it as something essentially different from what he is teaching. For the value of mysticism can never be measured by any psychological process nor can any such process be the norm of its authenticity. Its value lies in its being an expression of love. Put in another way, the value of Christian mysticism stems mainly from its motivation: as the same action can be virtue or vice, good or bad, heaven or hell according to the motive, so the psychological state of silent supra-conceptuality derives its religious value from the motive underlying the whole process. That some modern scholars have tended to say that all forms of mysticism are the same because of similarity in psychological process merely points to the fact that our generation, enamored with the seductive charms of its own psychiatry, tends to look at everything psychologically to the detriment of other (and more important) aspects of human activity.

Yet in the realm of supraconceptuality, distinctions are admittedly difficult to make. If Zen and *The Cloud* seem to follow a similar psychological pattern, so also do Christian mysticism and Quietism. Passages from Michael de Molinos and Madame Guyon are so strikingly similar to St. John of the Cross that the superficial, or even the intelligent reader can easily fall into the all-the-same error. Yet they are not the same. Nowhere is acute discretion more necessary than here; nowhere are we in greater danger of rushing in, like the proverbial fools, where angels fear to tread. " Beware of error here, I pray thee, " writes the prudent author of *The Cloud*, " for ever the nearer men touch the truth, the more wary must men be of error. " (C. 69:17)

We can conclude that " the sovereign point of the spirit, " " the lowest point of the wit, " " the naked being, " and so on are all parts of a terminology that does not deny but supplements an Aristotelian psychology scarcely equipped to explore that part of the human psyche brought into play not only in Christian mysticism but also in other kinds of mysticism, like Zen, and even in certain philosophical intuitions. This terminology goes back to the early days of Christianity (with variations in usage) and is not unlike the way of speaking of modern depth psychology. The English author uses it firstly, to stress the totality of the soul's union with God: not a union of parts or faculties but a total merging of one into the other; secondly, he uses it to emphasize the existential (as opposed to essential) nature of the union: it is a union of being with being; thirdly, he uses it to show that the union is not horizontal but vertical, not in motion but in rest, not in time but in timelessness. In this way is he able to describe the most complete union of man with God.

THE PROBLEM: THE MEANING OF UNION

From the above analysis two things are clear. Firstly, the mysticism of *The Cloud*, like all mysticism, is wholly concerned with union; secondly, this union is achieved by, and finds its consummation in, love. The difficulty arises, however, when one comes to analyze the exact nature of this loving union. What is meant by union? What is union with God? This is a problem fundamental to all mysticism.

Mystical union is never easy to understand; and when an author speaks of the total forgetfulness of one's own existence and about destroying the sight and the feeling of self, it is not surprising that a variety of interpretations should be forthcoming.

With Aldous Huxley it is possible to take the doctrine of the English author as an escape from the intolerable burden of the ego. Telling us that " the urge to transcend self-conscious selfhood is... a principal appetite of the soul, " Huxley continues:

> When, for whatever reason, men and women fail to transcend themselves by means of worship, good works, and spiritual exercises, they are apt to resort to religion's chemical surrogates—alcohol and " goof-pills " in the modern West, alcohol and opium in the East, hashish in the Mohammedan world,

alcohol and marijuana in Central America, alcohol and coca in the Andes, alcohol and barbiturates in the more up-to-date religions of South America... Ideally, everyone should be able to find self-transcendence in some form of applied religion. In practice it seems very unlikely that this hoped-for consummation will ever be realised. [14]

In this way, the cloud of forgetting is a means of transcending self, of escaping from the misery of one's own existence.

More plausible than the above, however, is the monistic interpretation of the doctrine of the English author. The Zen mystic, too, thinks vertically, reaching down to the sovereign point of the spirit; and here he claims to find a union devoid of all distinction whatever, a union in which there is no subject and object, no " I " and " Thou "; hence his insistence that Zen *is*: analysis does violence to its very nature.

Or again, viewed in an Oriental context, the author's doctrine might seem remarkably similar to that of the *Upanishads*: the whole of reality is God (or Brahman) from whom the world flows and to whom it returns; the ego (atman) is identical with God, and man by true wisdom is liberated to find his true identity with God in the total destruction of self. Thus he destroys, like the author of *The Cloud,* " the sight and feeling " of his own being.

Or, once again, in a Buddhist context, this destruction of the knowledge of self might look like the doctrine of Nirvana entailing the extinction of individuality—the " de-individualization " of man. Thus the English author would base his doctrine on the fact that the ego is simply a fiction of the mind, the cause of man's useless suffering, corresponding to nothing real—and, logically, something that has no real existence can be, and ought to be, eliminated from consciousness.

Such interpretations might seem far-fetched were it not for the fact that monism, far from being an Oriental phenomenon alone, had tortured the Western mind since Parmenides attempted to solve the problem of " the one and the many " with the assertion that all things are being. Only one thing exists: being—yet there are many beings. Analogy, so highly

[14] Huxley 2], p. 56.

developed by St. Thomas, gave a Christian solution; and yet in the centuries preceding the composition of *The Cloud* not a few Christian mystics had succumbed (at least in word, if not in thought) to the alluring fascination of monistic systems. Pantheistic trends had stemmed from neoplatonism with its doctrine of a God who (unlike the Creator of *Genesis*) *necessarily* created a world, flowing inevitably from His essence as the rays flow from the sun: man had only to empty his being of all self-hood, and the goodness of God would flow in—not as the gratuitous gift of a merciful Father, but with mechanical inevitability. The appeal of neoplatonism had proved too much for Eckhart (whose heart, however, was more orthodox than his head) and the pantheistically inclined vocabulary of John Scotus Erigena; the Beguardi and Beguinae and others had stimulated the Church into taking a clear dogmatic stand against pantheism in favor of the scriptural doctrine of God the Father, Creator of the world, utterly free to create or not to create, to give His grace or withhold it.

Now the English author was aware of all this history. A man of his theological learning could not escape it; and, moreover, many allusions (especially in *Privy Counsel*) to the unkind interpretations of critics indicate that he has been misunderstood. Probably the critics saw pantheistic tendencies like those of Eckhart; and the English author, making rapier-like distinctions, is determined to maintain an accurate doctrine. Some passages of *Privy Counsel* have even a bitter note, reflecting the indignation of one hurt by unjust criticism. Yet six centuries later we cannot but be grateful to these critics whose harsh words engendered his rigorously accurate theology.

That the English author is no monist could be shown by numerous instances. Whereas pantheism denies creation in time, he refers frequently to how man, once nothing, was created; whereas in pantheism there can be no adoration (for man is part of the whole), the entire mystical life of *Privy Counsel* consists of *offering* oneself to God in adoration; whereas pantheism cannot logically speak of love, the English author builds his whole doctrine on the blind stirring of love. Then, lest there be any doubt about his doctrine, he tells us explicitly that he wishes not to destroy self but to destroy the sight and the feeling of self. " And when thou covetest so earnestly, not to un-be—for that were madness and despite unto God—but to forego the knowing and feeling of thy being... " (C. 157:3) And these words of *Privy Counsel* re-echo a passage in *The Cloud* where, speaking of the terrible sorrow that accompanies the knowledge and feeling of self, and describing how the contemplative " weepeth and waileth, striveth, curseth, and denounceth himself, " he continues:

> And yet in all this sorrow he desireth not to un-be; for that were devil's madness and despite unto God. But he liketh right well to be; and he giveth full heartily thanks unto God for the worthiness and the gift of his being, although he desire unceasingly for to lack the knowing and the feeling of his being. (C. 84:20)

So the contemplative must be grateful for the gift of being. To " un-be " and to " lack the knowing and the feeling " of one's being are different things.

If further proof were needed that the author studiously avoids all trace of monism, one could quote the Mary Magdalen passages of *The Cloud*. Total forgetfulness of self and absorption in the divinity of Christ does not rob Mary of the " I-Thou " relationship with her God. While in metaphysical language the dividing line between the author's doctrine and pantheism is fine, the literary style of the Magdalen motif brings out the intensely human aspect of the height of mysticism. [15]

And yet, granted that the author of *The Cloud* is no monist, it would be idle to pretend that his words present no difficulty. Here we are faced with the gigantic problem that rises out of the writings of even the most orthodox mystics such as St. John of the Cross. It is that problem expressed by Teilhard de Chardin when he speaks of " the essential aspiration of all mysticism: to be united (that is, to become the other) while remaining oneself. " [16] The aim of the author is to lead the disciple to a point where he will be one with the Infinite Being of God while remaining himself in the most perfect way possible. How solve this antinomy?

[15] See *The Cloud*, pp. 44-49.
[16] Teilhard de Chardin, p. 93.

It is scarcely possible to find a solution in the author's psychology—that is to say, in his *description* of union; for, as the above analysis may have shown, while he does say something about the psychological state of the mystic himself, this reticent Englishman staunchly refuses to give details of the more important Actor in this drama; namely, God. In short we are given no details about *the object* of contemplation.

From psychology, then, one must turn to theology, examining what the author says about mystical union from his study of Scripture and tradition and from his metaphysical background. For him the basis of mysticism is theology—enlightened, of course, by his own experience and that of others.

The following chapters, then, will discuss his doctrine of mystical union. They will show, I think, an author who has mastered the scholastic metaphysics of his day and who is no small theologian.

16

GOD AND CREATURE

DEGREES OF UNION

In a passage of *Privy Counsel* that, he says apologetically, may be " little pertaining to our matter, " the English author outlines the various degrees of union between the creature and God by commenting on the scriptural text, " Without me you can do nothing. ". [1] Following the orthodox theology, he asserts that these words are applicable to all men, whether they be sinners or saints; for without God man is powerless even to sin.

God, says the English author, is actively present in every man in the world from the very fact of creation, but His action differs according as one is sinner, active, or contemplative. [2] In the sinner God is present by " sufferance "; yet this is real union for " in all our doings *lawful and unlawful*... without him we may do nothing. " God works in the heart of the sinner whether his action be " lawful or pleasant to him or not. " In short, the sinner cannot sin without God; but (and here again comes the accuracy) God does not consent to the sin—much less does He cause it; He is there " only suffering and not consenting. "

[1] Jn 15:5.
[2] See P.C. 163:12.

In the just man God is present not only by suffering but also by consent; yet while he is still an " active " the divine work is slight and natural and human activity predominates. But as contemplative grace grows stronger, human actions lessen while divine action increases. The contemplative is increasingly passive beneath the action of God " who is principally stirring and working. " And this is " great perfection "; this is the " ghostly oneing of our soul unto him in perfect charity. "

In all this, one of the most significant points is the union of God with the sinner. This is of special interest as indicating how the mystical union of *The Cloud* is built upon a natural basis, built upon a union with God common to all men. In this way, mysticism becomes something truly human: God does not unite Himself to the contemplative like a *deus ex machina*, descending into a realm in which He never was before; rather does He intensify, by supernatural gifts, a union already existing in the order of nature. For God is united with all men, including sinners, precisely because they *exist*. God is one with all that He has created in such wise that the author can address his disciple with the words: " He is thy being... " (P.C. 136:9) These latter words keep turning up like a refrain in the author's work; so now it is necessary to consider their exact meaning.

" HE IS THY BEING... "

Man, in common with all created things, shares in the being of God. It is when he comes to speak of this union in being that some of the authors' phrases have a dangerously pantheistic ring; yet he is always careful to add the saving phrase that makes his doctrine truly Christian.

At the beginning of *Privy Counsel*, it will be recalled, he tells the contemplative to empty his mind of all thoughts, even of good thoughts, even of the thought of self. But why should one forget the qualities of self and of one's own being? His answer is logical: God is more our being than we are our own being— and that is why we should forget self to concentrate on the being of God. This is put in the terse phrase: " For he is thy being, and in him thou art what thou art. " (P.C. 136:9) God *is* our being. This might sound like a pantheistic identification

of man with God, were it not followed a little later by the
saving clause:

> ...evermore saving this difference betwixt thee and him, that he
> is thy being and thou not his. (P.C. 136:15)

There is no question, then, of perfect identification between
God and creature, but of the closest of unions.

Such is the leading idea of *Privy Counsel*. God is my being;
but I am not His. God is all things; but all things are not God.
Here is one of the texts:

> For he is thy being, and in him thou art what thou art, not
> only by cause and by being, but also he is in thee both cause and
> thy being. And therefore think of God in this work as thou
> dost on thyself, and on thyself as thou dost on God... For
> though it be so that all things be in him by cause and by being,
> and he be in all things their cause and their being, yet in himself
> only he is his own cause and his own being. For as nothing may
> be without him, so may he not be without himself. He is being
> both to himself and to all. And in that only is he separated
> from all, that he is being both of himself and of all. And in that
> is he one in all and all one in him, that all things have their
> being in him, as he is the being of all. (P.C. 104:9) [8]

God, then, is the cause of all things and the being of all
things: to think on oneself, in the true sense of the word is to
think on God. Yet, as the last two sentences make clear, God
who is one with all things is also *separated* from them all.
He is separated because he is the cause or the source; He is
one because all things have their being in Him. So there is both
unity and separation.

As for the phrase, " in him thou art what thou art, " this
seems to mean that man *is* man precisely because God is united
with him. That God is the very being of man is again indicated
later when the author, urging the contemplative to existential
prayer in utter forgetfulness of essences, to a prayer in which
the existence of God and man are fused into one, he continues:

---

[8] The same idea is found in *The Cloud*: " For in him is everything, both
by cause and by being. " (C. 79:7)

...do worship to God with thy substance, all that thou art as thou art, unto all him that is as he is, the which only of himself and without more is the blissful being both of himself and of thee. (P.C. 144:15)

The theme is the same: God is not only His own existence, He is also yours; for He " is the blissful being both of himself and of thee. " So close is the unity of man with God that in contemplation one can be said to " worship God with himself " —and yet (saving clause again) man is nothing, possessing everything from Him:

And thus shalt thou knittingly, and in manner that is marvellous, worship God with himself. For, that that thou art thou hast it of him and he it is. And although thou hadst a beginning in thy substantial creation—the which was something nought—yet hath thy being been evermore in him without beginning and ever shall be without ending, as himself is. (P.C. 144:9)

Man from eternity has existed in the essence of God; and evermore will exist therein—and it is in this essence that he must view himself to get a true picture of what he is. Yet in his " substantial creation " he was drawn out of nothing. It is surely no accident that the English author introduces creation in time; this being one of the points always stressed by the Church in her opposition to pantheism.

Many more examples of this fundamental principle that man partakes in the being of God could be quoted. " For if any manner of special thought, " he writes, " of anything but only of thy naked being—*the which is thy God and thine intent*—come to thy mind then art thou away. " (P.C. 147:11) Here again he is telling us that the naked being of man *is* God. It is for this reason that he urges the contemplative to forget all essences and so to come down to the only reality that really *is*; it is for this reason that he stresses the forgetting of self:

And for this reason I proved thee in the beginning that God is thy being. (P.C. 156:2)

Thus is justified a cloud of forgetting that envelops even the thought and the feeling of self.

But to understand this ontological union more clearly it is necessary to glance at the background of scholastic thought in the fourteenth century.

GOD AND CREATURE IN SCHOLASTIC THOUGHT

" He is thy being. . . " A study of the metaphysical background of the fourteenth century reveals numerous ways in which these words can be used without falling into the abyss of self-annihilating pantheism.

From the earliest days of Christianity, the Fathers of the Church had taken a firm stand against pantheism, on the one hand, and dualism, on the other, affirming the existence of the One true God, Creator of heaven and earth, the merciful Father of all men. This developed into the scholastic metaphysic later to reach its perfection in a Thomism which asserted that God alone is Being in the full sense of the word: He alone possesses the plenitude of being, other things merely sharing by analogous participation in what properly belongs to God. He *is* existence; other things *have* existence. Therefore if we say that a thing other than God is being, our way of speaking is imperfect; for created things have not the fullness of being since they are *limited*. One indication of this limitation is the fact of change or motion; for the scholastics, following Aristotle, held that change or motion is nothing else but the acquisition of a new perfection. And anything that can acquire a new perfection is necessarily wanting in something, is necessarily limited. [4] This was generally stated in Aristotelian terms of act and potency. Every changeable being is an act, limited by potency—but all beings cannot be limited (since all cannot be acquiring new perfection unless there is a source from which to draw); so there must be a Being that is Pure Act. And this Being is God in whom there is no motion, no change, no acquisition of new perfection, He being the " Unmoved Mover " of Aristotle. And that is why it can be said (as the author of *The Cloud* says so

---

[4] For the scholastics, motion was the acquisition of a perfection *(acquisitio perfectionis)*; a being passes from *terminus a quo* to a *terminus ad quem* through intermittent stages, thus always *acquiring* something new. The definition of motion was, with Aristotle: " actus entis in potentia in quantum in potentia. "

often) that He is the Being of all—" all things have their being in him, and he is the being of all. " Only He really IS. Hence, " He is thy being... "

Then there is the union of God with creatures by causality: " all things be in him by cause and by being, and he be in all things their cause and their being, yet in himself only he is his own cause and his own being. " (P.C. 136:16) Here God is distinct from creatures in that He is uncaused (or, as the author puts it, He is His own cause) whereas they are caused by Him. And, once again, this has a familiar scholastic ring. The presence of efficient causes in the world leads to the discovery of a series of causes and thence to the uncaused source of all—and so God's existence is demonstrated as " *Causa Principalis Efficiens.* "

Causality, however, while demanding a distinction between cause and effect, thus denying pantheism, also demands an extremely intimate union. This is because when the effect is the very existence of a being (as happens in creation), then its dependence on the cause is total. And in scholastic thought, God's causality is creation; and not only creation but also conservation. So totally does the creature depend on God for its existence that without Him, its Cause, it would immediately fall into nothingness—in other words, the causality of God is a continuous inflow of existence itself into the being. Hence the doctrine of St. Thomas that God's conservation is not through any new action but is a continuation of that very creative act by which he gives existence. (*Conservatio rerum a Deo non est per aliquam novam actionem, sed per continuationem actionis qua dat esse.*) [5] Consequently, the dependence of the creature upon God is like the dependence of light upon the sun: " *Sic autem se habet omnis creatura ad Deum, sicut aer ad solem illuminantem.* " [6] This reminds one of the neoplatonic sun, except that the latter *inevitably* sends forth its rays whereas God, in Thomistic thought, is free. Yet, like the sun, He penetrates the very being of the creature; so that in saying that God is present by causality we are already saying: " He is thy being... "

[5] *Summa*, I, q. 104, a. 1, ad 4.
[6] *Ibid.*

Again, since God is Perfection itself, Pure Act, Unlimited Existence and the Source of all, it follows that God's act of creation *adds* nothing to Him nor to the sum total of reality. The scholastics expressed this by saying that after creation there are more beings but not more being—" *plura entia sed non plus entis.* " Being is one; the real Being is God; " He is thy being... "

Yet another sentence rich with scholastic overtones is that in which, stating that man was created in time, he adds: " Yet hath thy being been evermore in him without beginning and ever shall be without ending, as himself is. " (P.C. 144:12) That is to say, from all eternity we existed in the Divine Essence; then we were created in time; and we shall exist for ever in Him. Behind this there is quite a philosophical history. The diversity within the species of created things had led Plato to postulate a world of ideas, the exemplary cause of all existing things; and the Fathers of the Church (while with Aristotle they had rejected the world of ideas as such) had, so to speak, put the Platonic ideas into the mind of God, asserting that God is the exemplary cause of all things, a doctrine exposed in the so-called " fourth way " of St. Thomas. The Exemplary Cause of all things is the Divine Essence, God seeing from eternity that His own essence is imitable in creatures according to a decree of His will. From eternity, then, we (and all creatures) exist in that exemplary cause that is the mind of God; and this Exemplar will never cease to exist. Created in time, we come from the mind of God and go back to God upon whom we completely depend for every aspect of our existence. " He is thy being... "

And one more hotly disputed fourteenth-century problem lies beneath the author's words; namely, the problem of " pure love. " There had been much discussion about the commandment to love God above all things and to love God more than self. Unlike St. Bernard and Richard of St. Victor, who had greatly stressed the " violence " of divine love, St. Thomas had held that to love God more than self is according to nature. In an interesting passage of the *Summa* he points out how in the world of nature " everything that of its nature belongs to another is principally and more strongly inclined to that other to which it belongs, than toward itself. " [7] For example, " the part naturally exposes itself to safeguard the whole; as, for instance, the hand is without deliberation exposed to the blow for the whole body's safety; and in society " it behoves the virtuous citizen to expose himself to the danger of death for the public weal of the state; and if man were a natural part of the city, then such an inclination would be natural to him. " [8] Then he draws the conclusion:

> Consequently, since God is the universal good, and under this good both man and angel and every creature is comprised, because every creature in regard to its entire being belongs naturally to God, it follows that from natural love angel and man alike love God before themselves and with a greater love. Otherwise, if either of them loved self more than God, it would follow that natural love would be perverse, and that it would not be perfected but destroyed by charity. [9]

Here St. Thomas himself is as near to pantheism as the author of *The Cloud:* his doctrine is distinguished from pantheism only by his analogy: man is " part " of God not in a univocal sense but analogically.

Applied, however, to the mystical life, this leads to the conclusion (which the author of *The Cloud* logically draws) that the part must forget itself *as part* to see itself as *part of the whole.* We must never look upon self as a separate entity, independent of God; we must look at the totality of things. And here self, in the highest sense of the word, is not forgotten; rather is " self-love, " or the concentration on self to the forgetting of God, put aside. In short, the author is saying: See God as your true being and you see your real self.

Taken in this way, it can be seen that the destruction of the sight and feeling of self *as an independent entity* is no more than the climax of the work of the cloud of forgetting, no more than the climax of that nakedness he has always demanded. It is the perfect observance of that commandment he himself quotes: " Whoso loves me, let him forsake himself. " Self is forgotten in that intense love of God who fills both self and all things;

[7] *Summa*, I, q. 60, a. 5.
[8] *Ibid.*
[9] *Ibid.*

self is forgotten when the part forgets itself as part in order to love the whole.

Reading *The Cloud* against its historical background, one immediately sees that the author is applying the current metaphysics to the mystical life. If it is true that man has nothing of himself, that all his being is from God, that God is his real being, then he who thinks on his own being as something independent of God is in error. Guided by grace (for this is a work of God and can never be achieved by human endeavor alone) one should forget one's own being to see only God who fills both one's being and the universe, who is the source and origin of all things, who alone really IS in the full meaning of that word—and only then can one's vision of reality be said to be true. Looking into one's own being and seeing it as an analogous participation in the being of God is the only true vision of self.

And so one destroys the sight and the feeling of a false self in order to find that true self that is no more than an image of God. The greatest glory of self is to be filled with the being of God and thus be a copy or image of that exemplar which is the Divine Essence. Self has reached its perfection when it is conscious of the true fact that it has nothing of its own but is filled through and through with God. When we, as it were, look through self to see only God, we have found true perfection.

Thus is averted the error that we are our own being—which is ultimately to make self into God, an error that is at the root of inordinate self-love, of that " *amor sui usque ad contemptum Dei.* " In stressing that God is the being of all and that our being is nothing, the author leads to the " *amor Dei usque ad contemptum sui.* "

NATURE AND GRACE

In the above doctrine, the author of *The Cloud* prescinds from the gift of grace that (he also stresses) is the principal element in binding the soul to God. I have separated the metaphysical from the strictly supernatural element in his teaching in order to show that he bases his contemplation on a " natural

mysticism. " [10] This is not to say that there actually exists
a natural state of mysticism (for in the present order of God's
providence every man is either in grace or in sin); but the
Thomistic concept of a hypothetical " state of pure nature, "
a state in which man would have been were he not elevated to
the life of grace and, at the same time, had not sinned—this
notion cannot have been far from his mind. That is why he
speaks of the union with God that man has in common with
all creatures. As God is united with His whole material creation
by cause and by being, so He is united with man; the special
glory of man being, however, that he possesses intelligence
by which he can reflect on his own union with the Creator and
thus give glory to Him.

This point is of considerable significance because it shows
a doctrine according to which grace, far from doing violence
to nature, is adapted to it like a well-fitting glove to the hand. [11]
While the author knows too much theology to suggest that man
has an *exigency* for grace or that he has a right to obtain it
(repeatedly he speaks of the liberty of God to give or to
withhold), yet he grasps clearly, and emphasizes firmly, that
capacity to receive (the *potentia obedientialis* of the scholastics) by which the gifts of grace fit smoothly and easily into
human nature.

Moreover, reflection on the author's teaching on nature and
grace helps understand the phenomenological similarity between
his doctrine and that of non-Christian mystics. It has been
pointed out that he teaches a " vertical thinking " that has its
counterpart in Zen and that his " sovereign point of the spirit "
is paralleled in other mysticisms. All this is not surprising if
we reflect that the psychological processes at work in the order
of nature are never destroyed by grace—they are simply
" elevated " and their natural process is " divinized " by the
special life and light of God now infused into them. In other
words, the soul's union with God by the gift of grace is built

[10] Some authors speak of " natural mysticism, " that is, a mysticism based
on this *natural* union with God and prescinding from grace; but I have avoided
this terminology because others object to it on the ground that, in Catholic
theology, no man can concretely be a " natural mystic " since everyone is either
in grace or in sin, the Thomistic " state of pure nature " being purely hypothetical.
[11] Cf. P.C. 168:9.

upon a natural union existing in the order of nature—and this latter union prescinds so completely from grace that it can be experienced even by the sinner.

And this leads to another conclusion about Zen, which may be added by way of corrollary even though it may appear to be something of a digression.

In his survey of Zen Buddhism, Professor Dumoulin, giving examples of Buddhist contemplatives who looked into the " mirror " of their mind to find enlightenment, finally comes to analyze the nature of their liberating intuition. [12] Describing it as an " immediate perception of spiritual reality, " he goes on to say that " the soul which experiences its own spirituality in enlightenment, becomes aware, at the foundation of its own spiritual substance, of God's eternal creative spirit. " [13] He continues that if there is a pantheistic strain in Zen, this " stems, not from the experience, but from the philosophy of the Zen mystic. " [14] Whether or not this interpretation is correct is not for me to say here; what can be said is that such an interpretation is in keeping with that doctrine taught by *The Cloud* and in Ruysbroeck; namely, that any intelligent being, looking into the darkness of his own mind, can find therein supraconceptual silence that One True God who is the Ultimate Reality and who is the cause and the being of all things. [15]

---

[12] E.g., " The title ' Zen Master of the Great Mirror, ' which was bestowed on Hui-neng after his death, is indeed an apt designation of his genius. He experienced in sudden enlightenment and realized in daily life the mirror-nature of the mind and the spiritual nature of reality, which are the basic concepts of his metaphysics. All reality is Spirit (Mind). The mind is one and, like a mirror, is in motionless repose and yet perpetually active, for its brightness reflects continually. " (Dumoulin [1], p. 91)

[13] *Ibid.*, p. 287.

[14] *Ibid.*, p. 288.

[15] See also Lasalle-Enomiya: " The most typical trait of the activity of the pure spirit is the direct perception of self, and therefore is the nucleus of mystical life. This mystical intuition, however, can be not only supernatural, but also natural, and in the latter case, we would have natural mysticism. It is exactly this direct perception of self that takes place in the Satori Experience. " Lasalle then refers to Louis Gardet who " clearly explains the spiritual activity as it takes place in Enlightenment as quite a different one from the normal (or usual) and that it lies beyond the perceived state of consciousness. This is also confirmed by the fact that Satori is usually called ' the vision of the essence ' and this can only take place after normal spiritual activity has been wholly eliminated. " (Lasalle-Enomiya)

Also: " There remains the question if the Satori Experience somehow includes the knowledge of God. A Buddhist would scarcely believe that he

CONCLUSION

The conclusion is that the English author teaches various degrees or stages of union with God according to the state of sinner, active and contemplative. Most basic of these is the union of God with the sinner—a union possessed also by the saint. This is effected in the order of nature, God being united with all His creatures " by cause and by being " in such a way that nothing can lose this union and continue to exist. God is the being of all things, since He alone is Being in the full sense of the word; He is the being of all things because all thinge depend on him for every moment of their existence as the light depends on the sun. Since He is our being, it is right and proper (when guided by grace) to forget all things, even one's " self, " in order to see and love all things (and self) in the totality, in the One Being who alone really is: God. This is not to deny the real existence of self: it is to deny a self existing independently of God. It is not to propound pantheism because man's participation in the being of God is analogous and his existence in time depends on a free act of God.

Upon this basic union with God, common to saint and to sinner, the author builds his edifice. Having examined it, we shall now consider the next two stages; namely, that of the active and that of the contemplative. The union of God with the active is effected by grace building upon nature; the union with the contemplative, by love building upon nature and grace. Thus the perfection of man is achieved not by destruction but a succession of divine gifts that complement one another, blending together to transform man more and more into the image of God.

---

sees in his Satori, God, as in a mirror. His whole philosophical outlook in which ' Thou ' is a priori excluded would not be in favor of such translation. The Satori is felt in accordance with his philosophical outlook as a oneness with the universe. But this universe has for him the note of infinity and absolute, perfect happiness. It is open to transcendence, and in so far, it is a religious experience. The feeling of oneness is emphasized because, consciously or unconsciously, proof of one's own philosophical outlook is sought for. Besides, this feeling even with Christian mystics has at times been so strong that they were in danger of Pantheism. " *(Ibid.)*

17

THE DIVINIZATION OF MAN

The last chapter tried to show that the most basic union between man and God is found at the level of existence: man is one with God by reason of his creaturehood, precisely because he *is*.

When, however, the author of *The Cloud* writes of the union between man and God in being, when he urges the contemplative to existential prayer in rejection of essences, he is thinking not only of a union effected in nature but also of one effected by grace. He uses the word " being " because it connotes a totality no other word can convey. For, as was indicated in the first section of this work, " being " is all embracing; that is to say, when I say that something is a " being, " I do not abstract one quiddity as when I say that something is " good " or " heavy " or when I say that someone is " a man " (for here, too, I single out for mention the quiddity " humanity "). When I say that something is a being, this " being " refers to the thing in its totality, including color, weight, shape, size, and every quiddity it possesses. In short, " being " is equated of things with identity: there is nothing that is not being. And in the same way union with God in being implies an identity covering every aspect of man: it means that man is one with God with everything he possesses both by nature and by grace. For the

gifts of grace, also, are being; the scholastics spoke of them as
" *ens supernaturale.* "

The author of *The Cloud* states this quite explicitly in several
places. In *Privy Counsel*, for example, when emphasizing the
totality with which the contemplative must offer himself to God
and urging the disciple to offer his " fruits " to God, he explains
himself by saying: " All the gifts of *nature and grace* that ever
God gave thee, I call them fruits... " (C. 140:28) And then he
teaches us the perfect contemplative prayer:

> That that I am and how that I am,
> as in nature and in grace,
> all I have it of thee Lord,
> and thou it art. (C. 141:20)

Superadded, then, to the gifts of nature is the gift of grace.
And God is all this being—" thou it art. " But what is this
grace of which the author speaks?

THE WORK OF GRACE

Following the ordinary terminology, the author reminds his
disciple that grace is that gift given by Christ who " bought
thee with the price of His precious blood when thou wert lost
in Adam. " (C. 14:1) It is a gift obtained at Baptism and
restored to the sinner by Penance; that is why the author has
insisted that the first step in the contemplative life is made by
those who have " cleansed their conscience of all their special
deeds of sin done before, according to the common ordinance of
Holy Church. " (C. 63:9) By confession one receives that grace
which distinguishes the active from the sinner and constitutes
the first stage in the journey from sin to Christian active living—
whence one arises to the passivity of contemplation.

Grace does not destroy but perfects; it blends with nature to
form a harmonious whole. The last chapter has treated of the
author's respect for nature; and it is precisely because he values
the natural gifts of man that he keeps telling the contemplative
to take care of his health, not to strain nature, and so on.
For without nature there can be no grace; and grace is, as

Ruysbroeck well puts it, a " God-formed light " piercing through
nature. Here are the words of the Flemish mystic:

> For, that man has been made after the likeness of God, means
> that he has been created in the grace of God; the which grace
> is a God-formed light, which shines through us and makes us
> like to God; and without this light, which makes us God-like,
> we cannot be united with God supernaturally, even though we
> cannot lose the image of God nor our natural unity with Him.
> If we lose the likeness, that is, the grace of God, we are damned.
> And therefore, whenever God finds within us some capacity for
> the reception of grace, it is His pleasure and His free goodness
> to make us, through His gifts, full of like, and like unto Him. [1]

So man is like God in two ways. By nature he has a likeness
he cannot lose; by grace (this beautiful light, penetrating and
transforming and making God-like) he is united to God in
a new way—which, however, can be lost, thus causing
damnation.

Like Ruysbroeck, the author of *The Cloud* tells us that,
however weak, we may approach God " by the worthiness of
our creation to his image and likeness. " (C. 18:14) And this
likeness makes our soul " the ghostly temple of God. "
(C. 126:24) That is to say, the author builds his doctrine on the
scriptural and patristic teaching of the indwelling of the
Holy Spirit and the divinization of man thereby. By grace man
is so wonderfully reformed that he may " truly be called a god "
—and, lest this may appear to be his own doctrine, he adds:
" as Scripture witnesses. " Here is the passage in which he
asserts that the Christian is " a god in grace ":

> Thou attainest to come thither by grace, whither thou mayest
> not come by nature. That is to say, to be oned to God, in
> spirit and in love and in accordance of will... although it may
> be said in a manner that in this time God and thou be not
> two but one in spirit—inasmuch that thou or another that
> feeleth the perfection of this work may, by reason of that
> onehead, truly be called a god, as Scripture witnesseth—
> nevertheless thou art beneath him. For he is God by nature
> without beginning; and thou sometime wert nought in sub-
> stance; and afterwards, when thou wert by his might and his

[1] *Adornment of the Spiritual Marriage*, c. LVIII.

love made aught, thou wilfully with sin madest thyself worse than nought. And only by his mercy without thy desert art thou made a god in grace, oned with him in spirit without separation, both here and in the bliss of heaven without end. So that, although thou be all one with him in grace, yet thou art full far beneath him in nature. (C. 120:6)

This is accurate theology: it reflects a play on the notions of nature and grace that keeps appearing in the author's work. First of all there is the affirmation of the gratuity of God's supernatural gifts and man's utter incapability to attain to God by nature:

> thou attainest to come thither by grace,
> whither thou mayest not come by nature.

By grace, man comes to union with God, a union of a special kind:

> to be oned to God,
> in spirit
> and in love
> and in accordance of will.

It is because of this loving union of wills that man may truly be called a god since " in this time God and thou be not two but one in spirit. " Yet there is no question of a pantheistic identity of natures because

> he is God by nature...

whereas you were once nothing; you were drawn out of nothingness; you sinned and made yourself worse than nothing; you were redeemed

> And only by his mercy
> without thy desert
> art thou made a god in grace.

And so the play on nature and grace ends up with the clear assertion that

> although thou be all one with him in grace,
> yet thou art full far beneath him in nature.

All this is the traditional theology; and the " one in spirit " re-echoes the Pauline " he who unites himself to the Lord is one in spirit with Him, "[1] which is quoted and commented upon again and again by the Fathers, by St. Thomas, and finally by St. John of the Cross.

The nature-grace motif keeps recurring, the author distinguishing various stages: (1) The nature of man as such, i.e., the " state of pure nature. " (2) The fallen nature of man, i.e., man as wounded by sin. (3) Man who is a god by grace. (4) God who is God by nature. Lest these last two stages be confused (for this is always the delicate point), he reminds us:

> that thing that is had by nature
> is nearer to each thing
> than that which is had by grace. (C. 76:17)

This is a quiet reminder that God is nearer to Himself (since He is God by nature) than we are near to God (since we are only gods by grace); yet, in the union of man with God, distinctions are now becoming fine. The author, however, sticks to the same refrain:

> we should be perfect by grace
> as he himself is by nature. (C. 44:14)

And yet another beautifully accurate statement of his doctrine of nature and grace is found in the following words:

> For Christ went before by nature, and we come after by grace
> His nature is more worthy than grace,
> and grace is more worthy than our nature. (P.C. 154:28)

Here the ascending scale is clearly stated: (1) Our nature, (2) Grace, (3) The nature of Christ, which is divine.

Thus the union of man with God by grace, though different from the onehead of God with Himself, is somehow comparable with that very union:

> So that as God may not be from his being, *for onehead in nature,* so may not that soul... be from that thing that he thus seeth and feeleth, *for onehead in grace.* (P.C. 170:1)

[1] 1 Cor 6:17.

These words are used by the author of the summit of the mystical life when he declares that the soul experiences its union with God by grace: the " that thing that he thus seeth and feeleth " is the presence of God in the soul by grace.

CONTEMPLATION AND OFFERING

Grace, then, is the gift of God that renders man God-like and transforms his nature; but (and now the paradoxes begin again) this gift, far from being something sterile and inactive, is tremendously dynamic. Received passively in the utter silence of the cloud of forgetting, it might seem that man is reduced to something like inertia—and then suddenly a total activity breaks out; not an activity of this faculty or of that, but of the whole being. But to understand this it is necessary to consider the author's teaching on worship and offering.

In *Privy Counsel* the author keeps insisting that his mystical doctrine leads not only to prayer (and not even primarily to prayer) but also to " sacrifice. " The contemplative is told to worship God with his entire being, to offer himself with a totality only attained to by him who nakedly offers his blind being. Thus he says,. " That that I am, Lord, I offer unto thee... " (P.C. 136:4) And this prayer is so important that it is reiterated:

> That that I am, Lord,
> I offer unto thee;
> for thou it art. (P.C. 137:1)

The contemplative who " offers " himself is obviously conscious of a duality (since normally people do not offer things to themselves), and yet the succeeding phrase indicates no duality but unity: " for thou it art " is a continuation of the " He is thy being " motif.

And this way of speaking continues through *Privy Counsel*. In the utter passivity of mystical prayer there is yet a fundamental activity of the *whole being* of man (as he is by nature and by grace) offering himself up to God. " Bear up thy sick self *as thou art* " and try to touch God as He is. Furthermore, the contemplative is told to *worship*; and the words of the author make it clear that the passivity of diverse faculties, the cessation from discursive reasoning, the abandonment of conceptual thinking, the darkness of the intellect and the nakedness of the will—all this has been no more than a means to unify the personality enabling it to worship God with the total activity of the being itself:

> Thou ghostly friend in God, look that, leaving all curious seeking in thy natural wits, thou do whole worship to thy Lord God with thy substance, offering up unto him plainly and wholly thine own self, all that thou art and such as thou art, but generally and not specially—that is, without special beholding to that that thou art... (P.C. 140:18)

So now the paradox is clear. Just as the nought is all, and as the darkness is light, and as knowledge is ignorance, so the most complete passivity is a total activity; that is to say, when the faculties are lulled to rest, when dispersion is no more, when everything in man is unified and concentrated on God—then the whole being of the contemplative is active, as he *offers* himself to God in existential wholeness, concentrating all his energy at the sovereign point of the spirit. The author decries the "curious seeking" of the natural wits as well as any "special beholding" in favor of "whole worship" and a "general" offering.

Moreover, this offering is not a purposeless one. It is redemptive; it is an offering made in love, as the offering of Christ was made in love; it is an offering made for the salvation of all men. Let us recall once again the perfect mystical prayer in its entirety:

> That that I am and how that I am
> as in nature and in grace,
> all I have it of thee, Lord, and thou it art.
> And all I offer it unto thee
> principally to the praising of thee,
> for the help of all mine even Christians
> and of me. (P.C. 141:20)

The mystic, then, offers himself totally to God with everything that he has both by nature and by grace; and he does so for three intentions: (1) For the praising of God, (2) For the help of all Christians, (3) For himself.

This offering is performed after the imitation of, and in union with, Christ " offering himself up in veriest sacrifice, all that he was in general and not in special, without beholding to any one man in this life, but generally and in common for all. " (P.C. 142:17) The existential strain running through the whole work of the English author, then, is just a means to a total sacrifice like that of Christ; the contemplative is offering himself up for all men and " he must strain up his spirit in this ghostly work, for the salvation of all his brethren and sisters in nature, as our Lord did his body on the cross. " (C. 61:2) And like Our Lord, the contemplative offers up every moment of his life. He does not run away from the world of men to a silent forgetfulness but offers up his every action in a dynamic union with God:

> For in this blind beholding of thy naked being thus oned to God, as I tell thee, shalt thou do all that thou shalt do: eat and drink, sleep and wake, go and sit, speak and be still, lie and rise, stand and kneel, run and ride, travail and rest. This shalt thou each day offer up unto God as for the most precious offering that thou canst make. (P.C. 147:17)

Where now is the passivity? The mystic is eating and drinking, going and sitting, running and riding; but all is done in union with God and all is offered up to Him for the salvation of the world. The individual faculties are passive or naked only to be filled with the dynamism of God.

Realize that the author's mysticism is a sacrifice in union with Christ for the praise of God and for the redemption of the world and you grasp something of its essence. Here it is radically different from the mysticism of any other religion; here it is truly Trinitarian. The core of everything is in words like the following: " And more charity may no man do than thus to sacrifice himself for all his brethren and sisters in grace and in nature. " (P.C. 142:23)

United or " oned " with Christ, the mystic offers himself up in sacrifice for the redemption of all men; he lives in his own personal life the redemption effected by the Son of God, a redemptive work that continues in the Chruch and will continue until the end of time. The cloud of forgetting and the nakedness are only means to ensure that the oblation of the Christian life be a total one, an existential one without any trace of self-seeking, like that of Christ who offered Himself on the cross not for His personal friends, not for this or that person— but for all men. Now, united with Christ, the contemplative does likewise. He offers himself to the Father in perfect sacrifice; and by his union with Christ he enters into the very inner life of the Blessed Trinity. As the Second Person of the Blessed Trinity became man and offered Himself up to the Father for the redemption of all, so shared His divine life with other men who, in turn, offer themselves to the Father for the continued redemption of the world.

But to see more in detail how this may be, it is necessary to consider the theology underlying all this teaching.

THEOLOGICAL BACKGROUND

Traditional theology, as it came to the author of *The Cloud*, could be summed up in the words of St. John, " God is love. " God is the source of love; He is the essence of love; He is love itself. And being love, He is also goodness: He is goodness itself and the source of all good.

St. Thomas repeats the Platonic axiom: " Bonum est diffusivum sui "; and he further states (with the orthodox theology) that God communicates His being in two ways. The first way of communication is through creation in which God freely shares His being analogously with those creatures that He calls out of nothingness. About this creative communication I have already spoken, attempting to show that God's causality is creative and conservative, and that from the very fact of such causality one can say with the author of *The Cloud*, " He is thy being... " This sharing of His being with creatures was called by the Scholastics God's activity outside Himself—"*ad extra*".

But there is yet another way in which God communicates His being; and this is a Trinitarian communication, called by the Scholastics God's activity within Himself—" *ad intra.* " Here the Father, possessing the plenitude of the divine nature, communicates this nature to the Son; and from the loving union of the Father and the Son there proceeds the Third

Person who is the Holy Spirit. Thus this communication *ad intra* is nothing else but the mysterious and ineffable life of God Himself: it is a hidden life of loving intercommunication between the Three Persons.

Now in addition to analogously sharing His being with creatures by the causality of creation, God (by a free act of His mercy) decreed to grant to intellectual beings a share in His own very interior life; that is to say, He decreed to introduce man into the life of the Blessed Trinity Itself—and this by a completely free gift. This is the gift of grace about which the author of *The Cloud* speaks so much: it is a sharing in the interior life of God Himself. By it, men become (in the words of the Second Epistle of St. Peter) " sharers in the Divine Nature, " thus entering into the Trinitarian life of the Father, Son, and Holy Spirit. That is why the English author can say that by grace we are " gods, " a statement which is only a re-echo of many similar passages of the Fathers (especially the Greek Fathers) and of the earlier spiritual writers. For the very life of God is given to man. But what method does God choose to grant this grace to the human family? How does He share His Trinitarian life with man?

With this we enter into another great dogmatic mystery: Incarnation and Redemption. For the Blessed Trinity decrees that this gift be granted by the Second Person's becoming man; and so " the Word was made flesh and dwelt amongst us." [3] By reason of the Incarnation, the Word becomes truly man, in all things like to us, sin alone excepted; and yet He is also God—" *Deum verum de Deo vero.* " As the Second Person, He is by right at the very center of that Trinitarian life that is love; and so we have the extraordinary situation by which a man (a true man, a member of the human family and our brother) enters that Trinitarian community that is God Himself. This Person, who hungers and thirsts and suffers, receives that Divine Essence from the Father at every moment of His existence so that He can say: " My Father has entrusted everything into my hands; none knows the Son truly except the Father, and none knows the Father truly except the Son,

[3] Jn 1:14.

and those to whom it is the Son's good pleasure to reveal him. " [4] And from this union of Father and Son proceeds the Holy Spirit, the Spirit of love, whom Christ possesses so completely that He is scripturally spoken of as "the spirit of Christ." [5]

And now we come to the doctrine so central to the doctrine of the English author: this man, who is also God, *offers Himself* to the Father on the Cross for the redemption of the human family. This was the most perfect sacrifice so that the author of *The Cloud* can speak of " Christ offering himself up in veriest sacrifice. " (P.C. 142:17) It brings redemption to the world, since those who are saved " shall be by the virtue of the passion of only Christ. " (P.C. 142:16)

Moreover, the sacrifice of Christ was not only for His " special " friends; it was not made only for this person or for that; it was made for all men since, as St. Paul tells us writing to Timothy, God wishes for the salvation of all men without exception. The author of *The Cloud* expresses this idea by saying that Christ offered Himself up " without special beholding to any one man in this life, but generally and in common for all. " (P.C. 142:18) Here he indicates, too, that Christ, the ideal man, had such a perfect love for all men in utter detachment that no cloud of forgetting was necessary to purify His desires.

From this it can easily be seen how all the English author has said about " worshipping God with Himself " is fulfilled in a special, pre-eminent way in Christ. Now it has a deeply Trinitarian ring. Christ worships God with Himself not simply because, as man, He shares with all created things the being of God communicated *ad extra*; but much more because He, as the Eternal Word, receives the Divine Essence that is flowing back to the Father in the Holy Spirit who is " the spirit of Christ. " " He is thy being... " How true is this of Christ who, as the Son, receives the Divine Essence from the Father. The identification of the Son with the Father is perfect in essence; but the two are distinct in person. The *self* of the Son is never lost; it is never annihilated; when the father and the son, united in one nature " breathe forth " (*spiratio* was the technical

[4] Matt 11:27.
[5] See Rom 8:11–16.

word) the Holy Spirit, the " we " entails an identity that does nothing to destroy, but everything to enhance, the " I " and " Thou " of the Persons.

With this we come to yet another vitally important dogma. Christ does not wish to make this offering alone. He is the *first-born* of many. [6] Christians, united with Christ, make their sacrifice with Him, trying to make it as perfectly as did He. Christians are brethren of Christ. He is the vine of which those who believe are the branches—and as the branches live by the life of the vine, so those who believe are one with Christ, receiving eternal life from Him. He is the head of that Body of which all who believe are the members; and these members become more and more united with their Head according as they receive that sacred bread that gives them Trinitarian life.

Such is the union with Christ of the believer who possesses His Spirit. And no static union this. The sacrifice of Christ on the Cross, far from being His sacrifice alone, is made by all those who, one with Him, offer themselves to the Father. " For Christ is our head, " writes the English author, " and we be the limbs if we be in charity; and whoso will be a perfect disciple of our Lord's, he must strain up his spirit in this ghostly work, for the salvation of all his brethren and sisters in nature, as our Lord did his body on the cross. And how? Not only for his friends and dear lovers, but generally for all mankind, without any special regard more to one than to another. For all they that will leave sin and ask mercy shall be saved through the virtue of his passion. " (C. 60:25) This is to say that the offering of the contemplative is only of value insofar as it is united with the offering of Christ in His Passion. And this contemplative offering is no mere exterior imitation of Christ, as though the mystic were looking at Christ from outside and modelling his conduct upon His. Rather is it made by the very identification of the contemplative with Christ, whose very life flows through his veins and whose voice rises up within his breast crying, " Abba, Father. " [7] Only in the light of this can we understand how the garment that clothes the naked contemplative is Christ Himself; for the English author has put in

[6] 1 Cor 15:21 ff.
[7] Rom 8:15.

the mouth of Our Lord the stringent words: " Let him spoil himself of himself, if he will be verily clothed in me that am the full garment of love and of lasting that never shall have end. " (P.C. 156:23)

Now it becomes clear how those phrases about worshipping God with Himself, about God being our being and so on... these words, true in the order of nature because of causality and analogy, and true in the nature of Christ because of His divine Sonship and role in the Blessed Trinity, are true in yet another way of man by reason of his introduction into the Blessed Trinity by faith and by grace. It is precisely because he is " oned " with Christ, the Word, by grace that the offering of his blind being to God is of such tremendous value; it is Christ, the Word, dwelling within who is offering to the Father yet another humanity in the Holy Spirit. The offering of the contemplative is not his own; it is part of the offering of Christ, the whole Christ, who is one with all who believe in Him.

In short, the offering of one's blind being to God with a passivity of the faculties that leads to a total and existential activity—this can be understood only in a Trinitarian context.

CONCLUSION

An analysis of the English author's doctrine shows that the gift of grace perfects man's nature, giving him a share in the divine life and making him a temple of the Holy Spirit. Thus man comes to possess by grace the life that God has by nature.

This life comes to man through Christ who is the Second Person of the Blessed Trinity. Becoming man, the Word introduces the human race into the Trinitarian life of God: not only is He Himself a member of this Trinitarian family but He shares this divine privilege with all those who believe.

As man, Christ offers Himself to the Father for the redemption of mankind, an offering that, however, is not made alone but in conjunction with all those united with Him by faith; for these latter, too, are called to offer themselves to the Father for the redemption of their brethren and sisters in Christ. And this offering is most like that of Christ precisely in the contemplative life. This is because the mystic offers up

his total being to God in existential prayer and in utter forgetfulness of (that is, detachment from) all creatures.

In this way, it can be seen, we come to the same conclusion
as in other parts of this work; namely, that the contemplative
life as taught by the author of *The Cloud* is no more than an
intense and perfect form of the ordinary Christian life. The
contemplative fulfills in an eminent degree that vocation,
accorded to every Christian at Baptism, to offer himself to God
in Christ for the salvation of men. If his life is different from
that of other Christians, it is only because he makes his offering
with a greater totality in existential nakedness. And far from
being a rejection of dogma it is the implementation of dogma
in daily life. It is true that the contemplative does not reflect
discursively on dogmatic truths in his silent mystical sleep; he
forms no pictures of the Blessed Trinity; he makes no mental
images of the humanity of Christ. But these very dogmas are
incarnate in him; they course through his veins and are the
marrow of his bones. He is not *looking at* dogmas: he is *living*
them. He lives the life of the Trinity by offering himself to the
Father in union with the Word; he lives the Redemption by
making this offering for the salvation of all men; he lives the
Mystical Body by being united with all who believe in Christ;
he practices the first, and the greatest, commandment by offering
himself to God in perfect love without any restriction in the
totality of his being and in the forgetfulness of all things; he
practices the highest love of his neighbor by sacrificing himself
not for any one person " in special " but for all men. For this
silencing of the faculties in love is no sealing off of self from
the world but a unification of the whole personality enabling
man to offer himself to God in existential totality for the redemption of all men who have been saved by the blood of Christ.

Nor is personality annihilated. For just as the Father
communicates the divine nature to the Son without losing
anything of His personality; and just as the Son is one in nature
with the Father without losing His; so the Christian receives
the divine life of grace without losing that personality which
is the most fundamental thing in him. Reception of divine life
perfects the human personality, destroying nothing but
transforming all.

18

THE SPIRITUAL MARRIAGE

The contemplative, then, entering into the very life of the Blessed Trinity, in union with the Son, offers Himself to the Father " for the salvation of all his brethren and sisters in nature, as our Lord did his body on the cross. " (C. 61:2) Such an offering, however, is not made by contemplatives alone but by every Christian who seriously attempts to fulfill his role as a member of the Mystical Body and a branch of the Sacred Vine. It remains, therefore, to make clearer what is peculiar to contemplation, what distinguishes the author's " contemplative " from his " active, " what is the precise element that makes for the intensity of the Christian life as manifested in contemplation.

Much has already been said about the author's ascending degrees of Christian living: by penance the sinner becomes an active, and by a special grace the active is invited by the Good Shepherd to enter the sheepfold of contemplation. The latter state is characterized by a growing passivity, indicating that man is doing less and less while God is gradually taking the initiative until, in the final stages, the mystic finds himself impelled by something he knows not what, for God is " principally stirring and working. " (P.C. 164:5) While the Blessed Trinity is united with everyone who is in grace, the contemplative has a vital consciousness of this union: lovingly he surrenders self to the guidance of God who fills his being and *is* his being.

THE VISION OF GOD

Yet to understand the peak-point of contemplation in this life, it is necessary to consider the crown of the Christian life; namely, the vision of God as granted to the blessed in eternity. This is the goal to which the author ultimately leads and which he constantly has in mind.

Prior to the fourteenth century, there had been a good deal of discussion about the possibility of seeing God face to face in this life. While many mystics had spoken of intellectual visions, of " touches, " and of " union, " theological tradition tended to distinguish such things from the vision accorded to the blessed. St. Thomas prefers to keep separate the state of man " *in via* " and " *in patria* "; though he is willing to admit that by a miracle the beatific vision may well have been granted to Moses and St. Paul, and he discusses the possibility of Adam having had a similar privilege. [1]

The author of *The Cloud* was no stranger to this tradition; he knew well enough the doctrine of Augustine and Aquinas. Probably he would have no difficulty in admitting that by a miracle the vision of the blessed could be accorded also to suffering man; but he was less concerned with miracles than with the ordinary run of things in the mystical life. Consequently, he constantly maintains the distinction between this life and the next. The beatific vision he will not even grant to Moses. Telling us that the great prophet, separated from the multitude, attained to the highest wisdom accorded to man in this life, he goes on:

> And yet in all this he was not with God, so as it accordeth to the perfection of this divinity: but he had in contemplation an object not himself, for he may not be seen by that eye. But the place where he was, that was his object. And that place betokeneth the highest godly beholding, passing above and having in

[1] *II Sent.*, d. 23, q. 2, art 1.

subjection all man's reasons, as the lady hath her maidens. (H.D. 5:3)

Moses, then, even though he scaled the heights, did not see God according to the perfection of his divinity; he only saw the place where God is.

In this life the cloud (in some shape or form) always remains. " For one thing I tell thee: that there was never yet pure creature in this life, nor yet never shall be, so high ravished in contemplation and love of the Godhead, that there is not evermore a high and wonderful cloud of unknowing betwixt him and his God. " (C. 47:17) This cloud renders obscure the contemplative contact with God, so that although one may, in a sense, " see " and " feel " Him, this sight and feeling is imperfect. " For if ever thou shalt see him or feel him, as it may be here, it must always be in this cloud and in this darkness. " (C. 17:7) That " clear " sight is never had in this life is openly asserted: " But be thou sure that clear sight shall never man have here in this life; but the feeling may men have through grace, when God vouchsafeth. " (C. 34:17)

Even when the beam of ghostly light pierces the cloud to reveal the " secrets " of God, the sight obtained is not clear, God being grasped " blindly and in part, as it may be here in this life. " (P.C. 136:28) Thus is always maintained the distinction between the vision that may be had " here " and that of eternity.

What is this vision of God attainable in the next life but inaccessible to man " *in via* "?

The current theology, in this context, constantly used the Pauline text that here we see darkly through a glass but in the next life we shall see " face to face. " [2] Analysis was especially made of the Pauline assertion that " now I know in part; but then I shall know as I am known. " To know God as He knows me; to know God, somehow, as God knows Himself—this is the great ideal of the Pauline beatific vision as interpreted by the scholastics.

[2] 1 Cor 13:8–13. Also much used by the scholastics was 1 Jn 3:2: " Beloved, we are Sons of God even now, and what we shall be hereafter, has not been made known as yet. But we know that when he comes we shall be like him; we shall see him, then, as he is. "

To the metaphysics of the author of *The Cloud* (which is substantially the same as that of St. Thomas) this presents one difficulty. It will be recalled that for him love goes out to God as He is in Himself; whereas knowledge, so to speak, draws God down to man's level, imposing upon Him the limitations of conceptualization: to think of God in terms of what we see and hear is to bring God down from His transcendent position. Hence the scholastic dictum: " *Cognitum est in cognoscente per modum cognoscentis.* " To see God as God sees us and as He sees Himself, one must go up to Him in knowledge just as one goes up to Him in love. And the scholastics asserted that to make this ascent in knowledge a special elevating light was required: thus to the saints in paradise was accorded the " *lumen gloriae,* " enabling man to see God face to face. But in this life man must be content with ordinary grace (called " *semen gloriae* "), giving a vision that is embryonic or blind. Hence, though *love* goes to God's essence here as in eternity, *knowledge* is here blind but in eternity it is perfected.

In view of this, it is easy to understand how the author of *The Cloud,* together with Ruysbroeck, keeps speaking of a " blind " union founded upon love. Yet love leads to a true *experience* of God, an experience that is a stage below clear vision. This supreme experience of " *homo viator* " is spoken of by the author of *The Cloud* in the traditional metaphor of mystical marriage.

MYSTICAL MARRIAGE [3]

In the *Epistle of Prayer*, the author has been speaking of the union of the soul with God in love, using the Pauline text so

---

[3] From the time of St. Bernard, the great majority of Christian mystics have spoken of mystical marriage as the apex of the contemplative life. Freudian interpretations of this have not been lacking, the assertion being made that mysticism is a sublimation of the sexual urge, a kind of substitution for sex. The scriptural teaching of St. Paul, however, is that marriage is a symbol of the union between Christ and the soul; that is to say, union with God is the reality of which marriage is the type or figure (cf. Eph 5:25 ff.). In short, the celibate mystic chooses the reality, whereas the married person chooses the sign; and all will ultimately be mystics at the resurrection when they will neither marry nor be given in marriage but will be like unto the angels of God (cf. Luke 20:35). Catholic theology has always taught (in opposition to Freudian trends) that the most fundamental urge in man's heart is his desire for God,

dear to the Fathers and St. Thomas, " He who unites himself to the Lord is one with them in spirit "; and then he goes on to say that " although God and he be two and separate in nature, nevertheless by grace they are so knitted together that they be but one spirit. " This is a union accomplished in love and in " accordance of wills, " and it is brought about by spiritual marriage:

> And in this onehead is the marriage made betwixt God and the soul, the which shall never be broken, though all the heat and the fervour of this work cease for a time, but by deadly sin. In the ghostly feeling of this onehead may a loving soul both say and sing, if it will, this holy word that is written in the *Book of Songs* in the Bible: " Dilectus meus mihi et ego illi. " That is, " My loved unto me and I to him " understood " shall be knitted with the ghostly glue of grace on his part, and the lovely consent in gladness of spirit on thy part. " (P. 56:21)

Incessantly has the author claimed that God, who cannot be known, can be loved. And now at the supreme moment of the mystical life, he reaffirms the supremacy of love: here it is love that is the principal element; it is love that gives knowledge; it is love that brings about the union. But what more can be said about this love, about this blind stirring that has filled the author's pages?

The contemplative life, it will be recalled, began with the rising of this " blind stirring of love " in the breast of the disciple. At first barely perceptible, it grew into a raging fire, taking possession of his life, guiding his every choice, telling him when to eat and when to fast and so on. This love had given wonderful wisdom, infinitely greater than anything accessible to the " natural wits. " What is this love?

a desire that reaches fulfillment in the beatific vision, is adumbrated in the mystical union, and again is adumbrated in God's sacrament of Matrimony. It is true, then, that the sexual urge and the urge to mystical union have something in common (as is clear enough from the language of the mystics), in that both are adumbrations of the deepest urge of all: the longing of man for the infinity of God. But this does not mean that mysticism is a sublimation of sex. It should be remembered that mystical marriage is enacted only when the whole personality has been purified and unified, when the sensual part of man has been subordinated to the spiritual (" my house being now at rest, " writes St. John of the Cross), and when there is no faculty that is not fixed upon God.

St. John of the Cross, the great apophatic successor of the
English author, teaches a similar doctrine. For him it is " the
living flame of love " that performs the whole work of contemplation. And for him this living flame *is* the Holy Spirit. That
is why, in ardent apostrophe, he personifies it in the words:

Oh, living flame of love   That tenderly woundest my soul in
its deepest centre.

And commenting on these words, the Spanish saint writes:
" The flame of love is the Spirit of its Spouse—that is, the
Holy Spirit. " [4]
Thus the soul is transformed in God by the love of the
Holy Spirit.
Now it is difficult to avoid the conclusion that the author
of *The Cloud* is teaching the same doctrine; not only because he
is in the same apophatic tradition, teaching a remarkably
similar doctrine in all things, but also because this alone can
explain his total passivity joined to a total activity—the passivity
is that of man: the activity is that of God. It is precisely the
Holy Spirit who is now blindly stirring the will; He it is who
teaches, comforts, instructs, tells the contemplative when to
speak and when to be silent, when to fast and when to eat and
so on. He it is who is lovingly transforming the soul in God.
It has been stripped naked to be clothed in God; it has forgotten
all to remember only God; and now, as the contemplative
offers himself to the Father in union with Christ for the salvation
of the human family, that same Holy Spirit, referred to in the
Scriptures as " the spirit of Christ, " is his spirit also (for whoso
cleaves to the Lord is one spirit); and he is lost in God. This is
the union of which St. John of the Cross can say that " the
soul seems to be God rather than a soul, and is indeed God
by participation; although it is true that its natural being,
though transformed, is as distinct from the being of God as
it was before. "
And now for one more interesting parallel. Just as the
author of *The Cloud* speaks of *worshipping* God with Himself, so

[4] *Living Flame*, Stanza I, 3.

in this high state, St. John of the Cross speaks of *loving* God with Himself. Stating that this is a " total transformation of her will in that of God wherein the two wills are united after such manner that they become one, " he continues:

> And thus there is equality of love, for the will of the soul that is converted into the will of God is then wholly the will of God. And thus the soul loves God with the will of God, which is also her own will; and thus she will love Him even as much as she is loved by God, since she loves Him with the will of God Himself in the same love wherewith He loves her, which is the Holy Spirit, Who is given to the soul. [5]

The Pauline influence is unmistakable. In this life, the soul " will love Him even as much as she is loved ": in eternity, she will know as she is known. In this life, the soul loves God " in the same love wherewith He loves her ": in eternity, she will know the same knowledge by which He knows her.

And this is one of the basic principles of the author of *The Cloud* who, untiringly asserting that love attains to God in this life but not knowledge, adds that *as far as love is concerned* there is no difference between the mystical life and the beatitude of the blessed. The difference is in knowledge, not in love.

THE INTUITION OF GOD

The highest union accorded to man in this life, then, is founded on love; and love imparts a degree of knowledge that, though less than vision, can be called intuitive, being contact with God as He is in Himself.

While the author claims that his fleshly blabbering tongue can give no details of this experience, all the indications are that his mysticism, if Trinitarian, is not that of the person who looks at a picture from outside; rather is it an experience of the Blessed Trinity from within. The contemplative has, so to speak, entered the Divine Community so that, united with Christ, he offers himself to the Father in the Holy Spirit. There

[5] *Canticle*, Stanza XXXVII, 2.

is one passage that on analysis throws light on this difficult subject. The author is speaking of the summit of mystical experience when the soul, purified by purgatorial trials, has attained to that chaste and perfect love that is the goal of all:

> And in this time is thy love chaste and perfect. In this time it is that thou seest thy God and thy love, and nakedly feelest him also by ghostly oneing to his love in the sovereign point of spirit, as he is in himself, but blindly as it may be here, utterly spoiled of thyself and nakedly clothed in himself, as he is, unclothed and not lapped in any of these sensible feelings—be they never so sweet nor so holy—that may fall in this life. But in purity of spirit properly and perfectly he is perceived and felt in himself as he is, far removed from any fantasy or false opinion that may fall in this life. (P.C. 169:17)

This passage being of considerable importance, I would like to analyze it word by word.

" *And in this time is thy love both chaste and perfect* ": The summit of mysticism in *Privy Counsel* is the chaste and perfect love of the *Epistle of Prayer:* it is the " *amor castus* " of tradition. This is the love which, the author has said, is motivated by only God as He is in Himself and by no other consideration however good and holy. It is not even motivated by thought of God's love *for me* (such love being like the green fruit not yet departed from the tree) but by the goodness of God as He is in Himself. This is the ripe and luscious fruit; this is the ardor of the chaste woman who loves her husband and none of his goods. Such love is only attained to by him who buries all creatures beneath the cloud of forgetting in utter detachment from all things and from all considerations except the goodness of God.

" *In this time it is that thou seest thy God and thy love* ": Here we find that the peak-point of the mystical life is a vision; for the contemplative *sees*. Yet he sees not only God but also his love for God. Perhaps this accords with Merton's description of union which states that " the soul, touched and inflamed and transfigured by the illuminative flame of God's immediate presence, is no longer the object of knowledge but the actual medium in which God is known. Hence, God as He is in Himself is the object of the soul's contemplation. The medium in which He is seen is . . . the soul itself burning and translucent in the flame of divine love. " [6] In this way, knowledge is direct or immediate; that is to say, it is knowledge of God as He is in Himself, but He is seen in the medium which is the soul. This is clear again in the next words.

" *And nakedly feelest him also by ghostly oneing to his love . . .* ": Naked in intellect because the cloud of forgetting has erased all forms from the mind and memory, naked in will because love of all creatures has been cast away, the contemplative lovingly rests in God: he *feels*, he *touches* him, he contacts Him immediately, for there is no bar between the two. And he feels God, again, by reason of a union in love: now it is His love that is highlighted.

" *In the sovereign point of the spirit* ": Discursive reasoning has been abandoned; successive images have been halted; the soul has silently gone down to that deep point of its psychic center where it secretly contacts God who is its being. For " the center of the soul *is* God, " says St. John of the Cross [7] in words recalling the English author's, " He is thy being. . . " At this sovereign point of the spirit, the diversified activity of a multitude of faculties has been reduced to mystic silence, and the soul in existential unity is joined to God with a totality that no words can express.

" *As he is in himself* ": Once again comes the theme. The contemplative stands above all creatures, as did Adam, and there is nothing between him and God. He makes no illation from effect to cause; he sees God Himself. Yet the next words make the familiar puzzling distinction.

" *But blindly as it may be here* ": It is blind sight and obscure vision. " Here " is " *in via* "; for this is not the beatific vision; it is not the vision of God " *secundum essentiam* " that no man on earth attains to. The soul, it is true, loves with the love of God; but it does not know with God's knowledge.

" *Utterly spoiled of thyself and nakedly clothed in himself* ": Here is the " alling and noughting, " the " *todo y nada* " refrain of the apophatic mystic. Self is reduced to nakedness only to be beautifully clothed in God Himself.

---

[6] Merton [1], p. 278.
[7] *Living Flame*, Stanza I, 12.

" *As he is* ": The same emphasis; no creature must intervene in this sacred union of man with God; all are trodden down beneath the cloud of forgetting. One sees God not " as he is in creatures " but as He is in Himself.

" *Unclothed and not lapped in any of these sensible feelings—be they never so sweet nor so holy—that may fall in this life* ": This strikes a somber note. The nakedness of mysticism has demanded the renunciation of all consolation—purification has been just this. All visions, all revelations, all sounds and sweetnesses, " all these sensible sweetnesses, these fervent feelings, and these flaming desires " (P.C. 168:19) have been ruthlessly cut away. For the blinding light of God is as night to the soul, depriving it of all comfort. The summit of the English author's mysticism is not for those who crave for extraordinary phenomena and spiritual delights, but for those who will walk in the dark suffering of a night illumined only by love.

" *But in purity of spirit* ": When all sensible comfort is abandoned, God is encountered in pure spirit. " For grace in itself is so high, so pure, and so ghostly, that it may not be felt in our sensible part. The tokens thereof may, but not it. " (P.C. 168:23)

" *Properly and perfectly he is perceived and felt in himself as he is* ": The author never seems to tire of making this same point: that this is an experience of God as He is in Himself; it is the most utter rejection of, and annihilation of, all creatures that might separate man from God. The emphatic words " properly, " " perfectly, " " in himself as he is " would indicate that there is no *plus ultra*, that this is the highest point to which one can reach, that it is the beatific vision itself, were it not for those other indications that it is still " blind " and " as it may be here. "

" *Far removed from any fantasy or false opinion that may fall in this life* ": Here (in words that, incidentally, illustrate the author's amusing fondness for alliteration) sensible imagery and conceptual reasoning are rejected. Reasoning, he has told us so often, will not bring the mind to God as He is in Himself and may even lead to error one who forgets that all conceptual knowledge, when applied to God, is only analogous. Man in this deadly body may think of God in images and concepts; but the further he gets away from these to the realm of dark faith and naked love, the nearer he comes to God.

Having thus described the summit of mysticism, the author proceeds to give a theological analysis that is no less interesting:

> This sight and this feeling of God (thus in himself as he is) may no more be separated from God in himself (to thine understanding that thus feelest or thus seest) than may be separated God himself from his own being, the which be but one both in substance and also in nature. So that as God may not be from his being, for onehead in nature, so may not that soul (that thus seeth and feeleth) be from that thing that he thus seeth and feeleth, for onehead in grace. (P.C. 169:27)

This is indeed a difficult passage. God, says the author, is united with Himself in nature and in substance; nor can He be separated from Himself—He cannot be separated from His own being. And the soul united to God can no more be separated from Him *by reason of grace* than He can be separated from Himself *by reason of nature*. The play on nature and grace, with its rejection of pantheistic identification of man with God, has already been referred to. Now, in transforming union, the mystic experiences God as united with himself by grace; and such a union, though different from God's union with Himself by nature, is somehow comparable with it.

In this way, love brings about such union that the soul may be called " a god. " This terminology is used also by St. John of the Cross, who adds that the soul's " natural being, though transformed, is as distinct from the Being of God as it was before, even as the window has likewise a nature distinct from that of the ray, though the ray gives it brightness. " The soul, looking into its own being, sees the ray of light (which is God) shining through the pane of glass (which is itself). So filled with sunlight is the window that the glass is scarcely visible—and the cleaner the glass (through purification), the more invisible it becomes and the clearer becomes the sun. Thus does the soul look into the depths of its own being to see God and its own love for God—" thou seest thy God and thy love "; it sees the ray of sunlight in the medium that is itself. Yet the sunlight fills the glass completely. " It is like rain falling from the heavens into a river or spring, " writes St. Teresa, " there is nothing but water there and it is impossible to divide or separate the water belonging to the river from that which fell from the heavens. Or it is as if a tiny streamlet enters the sea, from which it will find no way of separating itself. " [8]

The English author expresses this in yet another motif handed down from mystic to mystic in the tradition, always with a Trinitarian connotation; this is the motif of the mirror.

Looking into one's own soul, one can see God. " Let that meek darkness be thy mirror and thy mind wholly, " he has written (P.C. 136:7), as if to say that in the darkness of a mind, emptied of images and thoughts but filled with faith and love, the soul can see God as in a mirror. And the same image appears in the *Study of Wisdom* where the English author, borrowing from Richard of St. Victor, writes:

> And know well that he that desireth to see God, him it behoveth to cleanse his soul, the which is a mirror in the which all thing is clearly seen when it is clean. And when the mirror is foul, then mayest thou see nothing clearly therein. And right so it is of thy soul. When it is foul, neither thou knowest thyself, nor God... and therefore cleanse thy mirror. (S.W. 43:4)

The author speaks to the person who desires to " *see* " God, declaring that he can only do so when he has cleansed his soul at the well of Confession and when his spirit is purified by the cloud of forgetting and the purgatorial suffering of the passive nights. Then can he see God in the mirror of his soul.

Yet this spiritual mirror differs from an ordinary mirror in one extremely important respect. In the ordinary mirror we see the reflection of an object that may, in fact, be locally far removed from the mirror itself; but the soul of man actually contains the object it reflects, for God is present in it. Man's soul is " the ghostly temple of God "; there is no question here of local separation, for " He is thy being and in him thou art what thou art, " and the soul is " conformed by grace to the image and likeness of God, his maker. "

---

[8] *Interior Castle*, Mansion VII, c. 2.

The English author, however, has stressed so often that the mystical " sight and feeling " is of " God as he is in himself " that it is not easy to reconcile his words with the interpretation that God is seen in a medium. The explanation of St. John of the Cross given above, that God is seen as the ray in the glass, is of some help; and somewhat similar is the mirror theme as expounded by Gregory of Nyssa who writes: " It is just like men who look at the sun in a mirror. Even though they do not look up directly at the heavens, they do see the sun in the mirror's reflection just as much as those who look directly at the sun. " [9] Gregory seems to mean that the man who looks at the sun's reflection in a mirror is not looking at the mirror: he is really looking at the sun. Yet he sees the sun in a medium; and in the same way, the soul at the summit of the spiritual ascent in this life really sees God as He is in Himself, but his vision is still through a medium. " And what is this vision, " continues Gregory, " It is purity, holiness, simplicity, and other such brilliant reflections of the nature of God; for it is in these that God is seen. " [10]

For the vision of God is " blind, " it is " in part, " it is " as it may be here, " it is in a " mirror "; and to the end the English author remains staunchly apophatic. This is like St. John of the Cross who solemnly warns that the soul " must not think that that which it feels and understands is God in His Essence, however profound such experiences may be. " [11] For both these mystics the supreme union is not in vision but in love.

THE PRIMACY OF LOVE

And so the author of *The Cloud*, at the pinnacle of the mystical life, is faithful to the doctrine stressed from the first pages of his work: " For why, he may well be loved, but not thought. " (C. 26:3) God, he has told us, is incomprehensible to the knowing power " but to... the loving power, he is, in every man diversely, all comprehensible to the full. " (C. 19:6) In love is knit the ghostly knot that united the soul to God; and just

---

[9] Gregory of Nyssa, p. 102.
[10] *Ibid.*
[11] *Canticle*, Stanza I, 2.

as lovers share their goods and their all but, far from abdicating their personality, perfect it; and just as the Father and the Son share their all and, far from abdicating their personality, hold it in its infinite perfection; so the soul, in love with God by spiritual marriage, gives its all to God in utter nakedness, in existential rejection of quidditive knowledge, and in the total noughting of itself, in order to receive in love and in one spirit the nature of the Beloved while retaining its own nature and its own personality.

But one who would be faithful to the English mystic must stop here out of respect for his principle of writing only about what pertains to man. The action of God is too sacred, too sublime, too ineffable to fall beneath the working of a human pen. " For of that work that pertaineth only to God dare I not take upon me to speak with my blabbering fleshly tongue; and, shortly to say, although I durst I would not. " (C. 62:19) The most sublime Trinitarian union is hinted at but is not, for it cannot be, described in detail.

And so, with a note of reticence, which is not only Dionysian but also English, he leaves the most exalted realms of the mystical life beyond the cloud of unknowing.

19

GENERAL CONCLUSION

The principal point I have made in this work is that the English writer's doctrine leads to a form of prayer that is no more than an intensification of the ordinary Christian life.

The first section examined his enigmatic sentence from Dionysius that " the most godly knowing of God is that which is known by unknowing. " (C. 125:11) Viewed in a twentieth-century context, this can appear to be a *kōan*-like rejection of logic; it can look like some form of agnosticism; it can be interpreted as a rejection of dogma. This is especially so when it is taken in conjunction with the Englishman's broadsides against discursive thinking and his doctrine of the two clouds (that of unknowing and that of forgetting) that exclude all clear and distinct knowledge in favor of tranquil rest in existential silence, supraconceptual and dark.

A close examination of this doctrine against a background of fourteenth-century metaphysics, however, shows his meaning to be that God cannot be known *univocally* through concepts. In the words of the author, He cannot be known by logical discourse " as He is in Himself "; but that analogical knowledge attains to God the author does not doubt. As for the emptying of the mind of all images and concepts, this is done to pave the way for a higher knowledge of which the " ground " is faith—" Let belief be thy ground, " he says to the silent mystic (P.C. 135:24)—and this faith sends forth a " blind stirring of love " of which wisdom is " the fruit. " The cloud of unknowing is thus seen to be that mystical knowledge that fills the mind when, void of images and concepts, it is grounded in *faith*, stirred by *love*, and suffused with *wisdom*.

The Mary Magdalen motif makes the thing clear. Rapt in silent love, this great contemplative is so fascinated by the divinity of Christ that she no longer has even any image or thought of His physical body before which she kneels; she has " right little special beholding unto the beauty of his precious and blessed body, in the which he sat full lovely, speaking and preaching before her; nor yet to anything else, bodily or ghostly. " (C. 46:21) Yet she had faith by which she " regarded the sovereignest wisdom of his Godhead lapped in the dark words of his Manhood. " (C. 47:11) In this way, the contemplative sees the sovereignest wisdom of God lapped in the dark words of Christ in Scripture and the propositions of the Church, while love goes out to " touch " the realities thus darkly apprehended. But what is the nature of this " dark " knowledge?

In the course of this work I have distinguished two kinds of thinking or mental activity, one of which I have called vertical, existential, supraconceptual, as opposed to another called horizontal, essential, or conceptual. This latter moves in successive images, one picture being replaced by another in the human phantasm; thus it is quidditive, concentrating on *what* a thing is rather than *that* it is; and in it the mind is conscious of time and place. To this way of thinking belong logic, reasoning discourse: it is the conceptual process at work in the daily life of every man. The author of *The Cloud* himself uses this way of thinking in his logical exposition of mysticism.

The other way of thinking, existential or vertical, does not move in successive images but spirals down silently into the depth of one's being without concepts, without images, and (at its highest point) without consciousness of time. This tells us *that* reality is rather than *what* it is; and the English writer is leading to it when he bids the contemplative not to meditate on the qualities of God, reflecting on *what* he is but simply to hold himself in the existential realization of the fact *that* God is and *that* I am. This silent, supraconceptual activity of the mind is dark or obscure because, being without images and quiddities, there is nothing clear and distinct in the mind; it takes place at a lower level of the consciousness; and when it arises in the depths of one's being accompanied by mystical love, one's faculties are " hindered "—the contemplative is crying out in the darkness of the cloud to God whom he loves but cannot adequately know.

Now the point I have tried to stress is that in the darkness of this supraconceptual knowledge ordinary Christian faith, Christian charity, and Christian wisdom, far from being jettisoned, reach a high degree of perfection. And because he believes this the author's aim is to lead those called by God from the horizontal to the vertical line of activity where their faith and love will grow in intensity. But the object of Magdalen's knowledge and love is no different when she is rapt in forgetful contemplation than when she reasons meditatively. The difference is only one of intensity.

The second section deals more specifically with that " blind stirring of love " that burns mystically at a deep level of the personality in the passivity of supraconceptual silence. Highly experimental in nature, this tiny flame of love develops into a raging fire until, in the *Epistle of Stirrings*, we read of how it dominates the contemplative's life, guiding his actions and determining his decisions with an urgency that can be denied only at peril to peace of mind. Yet the author is quite clear in his teaching that this fire of love is no more than a development of the evangelical love taught by Christ, that love which is the center of Christian perfection and contains every virtue.

Moreover, this mystical stirring, far from being an irrational uprising in the heart of man, is the child of Rachel, who stands for reason; and it leads to an ineffable " high, ghostly wisdom, " a wisdom so glaringly bright that it dazzles the intelligence of man who, blinded by the " abundance of ghostly light, " remains in the ever-thickening darkness of the cloud of unknowing. Hence, to the outer man it is nought; to the inner man it is all. To the outer man it is darkness; to the inner man it is light. And whence this wisdom? Just as the burning candle, says the author, throws light both on itself and on everything around, so the burning of love reveals both our own wretchedness and the wondrous glory of God. In short, true wisdom is the fruit of divine charity.

And this again is the ordinary fourteenth-century theology as outlined by St. Thomas: true wisdom is not the product of human reasoning but a gift of the Holy Spirit given to all who are in charity.

The cloud of unknowing, then, is *dark wisdom*, grounded on *faith* and produced by *love*—it is a development of supernatural gifts accorded to all who are justified. [1]

The third section deals with the purificatory aspect of the two clouds. " Scattered " by sin, orginal and personal, man must, either in this life or in the next, undergo a purgatory of purification to attain to the " oneness " within himself and with God for which he was created. The cloud of forgetting detaches man from inordinate love of that created thing to which he is most attached; namely, knowledge. Abandonment of inordinate desire of knwoledge entails abandonment of desire of all things; and it causes great suffering for (as Aristotle has said) " a man naturally desires to know. " (P.C. 171:24) The natural " wits, " starved of their food, cry out like ravening dogs; the contemplative, severed from God by the cloud of unknowing and from creatures by the cloud of forgetting, is suspended in anguished darkness tortured by his own love.

For the blind stirring of love is the " sweet burn " and the " delectable wound " of St. John of the Cross, an admixture of joy and pain that penetrates deeply into the psychic life, cauterizing not only sin (which is washed away in the " well " of Confession) but also the roots of sin. It burns into that very part of the personality where concupiscence takes its origin; and as the roots are torn out, the psyche shakes and trembles in violent temptations wherein the outer senses, those windows of the house, rattle and rumble. The soul, meanwhile, confident in its God, sits tranquilly within in silent love. Yet as the roots are removed (though they never disappear completely in this

---

[1] I use the terminology " all who are justified " to emphasize that Christian mysticism is accessible to those outside the Church if they are justified by charity.

life) the work of contemplation becomes easier, the coming of " Jesu " is more and more " merry, " and the contemplative, in great liberty, is permitted to see and to remember creatures; for the cloud of forgetting has not annihilated knowledge of creatures but inordinate desire of knowledge of creatures.

In this way the contemplative passes through a purgatory of love in this life. But this is a purgatory that, the author holds, must be passed through by every man wounded by sin. In short, it is an intense form of that purification required of all men in their passage from the " scattering " of sin to " oneing " with God in eternal life.

The fourth section deals with union. By reason of his very creaturehood man depends completely on God who alone is being in the full sense of the word, other beings existing only because of their analogous participation in Him who alone really IS. Consequently, one can forget or " destroy " the sight and the feeling of self *as an isolated part* in order to know and love oneself *as part of the whole*, just as (in the metaphor of St. Thomas) the hand will sacrifice itself to protect the whole body. One thus forgets self to be conscious of self as part of that totality that owes its existence to God.

But over and above this metaphysical union with God is a higher union in grace; for God, through Christ, has offered to man His own eternal Trinitarian life by which man " may truly be called a god "—not a god in the full sense of the word, " for He is God by nature... and thou... only by his mercy without thy desert art thou made a god in grace. " (C. 120:12) Thus man is divinized and, stripped naked of self to be clothed in the garment that is Christ, he offers himself to the Father —" for the sake of all mine even Christians and of me. "

But, once again, this is no more than the vocation of every Christian who by reason of Baptism is called to unite himself with the sacrifice of Christ to the Father for the redemption of the world. It is only that the contemplative *experiences* at the deepest part of his psychic life and at the center of his being those great realities that make less experimental impact on the lives of other Christians.

In short, the mysticism of the author of *The Cloud* is a development of those supernatural gifts that, though totally beyond the reach of the unaided human powers, can scarcely be called " extraordinary " insofar as they are offered at some time to every member of the human family and extend their redemptive influence to every man. These gifts are now *experienced* at a new level of the personality that the author calls " the sovereign point of the spirit " or " the lowest point of the wit. " Here it is that the *faith, charity,* and *wisdom* of the Christian life reach their perfection.

But is this " ordinary " contemplation accessible to every Christian? Should charity normally develop into the blind stirring of love? Should the supernatural gifts of grace ordinarily penetrate into that deep sector of the psychic life called " the sovereign point of the spirit "?

To this the author answers in the negative. He is at great pains to show that " this working " is not for everyone but only for those called specially by God. The would-be contemplative is told to test his vocation with the evidence of Scripture and of counsel; warnings against illusion are reiterated; those not called are told humbly to wait outside the sheepfold until the Good Shepherd lovingly calls them to the intimacy of contemplative union.

However, distinguishing between *those called to salvation* and *those called to perfection,* the English author insists that those whom God would make perfect He invites to contemplative prayer. Man may be saved without this gift; but his virtue will not be perfect, for " have a man never so many virtues without it, all they be mingled with some crooked intent, for the which they be imperfect. " (C. 39:15) Hence in his hierarchy of ways of life within " Holy Church, " the contemplative life alone is allotted the highest position, nor does he seem to envisage any other path to perfection. Moreover, the " roots " of sin can be removed only by the purificatory blind stirring; and perfect love is found only when the cloud of forgetting has done its work perfectly and man, in total oblivion of his own being, is rapt in ecstatic love for God as He is in Himself. In other words, the only way to *perfection* is by entering the sheepfold of contemplative prayer.

This, however, is one of the few points on which I personally beg to differ for reasons that I shall briefly explain.

The English author is a man of his age; he is the child of a medieval world rich in a spirituality one might call " monastic, " envisaging Christian perfection only in a contemplative context. Those called to the most perfect service of God embraced the religious or eremitical state that was orientated to mystical experience (although all the monks did not necessarily attain thereto), passing through those stages of love and of prayer vividly described by the Victorines and reaching a climax in the high stages of infused contemplation. [1] Such was the recognized path to perfection.

But with the opening up of the so-called " New World " and the discovery of continents, there arose in the Church a spirituality that was less monastic, less neoplatonic, devoted to the apostolate with a totality the medieval world scarcely conceived of. Then the question arose: Is contemplation the only way to Christian perfection, or can evangelical charity find perfect expression in another form? The early Church, as it appears in Acts of the Apostles, found room for the highest sanctity in the active life and in the world; one can then wonder if this intensely experimental gift is completely necessary to reach the summit of perfection. Not that the rise in the status of Martha means a belittling of Mary, for no one denies that the majority of great apostles were guided by the mystical, blind stirring of love dominating their every action and choice. The only question is, Is this the *only* way?

" In order to obtain a proper view of this matter, " writes Joseph de Guibert, " the whole body of the Church should be taken into account, the whole complexus of fervent or perfect souls should be examined, special attention being paid to those who devoted themselves heroically to external works of zeal and charity. On this basis, it does not seem possible that anyone who has had even a little experience in directing souls can assert that all of them follow the path of infused contem-

[1] In *Christian Perfection and Contemplation*, Reginald Garrigou-Lagrange maintains that until the seventeenth century the traditional teaching of theologians and spiritual writers was that there is only one way to the summit of charity that is Christian perfection—and this way is a mystical one. Mystical union was considered the apex of the spiritual life, not in the sense that perfection consists precisely in this (for all agreed that perfection consists in charity), but that perfection cannot be reached without this mystical grace. (Garrigou-Lagrange [1], pp. 23 ff)

plation. However, the experienced director knows that among
them it is not rare to find souls who enjoy infused contemplation
in a high degree. " [3] This is an interesting a posteriori point of
view from a theologian of immense practical experience in
the guidance of dedicated religious. Facts indicate, he feels,
that people reach the highest perfection without that experimental gift the English author calls the " blind stirring. "
And theologically speaking it is possible to question the author's
thesis that perfect love is found only in utter and complete
forgetfulness of self and of all created things. De Guibert states
his own view: " The way or state of infused contemplation is
not the only normal way to perfect love although, apparently,
generous souls do not ordinarily arrive at perfection unless God
gives them some touches or brief participations in those graces
which constitute strictly infused contemplation. Therefore souls
can ascend to any degree of sanctity without habitually walking
in the way of infused contemplation. " [4] That is to say, ordinarily
perfection will demand touches of mysticism and stirrings of
love—though not so deep, not so violent, not so uncompromis-
ingly imperative as those described by the author of *The Cloud.*

My position, then, differs only slightly from that of the
English author. I believe that his contemplation is one way to
perfection—and an ordinary way; but I do not believe it is
the *only* way.

Again the mysticism of *The Cloud* may be called " ordinary "
because it follows a phenomenological pattern of supraconceptuality that, in its broadest outlines, is common to many
religions and to many cultures. If one defines mysticism as
that vertical or existential thinking of which I have spoken
at length, then there is surely a point of contact in the thought
of such widely different personalities as Plato, the author of
The Cloud, St. John of the Cross, Dr. Suzuki, and Thomas
Merton. And there is a mystical way of thinking that, no less
than logic, is ordinary in the sense that it is governed by certain
psychological laws, studied from the earliest times in the East
and more recently in the West with the great advance of depth
psychology.

[3] De Guibert, p. 350.
[4] *Ibid.*, p. 346.

I have stressed, however, that this does not mean that all are the same. Mysticism is an extremely broad genus in which there are many species of which the traditional, apophatic mysticism of *The Cloud* is one. Its specific features are that its " ground " is faith, its motivation is the blind stirring of love, and its object is the Blessed Trinity: " God that *made* thee and *bought* thee, and graciously *called* thee to his love. " (C. 26:17) The silent supraconceptuality of a mind void of images, however, can in itself be a natural phenomenon—through which may come the vocation of God to Christian perfection, a call often entering the human psychology with such imperceptible unobtrusiveness that its very existence is difficult to discern. Hence the tests and checks that the English author, in common with most Christian mystics, elaborates in detail lest the would-be contemplative fall into idleness or into a supra-conceptual state that will not lead him to God.

Finally, the mysticism of *The Cloud* and its accompanying treatises may be called ordinary because of the assiduity with which the author eschews all extraordinary phenomena. His contemplative is a very ordinary person; and the author devotes pages of ridicule to the would-be mystic who acts as if he had a worm in his ear or looks like a silly sheep that has been banged on the head. True contemplative grace gently tranquillizes the personality, giving a wonderful serenity and a calm self-dominion. About the physical repercussions of ecstasy the author says nothing; about visions, locutions, and revelations he is silent; about consolations he is unenthusiastic. The distinction between consolation and grace is firmly and clearly made: " For know thou right well, that though God sometimes withdraw these sensible sweetnesses, these fervent feelings, and these flaming desires, nevertheless he withdraweth never the rather his grace in his chosen. " (P.C. 168:14) Sensible feelings " in themselves be not grace but tokens of grace "; for " grace in itself is so high, so pure, and so ghostly, that it may not be felt in our sensible part. The tokens thereof may, but not it. " (P.C. 168:23) It is good to be left barren in the boat without sensible joy; for then one walks in the darkness of true faith.

In a century that, not yet freed from the influence of Schleiermacher and modernism, feverishly searches for " reli-

gious experience " with drugs and mescalin, it is refreshing to
find a mystic who laughs good-humoredly at those who strive
and strain for consolation like "a greedy greyhound,"
(C. 87:19) forgetting that the essence of all is supernatural
charity. In opposition to those who would look for phenomenological experiences, the author insists that true contemplation
is found in the total forgetfulness of self and preoccupation
with God; there is no search for experience, only a search
for God.

And so, from across the centuries, this English mystic
speaks to a wicked and adulterous generation looking for
signs and intoxicated with the mescalin of its own psychiatry,
quietly warning us with apophatic conviction that God is
above every sensible experience and that He must be loved
in the darkness of the cloud of faith; he is the forerunner of
a St. John of the Cross who will later fiercely sweep away all
visions, all revelations, all concepts, all sensible consolation as
being utterly incapable of bringing man to the essence of the
transcendent God who can be touched in love but never (in this
life) grasped in univocal knowledge, for "all visions, revelations
and feelings coming from Heaven, and any thoughts that may
proceed from these, are of less worth than the least act of
humility." [5] This is the lesson of apophatic mysticism; this is
the lesson of *The Cloud*. To go to God one must be naked;
one must offer up one's naked being. "But look, as I oft said,
that it be naked, for fear of deceit." (P.C. 171:18) The person
who looks for sensible religious feelings is already clothed:
he is in danger. [6]

For God is utterly transcendent. He is the mystery of
mysteries; He is night to the soul; He can be loved but not
thought; and even the mystic is like an anguished child crying
out in the darkness of the cloud to Him whom he loves but
cannot adequately know. God can be best found in the naked-

---

[5] *Ascent*, III, IX, 4. Note that St. John of the Cross speaks of "all visions,
revelations and feelings *coming from Heaven.*" He is not speaking here of
illusions but of real graces *gratis data*, which are of less value than the least
act of humility, which is *gratum faciens*.

[6] I speak here of sensible experiences and not of "the beam of ghostly light"
that is something of another order. Yet even from this must the contemplative
be detached: it is futile to strive for it, God being free to give or to withhold
it as He wishes.

ness of that dark faith that is the cloud of unknowing. Only then does this good mystic raise his voice in angry protest when he thinks of any man (wise theologian or learned philosopher) who has the audacious ignorance to think that his images and syllogisms represent God as He is in Himself; and the quiet smile that plays around his tranquil lips as he mocks the disciple for imitating others " on ape manner "—this smile gives way to shrill anger and heated protest at the effrontery of theologians who think they have adequate knowledge of God.

Yet the anger cannot last, nor can the bitterness endure. It is the mirth, the playful humor, and the gentle charity that prevail; and *The Cloud* ends with a blessing. " Farewell, ghostly friend, in God's blessing and mine! And I beseech Almighty God that true peace, whole counsel, and ghostly comfort in God with abundance of grace, evermore be with thee and all God's lovers on earth, Amen. "

APPENDIX

HORIZONTAL AND VERTICAL THINKING

A good deal has been said about essential thinking that is horizontal and existential thinking that is vertical; but it may be of interest to add a few words to make the matter clear.

In Occident and Orient, both these ways of thinking have been known from the earliest times. Existential thinking is already found in the Bible when God reveals Himself to Moses with the words: " I am who am "—the great Jewish lawgiver becomes then the prototype of subsequent Judaeo-Christian mystics. But apart from the mysticism that forms an integral part of the Christian spiritual tradition, there are clear indications of vertical thinking in Plato (as in the *Symposium* and the *Seventh Epistle*) and even more so in Plotinus and the ensuing neoplatonic thought-stream. This points to a tendency toward supraconceptual thinking both inside and outside Christianity in the West.

In the East, it is hardly necessary to say, this vertical thought has been practiced by thousands of contemplatives who have devoted themselves to the search for truth in existential silence since the time that Sākyamuni found enlightenment beneath the pipel tree at Buddhagaya in the fifth century B.C. Together with the practice of mysticism, the East has shown great interest in the functioning of those lower reaches of the mind to which Western depth psychology has recently come to devote such energetic attention. That is why psychologists like Jung have felt that they have much to learn from the religions of the Orient.

Now a point of considerable importance for my work has been that mysticism (taken in this wide sense of the word) is an ordinary phenomenon, largely the product of education, temperament, cultural background, and personal effort. It is a phenomenon that the world always has known, and presumably always will know.

If this is so, however, the question may arise as to why mysticism becomes surrounded with an aura of occultism and why it is such an object of suspicion. The author of *The Cloud*, we have seen, keeps wrangling with the theologians; obviously he is deeply conscious of bitter criticism from learned divines, and he warns his disciple that a similar fate is in store for him. He knows that somehow mystical prayer is not fully trusted.

On the other hand, it is also interesting to note that if the theologians criticize him, he also criticizes them; if they jibe at him, he jibes at them; he gives as much as he gets. But why the dispute?

The answer, it seems to me, is first of all the historical fact that people who incline to vertical thinking and those who devote themselves exclusively to discursive or logical thinking have always had the greatest difficulty in understanding one another. In East and West, not a few mystics (even the most humble like the good author of *The Cloud*) have tended to look down on the less-favored advocates of logic, despising them as poor, dull fellows who sit in self-satisfied ignorance within the dark and drab Platonic cave looking miserably at shadows when they should come out into the superb sunshine to contemplate the glorious reality. And in answer to questions about the nature of their vertical knowledge the mystics simply answer that only the person with experience is entitled to speak—and even he should be careful because existential knowledge is ineffable nor can concepts express it. Thus the " uninitiated " are cut off from any possibility of satisfying their curiosity or deepening their understanding. Furthermore, the mystic, in his enthusiasm for the silent state of supraconceptual emptiness, will sometimes use words that, taken at their face value, amount to a denial of the validity of logic. This has scandalized the discursive thinkers who have rightly felt that a denial of reason in favor of blind irrationality could be one of the most insidious human deviations. The only thing is that the greatest mystics (at any rate, the greatest Christian mystics) had no intention of denying reason, as I have tried to show at great length in regard to the author of *The Cloud*. The latter (who, in this respect, is typical enough) simply stresses that discursive reasoning with its dependence on imagery cannot give intuitive knowledge of God and, in this sense, it is useless; moreover, its knowledge *in comparison with* supraconceptual wisdom is a feeble thing: this is no denial of the validity of reasoning. Suzuki, on the other hand, clearly denies the validity of reason in words; but whether he really means to be taken literally is difficult to say. Perhaps, like so many others, he is merely emphasizing the richness of supraconceptual knowledge with hyperbolic intensity.

Furthermore, if the champions of horizontal thinking have always regarded the mystics with suspicion, this, it must be confessed, has often stemmed from an inability to understand what the mystics are talking about: for mystical experience in dark supraconceptuality is something of a closed book to those not temperamentally disposed to understand its silence and its paradoxes. This point is made by Jung who, when setting out to give a psychological explanation of Zen, makes the assertion: " For anyone who does not share or understand this point of view, the ' explanation ' will consist of nothing but words which have no tangible meaning for him. " [1] And it seems an undoubted fact that for many people *Privy Counsel* and the works of St. John of the Cross are just so much meaningless rigmarole. Not unnaturally, the mystical paradoxes and the contempt for discursive reasoning has ired these people, at whose hands the mystics have sometimes undergone a mild persecution; for in their heart of hearts they cannot get away from the fear that somehow or other the whole thing may be a hoax. And what is true of *Privy Counsel* can be said of Zen.

[1] Jung, p. 15.

While its enthusiasts are numerous, there are never lacking people who regard it as little more than the esoteric dreaming of some idlers who sit for hours looking at their navel in silent waste of time.

In Western culture the struggle between the mystics and their critics has been formidable. On the one hand, one finds the glorification of syllogistic thinking inherited from Aristotle and the Greeks, highly developed by the scholastics, and reaching a climax in the years prior to the composition of *The Cloud*. Later, this esteem for true logic is to wane and give place to the Cartesian criterion of truth: " the clear and distinct idea "—the very antithesis of the mystic contention that the highest wisdom is savored in the sapiential obscurity of supraconceptual darkness. And so against this there have always been reactionaries who, like the author of *The Cloud*, wish to shake off the shackles of an excessive Aristotelianism to look for truth in silent and existential repose.

Thus we have a conflict between two kinds of thinking. But I would like to repeat that both are ordinary; both are found in many cultures; both are found inside and outside Christianity.

In short, the above distinction of vertical and horizontal thinking is largely a cultural phenomenon, nor is it *directly* connected with the supernatural gifts of God that we call faith and charity; indeed (as we have quoted Ruysbroeck in saying), even the sinner can engage in silent, supraconceptuality and (at least theoretically) he could see God united with him in the order of nature. This is to say, whether one thinks vertically or horizontally is mainly a question of temperament, education, and so on—it is even conceivable that vertical thinking of some kind could be induced by drugs like mescalin. [2]

And now a word about the special characteristics of Christian mysticism.

---

[2] However, I say this very tentatively. The experiments of Aldous Huxley are not very convincing; and R. C. Zaehner, who himself made the experiment, concludes: " As far as I am concerned, mescalin was quite unable to reproduce the ' natural mystical experience ' I have described elsewhere. I half hoped it would. However, once the drug started working and I was plunged into a universe of farce, I realized that this was not to be. The two experiences were... totally different. " (Zaehner, p. 226)

The vertical way of thinking that goes down to what the English author calls " the sovereign point of the spirit " can be cultivated in many ways. One way is by the *kōan* with its utter rejection of logical thinking; another is by sitting for hours in the silent vacancy of Zen. But there is yet another way.

It so happens that with people of a certain temperament, an intense love of God, revealing Himself in Christ, will lead to this vertical thinking—a love of God that, impatient of discourse, goes directly to the object of its desire. In this way is induced vertical thinking; and then it is of immense value, not for any phenomenological reason nor because it is a source of great pleasure and effects the unification of the personality, but because it is an expression of divine love. And this is Christian mysticism. The Christian mystic (and here I use the word " Christian " for all those who, whether or not baptized by water, are "justified" by supernatural charity and are temples of the Holy Spirit) is he whose love has begun to burn with such ardor that he abandons discursive thinking (which is now distasteful to him, for love so seizes him that he *cannot* think) to plunge down to the sovereign point of the spirit in supraconceptual silence. Thus the call of God is intimately linked with his ordinary psychological processes. This mystic may love more passionately than other Christians, but his ontological situation is not essentially different; he possesses the same supernatural life; the Holy Spirit dwells in him as in all the justified. It is only that he loves so deeply (and the fact that we use this word " deep " for love is in itself significant) that horizontal thinking no longer satisfies him, so that his psychic life begins to work vertically, bringing about a situation in which the Trinitarian life within the soul and the guidance of the Holy Spirit, great realities in the life of all in grace, become increasingly experimental. Thus he is deeply *conscious* of that union with Christ whereby he offers himself to the Father in the Holy Spirit for the salvation of all men.

As an expression of divine love, then, and as a way of finding God in His mysteries under the guidance of grace, the Church has always had great esteem for mysticism. But, aware of the danger of illusion, she has insisted on protecting it with the check of dogma, always declaring that when true charity is absent it is no longer Christian prayer, however great its cultural or philosophical value.

And in this delicate matter the wise author of *The Cloud* maintains throughout a Christian balance. He propounds the existential without rejecting the essential. If he is partial to vertical thinking, this is because he regards it as the highest expression of a burning love like that of Mary Magdalen: his supraconceptual silence is a great fulfillment of that law of charity which is the center of Christ's teaching.

BIBLIOGRAPHY

EDITIONS

HODGSON, P.: [1] *The Cloud of Unknowing and The Book of Privy Counselling*, Edited from the Manuscripts with Introduction, Notes, and Glossary. Early English Text Society, Oxford, 1944 (reprinted 1958).

— [2] *Deonise Hid Divinite and Other Treatises on Contemplative Prayer Related to The Cloud of Unknowing, A Tretyse of the Stodye of Wysdome that Men Clepen Beniamyn, A Pistle of Preier, A Pistle of Discrecioun of Stirrings, A Tretis of Discrescyon of Spirites*, Early English Text Society, Oxford, 1955 (reprinted 1958).

COLLEDGE, E.: " The Book of Privy Counsel, " *The Medieval Mystics of England*, London, 1962.

McCANN, JUSTIN, O.S.B.: *The Cloud of Unknowing*, With a Commentary on *The Cloud* by Father Augustine Baker, O.S.B., London, 1952 (Westminster, Maryland, 1952).

PROGOFF, I.: *The Cloud of Unknowing*, Introductory Commentary and Translation by Ira Progoff, London, 1959 (New York, 1961).

WALSH, J., S.J.: [1] *A Letter of Private Direction*, London, 1963.

— [2] *Denis's Hidden Theology* (Unpublished work).

WOLTERS, C.: *The Cloud of Unknowing*, Translated into Modern English with an Introduction, London, 1961.

GENERAL BIBLIOGRAPHY

ALLEN, HOPE EMILY: *Writings Ascribed to Richard Rolle, Hermit of Hampole*, New York, 1927.

ANESAKI, MASAHARU: *History o Japanese Religion*, Tokyo, 1963 (Rutland, Vermont, 1963).

AKIYAMA, NORUI: " Ningensei, " *Dogen Zen* (4 vols), Vol. III, Tokyo, 1961.

BECKER, ERNEST: *Zen: A Rational Critique*, New York, 1961.

BENEDICTINE OF STANBROOK: *Medieval Mystical Tradition and Saint John of the Cross*, London, 1954 (Westminster, Maryland, 1954).

BENNETT, H. S.: *Chaucer and the Fifteenth Century*, Oxford, 1947 (New York, 1948).

BLYTH, R. H.: *Buddhist Sermons on Christian Texts*, Tokyo, 1952.

BOUYER, L.: *History of Christian Spirituality*, Vol. I: *The New Testament and the Fathers of the Church*, New York, 1963.

BUTLER, DOM CUTHBERT: *Western Mysticism*. Second Edition with Afterthoughts, London, 1926; reprinted 1958.

CAYRE, F.: *Manual of Patrology*, Vol. II, Trans. by H. Howitt, Tournai, 1940.

CLARKE, JAMES. M.: *The Great German Mystics*, Oxford, 1949.

COLLEDGE, E.: [1] *The Medieval Mystics of England*, London, 1962 (New York, 1961).
—   [2] " The English Mystics and Their Critics, " *Life of the Spirit*, XV (June 1961).
—   [3] " Early English Spirituality, " *The Month* (July-August 1963).

CONZE, E.: [1] *Buddhism*, Oxford, 1951; (New York, 1951).
—   [2] *Selected Sayings from the Perfection of Wisdom*, London, 1955.
—   [3] " Spurious Parallels to Buddhist Philosophy, " *Philosophy East and West*, XIII (July 1963).

CUNNINGHAM, FRANCIS L. B.: *The Indwelling of the Trinity*, Dubuque, Iowa, 1955.

D'ARCY, MARTIN: *No Absent God*, New York, 1962.

DAVIS, CHARLES (ed.): *English Spiritual Writers*, London, 1961.

DEDEK, JOHN F.: " *Quasi experimentalis cognito :* A Historical Approach to the Meaning of St. Thomas, " *Theological Studies*, 22 (September 1961).

DUMOULIN, HEINRICH: [1] *A History of Zen Buddhism*, Trans. Paul Peachey, New York, 1963.
—   [2] " Technique and Personal Devotion in the Zen Exercise, " *Studies in Japanese Culture*, ed. by J. Roggendorf, Tokyo, 1963.
—   [3] *The Development of Chinese Zen*, New York, 1953.

ECKHART, MEISTER: A Modern Translation by R. B. Blakney, New York, 1941.

ELIOT, T. S.: *Four Quartets*, London, 1944 (New York, 1943).

EVANGELISTA, GARCIA A.: *La experiencia mistica de la inhabitacion*, Granada, 1953.

GABRIEL OF ST. MARY MAGDALEN, Father: *Visions and Revelations in the Spiritual Life*, Trans. A Benedictine of Stanbrook Abbey, Cork, 1950 (Westminster, Maryland, 1950).

GARDEIL, A., O.P.: *La Structure de l'âme et l'expérience mystique*, Paris, 1927.

GARDET, L.: *Expériences mystiques en terres non-chrétiennes*, Paris, 1953.

GARRIGOU-LAGRANGE, REGINALD, O.P.: [1] *Christian Perfection and Contemplation*, Trans. Sister M. Timothea Doyle, O.P., St. Louis, 1937, Ninth Impression 1951.

— [2] *The Love of God and the Cross of Jesus*, Trans. Sister Jeanne Marie, Vol. I, St. Louis, 1948.

— [3] *Idem*, Vol. II, St. Louis, 1951.

— [4] *The Three Ages of the Interior Life*, Trans. Sister M. Timothea Doyle, O.P., Vol I, St. Louis, 1948; Vol. II, St. Louis, 1951.

— [5] *The One God*, Trans. Dom Bede Rose, St. Louis, 1946.

— [6] *Christ the Saviour*, Trans. Dom Bede Rose, St. Louis, 1950.

GILSON, ETIENNE: [1] *The Mystical Theology of St. Bernard*, Trans. A.H.C. Downes, London, 1940 (New York, 1955).

— [2] *The Spirit of Medieval Philosophy*, New York, 1936.

— [3] *History of Christian Philosophy in the Middle Ages*, London, 1955 (New York, 1955).

GRABMANN, MARTIN: *The Interior Life of St. Thomas Aquinas*, Trans. N. Ashenbrener, Milwaukee, 1951.

GRAEF, HILDA: *The Light and the Rainbow*, London, 1963 (New York, 1963).

GRAHAM, AELRED: [1] *The Love of God*, London, 1939 (New York, 1959).

— [2] *Zen Catholicism*, New York, 1963.

GREGORY OF NYSSA: *From Glory to Glory* (Texts from Gregory of Nyssa's Mystical Writings), Ed. Jean Daniélou and Herbert Musurillo, New York, 1961.

GUIBERT, JOSEPH DE, S.J.: *The Theology of the Spiritual Life*, Trans. Paul Barrett, New York, 1953.

HAPPOLD, F. C.: *Mysticism, A Study and an Anthology*, London, 1963 (New York, 1964).

HILTON, WALTER: *The Scale of Perfection*, Trans. Dom Gerard Sitwell, London, 1953 (Westminster, Maryland, 1953).

HUMPHREYS, CHRISTMAS: *Studies in the Middle Way*, London, 1940.

HUXLEY, ALDOUS: [1] *Grey Eminence*, New York, 1941.

— [2] *The Doors of Perception and Heaven and Hell*, London, 1954, 1956 (New York, 1954). Published in one volume in Penguin Books, 1959.

— [3] *The Perennial Philosophy*, London, 1946 (New York, 1945).

INGE, WILLIAM RALPH: *Christian Mysticism*, London, 1899.

JOHN OF THE CROSS, SAINT: *The Complete Works of Saint John of the Cross, Doctor of the Church*, Trans. and ed. by E. Allison Peers from the critical edition of P. Silverio de Santa Teresa, C.D., 3 vols, London, 1953 (Westminster, Maryland, 1949).

JULIAN OF NORWICH: *The Revelations of Divine Love*, Trans. James Walsh, S.J., London, 1961 (New York, 1961).

JUNG, CARL GUSTAV: Foreword to *An Introduction to Zen Buddhism*, by D. T. Suzuki, London, 1949; reprinted 1960

KING, W. L.: *Buddhism and Christianity*, London, 1963.

KNOWLES, D.: [1] *The English Mystical Tradition*, New York, 1961.
—   [2] *The Evolution of Medieval Thought*, Baltimore, 1962.

LASALLE-ENOMIYA, H., S.J.: " Are There Similarities in Eastern and Western Mysticism?" *Ars et Mystica*, 13, Hiroshima, 1964.

LECLERCQ, J., F. VANDENBROUCKE, and L. BOUYER: *La Spiritualité du Moyen Age*, Paris, 1960.

LEHODEY, V.: *Les Voies de l'oraison mentale*, Paris, 1927.

LEONARD, A., O.P.: " Studies of the Phenomena of Mystical Experience, " *Mystery and Mysticism*, New York, 1956.

LOSSKY, V.: *The Mystical Theology of the Eastern Church*, London, 1957.

LETTER, P. DE, S.J.: [1] " The Encounter with God, " *Thought*, XXXVI (Spring 1961).
—   [2] " Reflecting on Purgatory, " *Cross and Crown* (March 1964).

LUBAC, HENRI DE: *Aspects of Buddhism*, Trans. George Lamb, London, 1954 (New York, 1956).

McCOOL, G.: " The Primacy of Intuition, " *Thought*, XXXVII (Spring 1962).

MARÉCHAL, J., S.J.: *Études sur la Psychologie des Mystiques*, Paris, 1938.

MARITAIN, JACQUES: *The Degrees of Knowledge*, Newly translated from the fourth French edition under the supervision of Gerald B. Phelan, London, 1959 (New York, 1959).

MARMION, C., O.S.B.: *Le Christ, idéal de moins*, Maredsous-Paris, 1923.

MATHY, F. H.: *Kitamura Tokoku : Between East and West* (Unpublished work, 1963), appearing currently in *Monumenta Nipponica*, Tokyo.

MERTON, THOMAS: [1] *The Ascent to Truth*, New York, 1951.
—   [2] *The New Man* (Paperback), New York, 1963.

MOKINARI, P.: *Julian of Norwich*, London, 1958.

NAKAMURA, H.: *The Ways of Thinking of Eastern People*, Tokyo, 1960.

NEMESHEGYI, P.: [1] *De Deo creante*, Tokyo, 1961.
—   [2] *Tractatus de gratia*, Tokyo, 1962.
—   [3] *Tractatus de SS. Trinitate*, Tokyo, 1963.

PEPLER, CONRAD, O.P.: [1] *The English Religious Heritage*, London, 1958 (St. Louis, 1958).
—   [2] *The Three Degrees*, St. Louis, 1957.

PIOVESANA, G., S.J.: *Recent Japanese Philosophical Thought*, Tokyo, 1963.

POULAIN, A., S.J.: *The Graces of Interior Prayer, A Treatise on Mystical Theology*, Trans. Leonard L. Yorke-Smith, London, 1912.

POURRAT, P.: *Christian Spirituality*, Vol. I, trans. W. H. Mitchell and S. P. Jacques. (Rev. ed.) Westminster, Maryland, 1953; Vol. II, trans. S. P. Jacques, London, 1924 (Westminster. Maryland, 1953).

POWELL, R.: *Zen and Reality*, London, 1961.

REINHOLD, H. A.: *The Soul Afire, Revelations of the Mystics*, New York, 1944.

RICHARD OF ST. VICTOR: *Selected Writings on Contemplation*, Trans. with an Introduction and Notes by Clare Kirchberger, London, 1955 (New York, 1957).

ROBINSON, J. A.: *Honest to God*, London, 1963 (Philadelphia, 1964).

ROQUES, RENÉ: *L'Univers Dionysien*, Paris, 1954.

RUYSBROECK, JOHN OF: *The Adornment of the Spiritual Marriage, The Sparkling Stone, The Book of Supreme Truth*, Trans. C. A. Wynschenk. Ed. with an Introduction and notes by Evelyn Underhill, London, 1916.

S. M. C.: *Henry Suso, Saint and Poet*, Oxford, 1947.

ST. AUSTIN, MOTHER MARY OF: *The Divine Crucible*, London, 1948.

SENZAKI, NYOGEN, and RUTH S. MCCANDLESS: *Buddhism and Zen*, New York, 1953.

SITWELL, DOM GERARD: *Medieval Spiritual Writers*, London, 1961 (New York, 1961).

SPENCER, S.: *Mysticism in World Religion*, London, 1963.

STAEHLIN, C. M., S.J.: *Apariciones, essayo critico*, Madrid, 1954.

SUZUKI, D. T.: [1] *Essays in Zen Buddhism* (I), London, 1927.
—   [2] *Essays in Zen Buddhism* (II), London, 1933.
—   [3] *Essays in Zen Buddhism* (III), London, 1934.
—   [4] *An Introduction to Zen Buddhism*, Kyoto, 1934. New edition with a foreword by C. G. Jung, London, 1949, 1960.

TANAKA, TADAO: " Shingakudo, " *Dogen Zen* (4 vols), Vol. II, Tokyo, 1960.

TANQUERAY, A.: *The Spiritual Life*, Trans. H. Branderis, Westminster, Maryland, 1947.

TEILHARD DE CHARDIN, P., S.J.: *Le Milieu Divin*, New York, 1960.

TERESA OF JESUS, ST.: [1] *Life, Written by Herself*, Trans. David Lewis. London, 1916.

— [2] *The Interior Castle or The Mansions*, Trans. P. Zimmerman, London, 1921.

THURSTON, H., S.J.: *The Physical Phenomena of Mysticism*, ed. J. H. Crehan, S.J. London, 1952 (Chicago, 1952).

UNDERHILL, E.: [1] *Mysticism*, London, 1911.

— [2] *Mixed Pastures*, London, 1933.

— [3] *The Mystics of the Church*, New York, n.d.

VERNET, F.: [1] *La Spiritualité médiévale*, Paris, 1929.

— [2] " Anglaise, Ecossaise, Irlandaise " (Spiritualité), *Dictionnaire de Spiritualité* (Paris, 1937), 1, cc. 625-659.

WACH, J.: *Types of Religious Experience, Christian and Non-Christian*, London, 1951.

WALSH, J., S.J.: " The Cloud of Unknowing, " *The Month*, CCXVI (December 1963).

WATKIN, E. I.: *Poets and Mystics*, London, 1953.

WATTS, A.: *The Way of Zen*, New York, 1957.

WIESINGER, A.: *Occult Phenomena in the Light of Theology*, Trans. Brian Battershaw, London, 1957 (Westminster, Maryland, 1958).

WULF, MAURICE DE: *Philosophy and Civilization in the Middle Ages*, Princeton, 1922.

ZAEHNER, R. C.: *Mysticism Sacred and Profane*, Oxford, 1957.

INDEX

Abbot of St. Victor, *see* Gallus

Abraham, 58

Acts of the Apostles, The, 263

Adam, 108, 112, 145-147, 149, 156, 230, 244, 251

affirming divinity *(theologia affirmativa)*, 34, 45, 49, 50

agnosticism, 257

Akiyama, Noriji, 24n

Albert, St., 32

Angela de Foligno, 10

angelism, 68, 79

anthropomorphism, 45, 89

apophatic mysticism, 1, 31, 36, 58, 59, 133, 200, 266

  apophatic mystics, 27, 28, 34, 50, 251

  — current, 11

  — doctrine, 132-133

  — tradition, 57-59, 248

Aquinas, *see* Thomas

Aristotle, 9, 12-13, 25, 26, 27, 32, 131n, 161, 202, 205, 221, 223, 260, 272

  Aristotelianism, 93, 203, 272

  Nicomachean Ethics, 26

ascesis, 161, 162-166

Asser, 127

astronomy, 204

Augustine, St., 10, 11, 13, 26, 28, 45, 70, 71-72, 82, 91, 148, 150n, 202

  Commentarium in Evangelium Joannis, 72n

  Sermons, 72n

  Soliloquies, 198n

Aurobindo, Sri, 208n

  Bases of Yoga, 208n

author of *The Cloud of Unknowing*, the

  identification of —, 1-3, 4

  traditionalist character of —, 10-11, 93

  similarity of — to St. John of the Cross, 11

  characteristics of —, 40-43

  Denis Hid Divinity, 2, 3, 34-37, 45, 56, 61, 63, 111-112, 177, 197

  Discretion of Spirits, A Treatise of the, 2

Epistle of Discretion of Stirrings, 2, 3, 117-118, 119-124, 127, 128, 184, 259

Epistle of Prayer, 2, 79n, 86, 105-108, 109, 111-112, 163, 166, 197, 246-247, 250

Privy Counsel, The Book of, 1, 2, 3, 39, 42-43, 45, 59, 86n, 99-100, 110, 111-112, 119, 129, 131-132, 136, 165, 173-174, 193-197, 208, 213-214, 218-220, 230, 234-236, 250, 271

Study of Wisdom that Men Call Benjamin, A Treatise of the, 2, 3, 69, 119, 127-131, 168, 197, 254

Baker, Augustine, 4, 6, 12, 58-59, 93, 99, 176-177

Bala, 127-128

Baptism, 86, 88, 92, 102, 114, 140, 230, 242, 261

Bartholomew the Apostle, St., 63

Bartholomew of the Martyrs, 209n

beatific vision, 28, 108, 194, 198, 244-245, 247n, 251, 252

Beguardi, 213

Beguinae, 213

Benjamin, 100-101, 119, 127-130

Bernard, St., 2, 10, 26, 28, 69-70, 107n, 223, 246n

blind stirring of love, 3, 18, 36, 38-39, 40, 50, 64, 69, 87, 90, 97ff, 105ff, 117, 119-123 *passim*, 125, 136, 139-140, 147, 148, 155-156, 157, 160-161, 167-172 *passim*, 180, 184, 186, 206, 213, 247, 258-265 *passim*

Boethius, 45

Bonaventure, St., 26, 28, 32

Buddha, 23, 67

Buddhism, 9, 31n

Canticle of Canticles (Book of Songs), 52, 247

Catherine of Siena, St., 10

Chapman, Dom, 11n

Chardin, Teilhard de, 184, 214

  Teilhardian vision of the universe, 181